A HISTORICAL WALK AROUND

GRAVESEND AND NORTHFLEET

OR

A HISTORICAL PERAMBULATION
OF
GRAVESEND AND NORTHFLEET

by

JAMES BENSON

Revised and Edited
by

ROBERT HEATH HISCOCK
LL.B., F.S.A.,

GRAVESEND HISTORICAL SOCIETY

First published 1976, reprinted 1981 under the title *A History of Gravesend* by Philllimore & Co. Ltd., London and Chichester

This is a new fully revised edition

ISBN: 0-9548137-3-1

Printed by Northfeet Press, 5 and 6 Stonebridge Road, Northfleet, Kent. DA11 9DR. Designed and set by The Publications Committee of the Gravesend Historical Society. Published by the Gravesend Historical Society, Hon. Secretary, 58 Vicarage Lane, Chalk, Gravesend, Kent. DA12 4TE.

CONTENTS

Thamesgate Centre, Lloyds and Midland banks, coaches, *Nelson* and *Prince of Orange*, King Street, Free School, *Mitre*, National Westminster bank, David Greig's, cab rank, County Court

Part Three

Part Four

ILLUSTRATIONS

Illustrations in this book are included within the chapters dealing with their area.

Acknowledgements

The Gravesend Historical Society would like to record its sincere gratitude to the following people for their kind permission to use more than a few of their illustrations within this book: Mr. Robert Hiscock, Mr. Eric Green, Gravesham Heritage Association, Mr. Tony Bontoft, Mr. David Jewiss, plus those who have contributed individual illustrations, Mr. Ian Bouchard, Mr. F. Hutchins, Mr. and Mrs. Turner, the late Mr. Richard Palmer, Miss Brenda Lawrence and Miss Joan Colston.

The Society would also like to thank those who have contributed to the Society's own Archive from which many of the pictures are also drawn: Miss Joy Barnes, the late Alderman Jack Bacon, the family of the late Mr. Ernie Tilley, Mrs. D. Parr, the family of the late Mr. R. Turk, the family of the late Mrs. M. Heppenstall and Gravesham Borough Council and Gravesend Library for allowing members of the Society, in the past, to photograph paintings within their possession.

The Gravesend Historical Society has done its best to identify where permissions for the inclusion of images seemed necessary. The Society apologises for any mistakes or omissions.

Mr. James Benson

Miss Frances Tunbridge

PREFACE

THE ORIGIN of this historical guide to Gravesend and Northfleet first published in 1976 and reprinted in 1981 lies in a manuscript first typed by James Benson in 1954. It then comprised the section relating to Gravesend, although a section on Northfleet with two or three appendices were planned. He was not altogether satisfied with it and put it aside to revise and complete, but other projects intervened. It was only after the death of his wife early in 1972 that, at my suggestion, he started work on it again, intending to give it to the Gravesend Historical Society for possible publication. At the time of his death on 4 June 1972 he had only revised a few sections.

The principle on which this history has been compiled has necessitated a thorough revision of all sections to bring it up to date, owing to the extensive demolitions and rebuilding which has taken place in the town during the last 50 years. In addition a section on Northfleet was added, making use in part of the material which Benson collected for his series of articles in the *Gravesend Reporter* on 'Northfleet through the Ages', and A.F. Allen added an Appendix on the piers.

On 1 April 1974 both Gravesend and Northfleet became part of the new Gravesham Borough Council. The name 'Gravesham' appears only in the Domesday Book 1086, and was probably an error of the Norman scribe. It was 'Gravesend' in the Domesday *Monarchorum* c.1100, and 'Gravesende' in the *Textus Roffensis*, c.1100. It is strange that the 'clerical error', was adopted for the name of the new Council.

Mr Benson, who was born on 12 December 1878, had lived all his life in Northfleet and Gravesend, and had quite a remarkable memory not only for events, but also for dates. His articles in the *Gravesend Reporter* on local history did much to stimulate interest in the locality and his researches into local archives and documents increased considerably our knowledge of the district. On his 90th birthday the Historical Society presented him with an illuminated address, the work of the late J.S. Kean, which is now in the local museum. It is hoped that the publication of this history may be some memorial to Mr Benson and the work he did for local history in this area.

The reprint is now long since exhausted and the Society felt that a new edition was necessary to bring the text up to date and this has now been done by a committee of the Gravesend Historical Society consisting of Messrs. R.H. Hiscock, E.R. Green, C.R. Bull, P.V. Bowles, V.T.C. Smith, K.McGoverin and D.Jewiss. Mr R.H. Hiscock has acted as editor of the Gravesend Section and Messrs. E.R. Green and C.R. Bull of that on Northfleet.

The publication has been made possible by:
1) a generous gift from Mr and Mrs William Worth and Philip Worth of Essex in memory of their aunt, Frances Caroline Tunbridge, a member of an old Gravesend family, who had lived in Gravesend all her life, latterly at 92 Parrock Street. Her grandfather, Edward Tunbridge, was a baker and confectioner at 41 High Street from 1868 until his death in 1888. In his *'Gravesend through the* eyes *of a Nonagenarian'*, William Smoker, who lived from 1881 to 1894, at 49 High Street, the shop in which Robert Pocock, Gravesend's first historian set up his printing press and who picked grapes from the vine planted by Robert Pocock, recalls their taking their Saturday joint with Yorkshire pudding below and potatoes around in a dish covered by a cloth to Tunbridge's baker shop to be cooked in a cooling brick oven for two hours for their hot dinner for which they paid two old pence.

Edward's widow, Fanny Tunbridge, carried on the Tunbridge's business until 1911 when it was taken over by their son Thomas Frederick Tunbridge (father of Frances Caroline Tunbridge) until 1934 when he retired. He died five years later.
2) a generous loan from the Gravesham Borough Council of £5000 and the Society are indebted to Mr L.Beven M.I.L.A.M., Leisure Service Manager, for his help in negotiating this.

A further note is necessary in reference to the origin of Gravesend and Milton next Gravesend. According to Dr Alan Everitt's *'Continuity and Colonization: the Evolution of Kentish Settlement'* (Leicester University Press, 1986), Northfleet was the large Minster

Parish between Hoo and Dartford still comprising 3934.111 acres according to the 1863 Ordnance Survey at which time Gravesend comprised 564.049 acres and Milton 692.049 acres. Denton (437.956 acres) may also have come from Northfleet via Milton which at one time bordered them all to the south. It is interesting to note as evidence of this that Denton glebe land comprised an area of land to the south of Old Road East near Devonshire Road in Milton Parish. Milton Parish had only a tiny piece of glebe of its own. Chalk (1970.986 acres) probably came from Shorne (according to Dr Everitt, a sub-minster parish). The Parish of Ifield (312.940) acres is intermingled with Northfleet, the tract of Singlewell village to the south of old Watling Street (now Hever Court Road) and to the west of Church Road being in Northfleet, with a detached part of Ifield being to the west of Singlewell Road and the north of Watling Street. The Ifield Manor House of Hever Court lay to the north of Watling Street opposite Orchard Farm, itself in Northfleet. Ifield Court, however, was also in Northfleet Parish with the road between its entrance drive and Ifield Church and the triangular green in front of the church also in Northfleet. Ifield, however, had a short stretch of Watling Street leading to its detached portion, with Northfleet Parish on either side.

The Parish churches of Gravesend and Denton were both near their western boundaries that is, in the direction of Northfleet, and dedicated to St. Mary, an early dedication. Milton Church, dedicated to SS. Peter and Paul, was nearer its eastern boundary but adjoining an ancient site, namely the mill.

The origin of the town was undoubtedly the river traffic, growing as the first place up the Thames where there was firm land and chalk cliffs near the tideway. Prior to the building of the sea walls the marshes beneath the town would have been saltings, under water at high tides. The town straddled the boundary between the Parishes of Gravesend and Milton (the boundary is now High Street, Windmill Street and Singlewell Road) and it was here that the settlement grew up. Both parishes at the time of the Domesday Book had hythes or landing places and it has been suggested that Milton's hythe, below the present Town Pier, was the landing place for the Long Ferry to Billingsgate, London and that Gravesend's hythe, probably on the site of the later Three Crowns Causeway, was that of the Short Ferry to a point near the later World's End, Tilbury, from whence there was a causeway across the marshes into Essex.

Many people are interested in place names. Lambard, the Kent County Historian who was a scholar of the Anglo-Saxon language, derives Gravesend from Portgereve (ruler of the town) (possibly London) and the end of his jurisdiction (see Lambard, 1826 edition, p.435). Judith Glover ('*The Place Names of Kent*' 1976, p.83) derives Gravesend from the end of a grove of trees possibly at the end of a park. It has **nothing** to do with the Great Plague of 1665, although there are a number of entries relating to this in the local registers, or the notion that it was the last place down river where you were buried in a grave if you died on board ship; below the town you were buried at sea.

This is not a history of Gravesend but merely a perambulation round the built-up areas of the old parishes of Gravesend, Milton next Gravesend, Denton, Chalk, Ifield and Northfleet, describing the history of the roads and buildings and what, if anything, was there before them. For this reason we have decided to use the title '*A Historical Walk through Gravesend and Northfleet*' and the sub-title '*A Historical Perambulation of Gravesend and Northfleet*' which was Benson's original proposed title. There is ample room for a new full scale history of the town if funds and time should ever permit. Robert Peirce Cruden's '*History of the Town of Gravesend and the Port of London*', 1843, is still the only comprehensive history of the town but, of course, long out-of-date and does not cover the very interesting nineteenth and twentieth century development since 1843, for which the only sources are J.A. Mansfield's '*History of Gravesend*', 1922, reprinted by Rochester Press, 1981; A.J. Phillip's '*A History of Gravesend and Its Surroundings*', 1954, many of the ideas in which are now out-of-date, and Sydney Harker's '*The Book of Gravesham*', 1979.

I must thank Mrs Sandra Soder for all her help in producing this new edition and preparing the same for the printers.

Robert H. Hiscock
Hon. Member Gravesend Historical Society

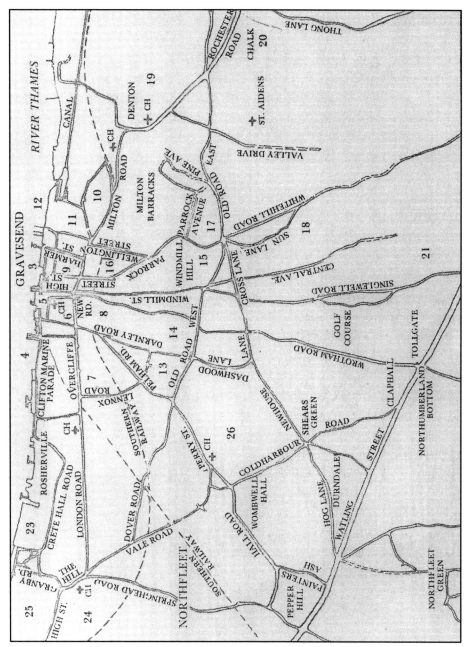

The numbers on the above map are a guide to chapter numbers

3

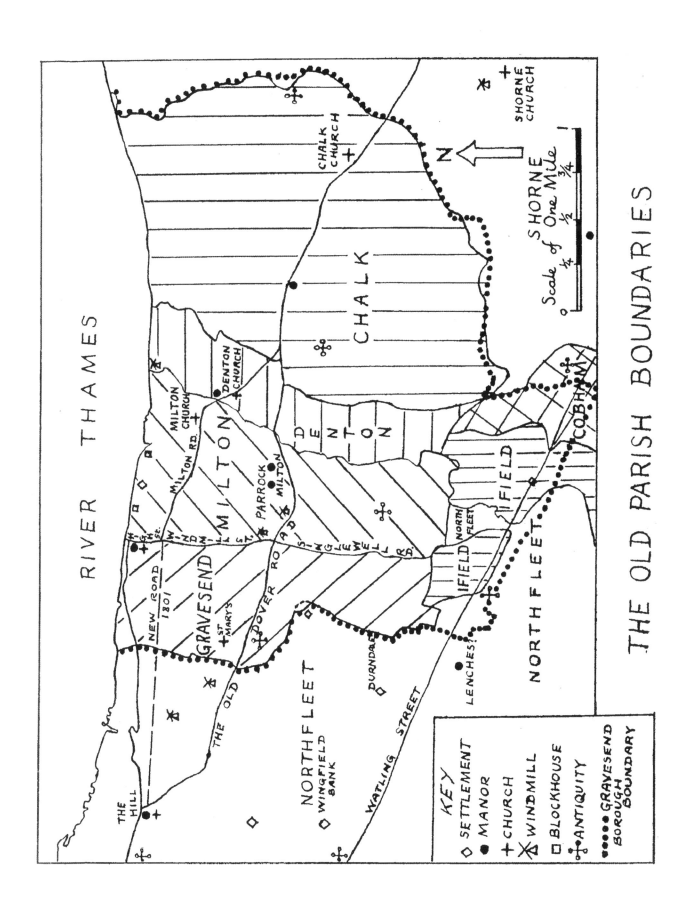

THE OLD PARISH BOUNDARIES

RIVER THAMES

CHALK

SHORNE CHURCH

CHALK CHURCH

DENTON CHURCH

MILTON CHURCH

DENTON

MILTON

MILTON RD.

PARROCK

MILTON

SWANGEWELL RD.

GRAVESEND

NEW ROAD 1801

DOVER ROAD

THE OLD

COBHAM

IFIELD

NORTH FLEET

IFIELD

NORTHFLEET

ST. MARY'S

THE HILL

WINGFIELD BANK

NORTHFLEET

DURNDALE

WATLING STREET

LENCHES?

Scale of One Mile
0   ¼   ½   ¾   1

KEY
◇ SETTLEMENT
● MANOR
✝ CHURCH
✳ WINDMILL
▢ BLOCKHOUSE
⚑ ANTIQUITY
●●●● GRAVESEND BOROUGH BOUNDARY

PART ONE

Chapter 1

SURVEYING THE GROUND

THOSE UNFAMILIAR with the town of Gravesend, its situation and the contour of the district may not readily appreciate the reason for the choice of the summit of Windmill Hill as the starting point of this perambulation of the town. The Hill has little discoverable history earlier than the 16th century, and that very meagre, but its height above the surrounding country provides a vantage ground from which to view the district as a whole before visiting at closer quarters the buildings and streets possessing historical associations. When this survey was first contemplated around 1952 the view to the north from the Hill presented a homogeneity which the last 50 years have destroyed. Then, most of the roofs were grey Welsh slate covering houses built between 1830 and 1860 in a fairly regular pattern of through roads with houses of three or four storeys, usually with basements, and smaller houses in between. The clearance of the area between Windmill Street and Parrock Street and the erection of large blocks of flats with the multi-storey car park and municipal buildings completely altered the view, and the enormous chimneys of the power stations and cement works have provided a new dominant feature in the landscape, although the Northfleet Power Station and two of these chimneys have gone since 1976.

Looking northwards one is conscious of the important part played by the River Thames in England's history. With the closure of the London docks, the traffic on the river has diminished, but the presence of shipping and container ships in Gravesend Reach still provides a reminder of the link which has so long existed between the Thames and the continent of Europe, as well as the remotest seaports of the world. There can have been fewer grander maritime sights than to witness from the summit of the Hill in the mid-years of the 19th century the stately towers of square sail of the numerous clippers making their way up the river with cargoes of tea, grain, wood, or spice, having been blown across the oceans of the world: a scene now occasionally enacted when the tall ships come up to the Pool of London.

The flat Essex shore, rising a mile or so back to a ridge upon which modern dwellings and blocks of flats have been built, provides a background for the scene: slightly more to the left, Tilbury docks (opened in 1886 and since enlarged and now a container port) remind us of the many processes entailed in a maritime nation's economy. The liners with their regular sailings for mail and passengers to Australia and elsewhere have now gone. Only cruise ships and pleasure liners now use the landing stage at Tilbury. The docks were opened in 1886 and the Orient Pacific transferred their sailings to Australia here from Liverpool on 15 January, 1887, their first liner, then the biggest to come up the Thames, being the R.M.S. *Ormuz* (6387 tons). The last was the *Himalaya* (28000 tons), the line moving to Southampton on 10 September 1969.

On the Essex shore can be seen 'The World's End' with what was formerly the causeway for the cross ferry in front and to the right of Tilbury Fort with its Carolean Water Gate built in 1682. The first defences here were provided during the reign of Henry VIII when a blockhouse was erected by the side of the river. The present bastioned fort (which is in the care of the Department of the Environment) was built between 1670 and 1683, according to a design by Sir Bernard de Gomme. To the east stands the Tilbury power station, built in the 1950s and considerably extended thereafter.

It will not be amiss at such a point in our thoughts to conjecture why Gravesend came to be the outer port of the firmly established city of London. Was it not that, in very early days, when the river, unembanked, spread at high tide over the marshes east and west of Gravesend, the chalk spur reaching out to the tideway itself provided the first hard landing-ground upon which incoming sailor men could find firm foothold? In addition to this, the landing-place was exactly a tide away from London, so that whether the wind were fair or foul quick passage and a safe anchorage were available, with shelter under the lee of the Kent and Essex shores. The hythe which existed at the foot of the present High Street in the 11th century was even at that date a landing-place with a few centuries' history behind it. Travellers to the New World in Tudor and later times frequently spent their last night in England at Gravesend at one of the local inns, such as the *Christopher*. The great East India company, founded in the 16th century, provisioned their ships at Gravesend, and had their own camp for their soldiers and sailors and their own hospitals here.

If one turns towards the south, one sees today a large built-up area, much of it roofed with clay tiles, although some mostly older houses with slate, spreading into the countryside, where 90 years ago one looked upon wheat fields, orchards and arable lands devoted to market garden produce. Until the last quarter of the 19th century, Windmill Hill lay to the south of the town, and Singlewell and Chalk were isolated villages.

The Hill rises to about 169 feet above high tide level and consists of an outlier or capping of Thanet Sands in the middle of surrounding chalk six hundred or so feet deep. It owes its present name to the windmills built upon its summit at various times from the 14th century onwards. It was previously known as Ruggen, Rogge, Rounden or Rouge Hill. Until the end of the 18th century it was rough, untilled ground, and the earlier name may have been a spelling of 'rough'. Beacons giving warnings of the approach of invading forces were erected on the Hill in 1377 and again in 1588, and one was standing there in readiness for use in 1719, according to Dr Harris's *History of Kent.* A new beacon was erected in 1988 in connection with the Armada anniversary celebrations.

Whether the Hill was used in Roman or Saxon times as a look-out is unknown. No evidence in the shape of pottery, coins or domestic articles has ever been found. The important Roman town of Vagniacae was some two miles away to the south-west at Springhead, although evidence of Roman occupation has been found near the riverside.

In the early 19th century, Windmill Hill became the playground of London residents, who spent summer holidays in Gravesend or made day trips by steamer, engaging in donkey-rides and the fun-fair activities of the period, mounting the old mill. This was erected in 1764, the previous one having been burnt down in 1763, when the sail became loose in a gale. There is a record of 'A new windmill by John Young, millwright and carpenter in 1373' The last millers, Alexander Deakin and John Fiveash, were moved to Perry Street. In the 19th century, a camera obscura was erected on top of the mill and it was used as a means whereby a better view might be had of still farther horizons. A gallery at the height of 20 feet above the ground provided a look-out for visitors. A proposal to erect a tower as a memorial to the Battle of Alma in 1855 did not proceed, although architects' plans were prepared. Refreshment houses, the *Tivoli,* the *Belle Vue* on top of the Hill, the *Miller's Cottage* and *The Windmill* in Shrubbery Road, and other licensed houses carried on a thriving trade. With the decay of Gravesend as a holiday resort, the mill became derelict and was finally pulled down in 1894. The last remnant of the town's heyday, the *Belle Vue,* (then closed) was destroyed by fire during the boisterous celebrations of Mafeking Night in 1900, the firemen's hoses being cut when they attempted to save it, The *Tivoli* hotel, to be noted when reaching Windmill Street, became an academy for Jewish youths and a synagogue in 1856, and remained in this use until the outbreak of war in 1914, when the school was removed elsewhere. Later, it has been employed as a social club and as an auctioneer's saleroom, and as a bingo club. It is now in 2005 being developed as domestic units.

The Hill was purchased in 1843 by the Corporation, and in 1889 the lower slopes were acquired also. This enabled the foot of the Hill to be terraced and turned into pleasure and sports grounds. They were opened by the Lord Mayor of London in May, 1902, by Sir Joseph Cockerdale Dinsdale Bart. who also opened the Promenade extension.The War Memorial was dedicated on 11 June 1922 and unveiled by Gen. Lord Horne, architect F.W. Doyle-Jones. This was damaged by enemy aircraft during the 1939-45 war, and re-erected afterwards. Here a service of remembrance is held each year on the Sunday nearest to 11 November. The small granite stones on the Hill mark the site of the first bombs dropped on the town from a German zeppelin, L.2.38, on 31 May 1915, when numbers 99 and 100 Windmill Street and houses in Brandon Street were also damaged.

As we turn west from the Windmill Gardens we shall pass the Veterans Club, erected and opened in 1954 as a social meeting-place and games centre for men above 60 years of age. It occupies the site of the Maze, later Ashenden's early nurseries. The thoroughfare in which it

Windmill Hill and King's Cottages, oil painting, Gravesend Library Collection.

View from Windmill Hill area, circa 1825

Gravesend, 1662, from an old engraving

is situated, Clarence Place, was known earlier as Lacey Terrace at the east end, from the name of the builder of many of its houses, Edward Lacey, who was mayor of Gravesend in 1850.

In this thoroughfare there was erected in 1873 Milton Congregational Church (architect John Sulmar of London). It was intended to have a south-west tower and was the outcome of a split in Princes Street Congregational church (see Chapter 6). It maintained a separate and useful ministry until 1955, and, after closing, was used as a warehouse. In 1968, it became a Sikh temple for the local Indian community, who had previously had a temple at 55 Edwin Street. A new temple costing nine million pounds is being built in Khalsa Avenue on the old Barracks site.

War Memorial, Windmill Gardens
Clarence Place

Chapter 2

WINDMILL STREET AND HIGH STREET

WINDMILL STREET is the dividing line (with Singlewell Road, its continuation southwards, and High Street northwards) between the ancient parishes of Gravesend and Milton (which, with the addition of Denton and Chalk and parts of Ifield, Cobham and Northfleet in 1935) made up the municipal borough of Gravesend as it existed until 1974. The majority of the houses in this street to the north of Clarence Place date back to the 1830s and 1840s. On the west side, where Wingfield Road is, and extending to Darnley Road, is the site of a vast market garden in the 19th century known as Clark's, extending 200 yards north and south, and here was grown the Gravesend asparagus which was greatly sought after by West End gourmets in the late 18th century. As we turn right we see two large semi-detached houses on the west side, 'North House' and 'South House'. At one time they had iron fencing, the gate standards of which were decorated with the town arms. These were originally part of the railings in front of the town pier (see Chapter 3). Next to them is Sheppey Place, which formerly led to Baynard Castle, a castellated Gothic house, once called Lacey Castle, built in the early 19th century by Edward Lacey, a former mayor, used later as the junior school for Milton Mount College. At one time Mrs. Gutteridge and later the Misses Shrewsbury ran a girl's school here. It was demolished in 1952 and the site is now part of Wrotham Road Schools.

Just below Sheppey Place, in which the houses were built by William Wood, the builder, for his workmen, including two for foremen, is 'Lodgewood' formerly 'Mariner's Cottage', 111 Windmill Street. Here lived William Mariner, brought up as a Tongan Chief's son. He was later a London stockbroker and drowned in the river (see Philip's history p.154). Later Dr. Robbs lived here as did Alex. J. Philip.

On the northern corner of Clarence Row was at one time the high-class boarding school known as Clarence House or Gutteridge's, where many lads of the district and beyond received an education for business and academic careers. Before becoming a school it was the *Clarence Hotel* (1832-1855), giving its name to the houses in Clarence Row. The school later moved to Wrotham Lodge, Wrotham Road and then Glen View. It was demolished circa 1906 when maisonettes were built on the Windmill Street frontage and a row of small houses on the playground.

The Old People's Day Centre was opened on a site opposite in Clarence Row in 1973, the houses on this side having been cleared circa 1965. They included a pair of rather attractive stucco cottages with small bow windows.

A store on the corner of South Street on the right demands attention as a former place of leisure and entertainment built in 1835 at Tulley's Bazaar. Here holidaymakers were welcome at all times of the day to listen to orchestral music free of charge, and to purchase, if so inclined, mementos of their visit, or presents for friends. Round the sides were illuminated views of Italy and Switzerland, seen through a porthole: refreshment could be obtained in the form of coffee and chocolate. In the evenings, concerts were given at prices ranging from about a shilling (10p) per person. Later, the building became the drill hall of the local Artillery Volunteers, with small cannon standing outside, and in 1890 a grocery and provision store known as Milton Hall Stores. There was once a date of 1859 after 'Milton Hall'. Tulley's had a similar bazaar in High Holborn. Their premises in Windmill Street was originally a wooden hall.

A few yards lower down is the Baptist church, erected in 1843, architect John Gould (junior). The builder was his father. Nearly opposite was the Gravesend fire station and police headquarters of the town, erected in 1940, demolished in 1973, and now rebuilt as the Police Station, opened on 30 June, 1975, by Sir John Hill, H.M. Chief Inspector of Constabulary, architect: D.F. Clayton, County Architect. Immediately to the south of this was the Kent County Council divisional offices, erected in 1965, now Cygnet House and part of the Borough Council Offices. To the north lies the new Civic Centre and Woodville Halls, opened by the Duchess of Kent in 1968. The architect was H.T. Cadbury-Brown. The site was formerly occupied by private houses, on one of which was the date 1837, and a little further up a date of 1849. In 1924, a charity erected a crèche for mothers and young children in the back garden of one of the houses in Woodville Terrace, and was the forerunner of the present child clinics.

Opposite the Civic Centre is Lord Street, named after its original builder, Mr Lord and now widened to form part of the east-west ring-road. The multi-storey car park was opened by the then Mayor, Councillor Dan McMillan in November 1972, the first in the town.

The *Queen's Arms,* erected in 1836 and demolished in 1963, stood at the junction of Windmill Street and Wrotham Road.

A very pleasantly laid-out public garden on a 'flat-iron' site, known as Woodville Gardens, was formerly a burial ground of the town, and a few of the old tombstones are still to be seen against the north wall. This piece of ground was acquired in 1788 by the Vestry and churchwardens of Gravesend to supplement the old graveyard of St. George's church. When the burial ground was first used it stood on the outskirts of the town. It was closed for burials on 1 January 1855 and laid out for gardens. Where now Windmill Street and Wrotham Road are joined, there once stood the 'pound': in 1864 it was the site for the election hustings.

The open space known as Railway Place was occupied before the coming of the South Eastern Railway in 1849, by wooden cottages and here, too, the donkeys which provided rides on Windmill Hill and the goat-drawn chaises for children were stabled. Manor Road, on the east side of the street, is stated to have been so called from the existence there of an office where manorial quit-rents were paid but the evidence of this is very meagre. Pocock informs us that the Court Baron for the Manor of Gravesend was opened (and then adjourned) in a piece of ground called the Pound Field, which was opposite the end of Manor Road. This may have been the site of the 'pound' mentioned above at one time. This field and Manor Road were both in the parish of Milton, although apparently part of the Manor of Gravesend. On a map of the early 19th century Manor Road is marked as 'The Land Way', the ground at its eastern end being then all open fields.

At the turn of the 19th century many of the shops on the east side of Windmill Street were private houses with gardens in front and, except for a cobbler's adjoining the bridge, there were no shops to the south of the railway until about 1925. Those on the western side have a longer history, and it is interesting to note that, in the 18th century, the street was known as Upper High Street. The building now occupied by the Halifax Building Society may have been a farm house but now rebuilt. Opposite was the Plaza Cinema, the first purpose-built cinema in Gravesend, opened in 1911 as 'The Cinema'. It is now a carpet shop with hairdresser at the rear.

Just before reaching the crossroad the public library deserves attention. Built of Ancaster stone and red brick, it was opened on 28 September 1905 by the mayor, G.M. Arnold. The cost of the building was obtained from a grant by the Scottish-American millionaire, Andrew Carnegie. The site was donated by subscriptions of £50 from each of ten local residents. The architect was E.J. Bennett. In addition to its ordinary function of lending books, providing computers and newspapers in the public reading room, its reference library possesses a wealth of reference books and material on local history.

Here and around the corner into King Street there stood until 1896 St. Thomas's almshouses, the successors of other gift houses bequeathed in 1624 by Henry Pinnock, Portreve of Gravesend in 1597, 1607 and 1613, for the benefit of the poor of Gravesend and Milton. Pinnock provided 'one and twenty dwelling houses and for a woman to employ the poor'.

The almshouses which the present buildings superseded were built in 1834 of red brick with stone set dressings on a plateau walled with brick and with a stretch of grass before. They replaced a group of weatherboard almshouses which appear in the earliest prints of King Street. When the Trustees disposed of the site the proceeds were used to build the first almshouses at the junction of Old Road and Upper Wrotham Road (see Chapter 14).

Hereabouts, where the streets cross, there was in earlier centuries what was known as St. Thomas's Waterings, where pilgrims to the shrine of St.Thomas à Becket stopped for rest and refreshment and to water their horses. This has caused the name of St. Thomas to be given to the almshouses. King Street, the road on the right, was known as late as the 18th century as St. Thomas's Street. In the 16th century it was known as Holy Water Street, as a house here, known as 'Holy Water' belonged to William Sidley or Sedley, who sold it to Henry Pinnock in 1624. Until 1801, when New Road was cut to provide a direct road to Northfleet, there was no break in the line of shops and houses on the western side from what is now Windmill Street to High Street.

The earliest mention of High Street, which we now enter, is of the year 1334, when property with houses thereon was conveyed to John Page the younger and Helen his wife, of Gravesend. This was in the parish of Milton and was stated to be 'abutting upon High Street towards the west'. The High Street of that time was not a continuous line of houses as we see it to-day. Between what is now the site of the old Town Hall and the river there appears, according to a document of 1456, to have been only two houses on the Milton side of the street, until the riverside was reached, with one or two tenements on the Town Quay. It is probable that a channel ran down the middle of the street and that down its course went the unwanted domestic rubbish, washed by rains or periodical swillings with well water. The Town's Second Charter of Incorporation, dated 1568, required every inhabitant 'to weekly cleanse before his door for the avoidance of evil odours' under a penalty of three shillings and fourpence.

Between the *Kent* public house and the junction with Royal Pier Road was a parcel of land belonging to the Abbot of the monastery of St. Mary Le Graces, Tower Hill, London. This was also part of the old manor of Parrock. The piece between the *Kent* and Bank Street was in the early part of the 15th century the site of Dame Anne's Hall. The other piece between Bank Street and Joe Coral's turf accountants, was called Beelings or Baldwin's Acre, and the rest of the land on the north was called Stonehawe or Stonehall.

William Bourne (c.1535-1581), innkeeper, mathematician, gunner and mercer, well-known for his writings on ordnance, inventions and navigation, owned messuages, tenements and gardens on the east side of the High Street.

By the late 18th century the street must have begun to assume something of the appearance it still had in the late 19th century, as Pocock, Gravesend's first historian (to whom reference will be made later), writes: 'almost every tradesman had a sign and in the night when the wind blew strong, a concert of squeaking music filled your ears with sounds not the most pleasant'. The demolition in 1928 of the *New Prince of Orange* (built in 1805 when the New Road was cut) which occupied the site of Burton's, the tailors, and of Bryant and Rackstraws, at one time the leading drapery and haberdashery store in the town, on the opposite corner (now Woolworths) in 1957 has completely altered the appearance of this corner. High Street has doubled in width. It was previously eight feet wide.

In 1963, the shoe shop at 43 High Street was demolished, and the late E.W. Tilley of the Gravesend Historical Society excavated the site from which it was apparent that a shoe shop had existed on the site for 150 years. From the contents of various rubbish pits, however, there was evidence that the site had been occupied continuously since the 13th century with slight slackening off in the 14th and 15th centuries, with extensive occupation beginning again in the 17th century.

Robert Pocock (1760-1830) was born and lived in High Street for many years and on the front of the house on the west side, where he carried on his trade of printer, and from which his *History of Gravesend and Milton* was published in 1797, a blue-enamelled iron tablet was affixed in 1888 by G.M. Arnold, mayor of Gravesend in 1890-92, 1896-7 and 1904-6. This records the fact that it was here that Pocock set up the first printing press in the town in 1786. Here, too, in Pocock's youth, John Wesley visited his friend the Rev. John Dolman, Vicar of Chalk, who had apartments with Mrs Pocock (Pocock's mother), spending the night here with his friend.

Robert Pocock was a man of wide interests, one of which was botany: he also badgered sailors to bring him natural history specimens from foreign lands. Ill-fortune overtook him towards the end of his life, his property being sold to defray his debts; later historians owe a great deal to his enthusiasm for recording historical events.

Passing Jury Street, the narrow opening on the left, it may be observed that until this was cut in 1846-7 there was no outlet from High Street other than pedestrian footways. A fire which occurred in the earlier year, and which destroyed much property in the street, provided the opportunity to cut through into Princes Street, and the name of the street commemorates the fact that a jury sat to assess the amount of damage and the cost of the change made.

Top picture: Windmill Street circa 1910.

Bottom picture: *Queen's Arms* public House, 1963.

Top picture: The *New Prince of Orange*, corner of High Street and New Road.

Middle picture: Bryant and Rackstraw, corner of High Street and King Street, circa 1951.

Bottom picture: High Street looking from just north of Bank Street, on the left of the picture, circa 1905.

To the north of Jury Street was *The Catherine Wheel,* which bore on its front the year of its erection, 1686. Half of this building remains and is now 56 High Street. The date stone is now in the local museum. The right-hand pilaster of the former entablature can still be seen above the shop front.

The old Town Hall stands in the parish of Milton, with the market at its rear. It was erected in 1764, C. Sloane, who designed St. George's church, being its architect. In 1836, the old front was removed and the present one substituted by Amon Henry Wilds (William Wood was the builder). Three large figures adorned the pediment until 1939, when they were removed, being thought unsafe in the event of air raids: these represented Minerva, Truth and Justice. This building was used as the Town Hall until 1968, when the present Civic Centre was opened. It later housed the Magistrates Courts, closed in 2002. The old Council Chamber was used as the No.1. Court. It contained the portraits of former members of the council and town clerks. Until 1940 the police station was underneath, on the north side. These rooms now house the local museum and collections belonging to the library and the Gravesend Historical Society. The No.2. Court was part of the original building. The Coat of Arms came from St. George's Church. Gravesend had a separate Commission of the Peace from 1848 and its own Quarter Sessional Recorder until 1974. The mayor, immediate past mayor and senior aldermen were ex officio JPs under the charter of 1632 and held petty sessions for the Borough prior to 1848.

Gravesend's first Town Hall was built in 1573, five years after the Borough received its second Charter of Incorporation. The First Charter was granted by Queen Elizabeth in 1562 and the second (which required one Portreve instead of two) in 1568. This Charter required that the Portreve, Jurats and Inhabitants meet in some convenient place to transact municipal business. The lease of the ground upon which the Town Hall now stands was then held on a 2000 year lease of the Manor of Parrock by William Child of Northfleet: the new Corporation acquired an under-lease, and the Town Hall was built.

The Common Market which the Charter required the Corporation to hold once a week was established between the new building and what is now known as Queen Street. At first an open space, in 1818 it was converted into two covered ways with stone columns supporting the roof, but with an uncovered centre area. The architect for this work was Charles Fowler, who was also responsible for Covent Garden and Hungerford Markets. The fish market was added on the site of the Shambles in 1829. This remained until the present market hall was built in 1897, when the columns were removed to the grounds of Milton Hall (see Chapter 17). The architect for the covered market was Edward J. Bennett and the builders Multon and Wallis. It was opened by the mayor, John Russell. on 18 December, 1898.

Before the new frontage was added to the Town Hall in 1836, and indeed from the first Town Hall's erection, space was provided for a 'cage' for the incarceration of prisoners, and stocks were set up here. The parish of Milton, in which the cage stood, had to provide fresh straw for it periodically, and keep it clean. This cage was on the north side of the Town Hall forecourt.

This place in our guide seems the most suitable to mention the first arms of the town, which, on the obtaining of the Second Charter was a device of a boat with one mast, its sail furled, rowed by five hooded rowers and steered by a porcupine. (A replica in metal can be seen on the south gate of Milton church.) The porcupine is held to be a compliment to Sir Henry Sydney, Steward of the Honour of Otford, in whose stewardship Gravesend and Milton were, and whose arms embodied a porcupine: the rowers denoted Gravesend's association with the waterside. When the town was granted its Third Charter in 1632, the Duke of Lennox was prominent in securing the charter, and the city fathers substituted the Duke's arms for the earlier one, viz: a castle with a buffalo's head in its centre, and the Latin words 'Decus et Tutamen', which are held to mean 'My Glory and Strength'. The Borough of Gravesham was created by statute in 1974 and a new Coat of Arms was granted by the College of Heralds on 15 July 1975.

Lower down the street on the east side is Bank Street, cut through in 1850 following another extensive fire, and so named from the bank that stood on its southern corner. Two early (1824) private banks were Messrs Brenchley Becket and Ride and Messrs Miller Twiss and Co. In 1823, Gravesend Vestry sustained a loss of £68 2s. 11d on the failure of Messrs Hills and Sons

Bank. The first branch of a joint stock bank was opened in Gravesend in 1837 at 17 High Street by the Surrey, Kent and Sussex Banking Company, later the London and County, and now the National Westminster. After the fire of 1850 the bank was rebuilt at 16 High Street. In 1864, they moved to new premises at 24 High Street, next to the old Town Hall and formerly the *Freemason's Arms,* and in 1901 the present branch in King Street was opened. The architect was A. Williams and Messrs Creaton and Co. were the builders, the work commencing in 1898 on the site of the old almshouses. Barclays Bank followed the London and County at 24 High Street, moving to King Street about 1930. The Bank moved to the New Road in 1987 when the King Street building was taken over by the Woolwich Building Society. The Gravesend Steam Carriage Works was established in Bank Street in 1838.

In the early 17th century the *Ship* inn stood just below the present Bank Street where, on his second visit to England in 1614, King Christian of Denmark dined with his nephew, the short-lived Prince Henry, son of James I, when they were passing through Gravesend to review the fleet in Chatham Dockyard. Pepys dined here on Sunday, 16 September 1668.

Farther down on the right there stood until the early years of the 20th century the *Bull* Hotel (No.6) (1445-1939), itself a successor of a licensed house where lived Henry Pinnock, whose will provided the almshouses mentioned above. In his will he speaks of 'My mansion house called the Bull in Milton' and, leaving it to Thomas Lord, requires that he should 'pay to our Sovereign Lord the King £3 every year for the wine licence out of the rent'. The *Bull* is also mentioned in a document of 1445.

Before leaving High Street, reference must be made of the Great Fire of 1727 which consumed the whole of the lower part of the street, much of West Street, and part of East Street opposite. It had its origin in a farm building just south of St. George's churchyard, near to Princes Street, where Wakefield Street later stood. On the early morning of 24 August of that year a doctor named Mann, who resided in High Street nearly opposite the Town Hall, was returning from a call and noticed a small fire which he said 'could have been covered by a hat'. He stabled his horse and when he returned the fire, fanned by a strong south-west wind, was beyond control. Inhabitants, roused from sleep, fought the flames, aided by soldiery, but they gained so rapidly that not only the streets mentioned above suffered destruction, but also the parish church. Dwelling-houses and shops to the number of 120 were laid in ruins, and the loss in money value was variously set between £120,000 and £200,000.

When rebuilding was carried out the shops and houses in the streets were again built mainly of timber and some of these fell a ready prey to other conflagrations in 1731, 1748, 1799, 1846, 1850 and 1857. There are still a small group of houses on the east side of the street, Nos. 77-83, which are the last of those built in the 1730s after the fire of 1727, although one of these has been damaged in a recent fire.

A scheme for widening West Street and East Street, carried out in 1958, has necessitated the demolition, among others, of the corner shop, whose predecessor on the site *The Chequer* (1570-1739) was bequeathed by David Varchell in 1703 to provide the annual gift of money and bread to the poor which used to be distributed in St. George's Church on the Sunday before Christmas, when the rector preached a charity sermon.

High Street, Windmill Street, Stone Street, Princes Street, Bath Street and West Street became 'one-way streets' in 1933, the first such scheme in the town, now replaced in part by the northern internal ring road.

Crowhurst & Willis shop, 9 High Street.

Gravesend Borough Police Force, pictured prior to the alterations to the Town Hall and the building of the new covered market hall in 1897/98. The shops that can be seen through the archway are in the High Street.

Top picture: A tilt boat.

Middle picture: Gravesend
Landing Place 1810

Bottom picture: The steam
ferry boat *Edith*
at the Town Pier

18

Chapter 3

THE TOWN PIER

IN MOST TOWNS there is an area where history is more closely packed than anywhere else, and Gravesend is no exception. Most often it is the market-place that can claim this distinction, but it is around the Town Pier square in this waterside town that the events of the centuries are most clearly seen. If it were possible to bring upon the square, as upon a stage, with their attendant circumstances, all the important historical characters known to have embarked at this spot, what a varied and colourful assemblage it would be!

How many of the 'noble lordes, Knyghtes, squyers and oother about the noombre of cccc (400)' who accompanied the Count de la Roche in 1467 when he came from Burgundy to joust with the Queen's brother, landed at Gravesend is unknown, but the 'rich-apparailde' ships that lay off the town must have provided a delightful sight for its citizens.

Of those known to have been ashore with a great retinue, Cardinal Wolsey, who had met the Emperor Charles V of Spain at Dover with a train of earls, knights, bishops, abbots and chaplains, with 100 gentlemen and 700 yeomen, came to Gravesend, where they embarked for Greenwich in 30 barges in 1522. Henry VIII, Wolsey's royal master, also landed in Gravesend from Erith in 1544 and, having dined here, rode to Faversham for an expedition in France that he afterwards abandoned.

Sebastian Cabot 'banketted' with others at the *Christopher* inn (where the *Pier* hotel now stands) in 1556; maybe also Martin Frobisher, who had a Gravesend man, James Bere, as his navigator on his second and third voyages in search of a north-west passage to China, and who with his crew 'received the Communion by the minister of Gravesend' aboard the *Ayde* in 1557. In May 1553, the first expedition of the Muscovy Company sailed from Gravesend under the command of Richard Chancellor, who was well received by Ivan the Terrible.

Later royal personages included King Christian of Denmark, brother of James I's queen, ships of whose fleets lay off Gravesend in 1606 while he was on a royal visit which he repeated in 1614. On that occasion he was accompanied by Prince Henry, James's short-lived son; James II, who as Duke of York occupied a house where now is the western part of the *Clarendon* hotel, and who, in flight in 1688, landed and passed through the town; Charles I, both as prince and king, first incognito on a prospective matrimonial venture in Spain, and later with his bride, Queen Henrietta, in 1625; the Count Palatine of the Rhine, who landed at Gravesend in 1612, to espouse the Princess Elizabeth, daughter of James I (the Winter King and Queen of Bohemia), whose grandson was George I; and the Prince of Orange who, after his marriage to Princess Anne, daughter of George II, stayed in Gravesend, weather-bound, for three days in 1734. The last monarch to land at the Town Pier was H.M. Queen Elizabeth II, in February 1953, when she visited the area affected by the flood of that year.

To these royal persons may be added Lady Deborah Moody (nee Dunch) who sailed from Gravesend for New Amsterdam (now New York) in 1643, where Dutch Director General Willer Kieft granted her a charter to found a new town called Gravesend, which included Coney Island and which she laid out on the first grid plan; Andrew Marvell the poet, accompanying Lord Carlisle on a diplomatic mission to Muscovy, in 1663; Pepys and John Evelyn in 1667; Hogarth, the painter, in 1732; and John Wesley, in 1734. A tablet formerly upon the Town Pier recorded the landing there in 1873 of August Strindberg, the Scandinavian playwright. The tablet is now in the local museum.

The beginnings of this part of the Thames shore as a landing-place lie beyond the reach of records. The first reference is to be found in Domesday Book, that monumental inventory compiled under the authority of William the Conqueror, the date of which is given approximately as 1086-1089. Here is to be found:

> Herbert, son of Ivo, holds Gravesham of the Bishop....[the 'Bishop' was the
> Bishop Odo of Bayeux, half brother of William the Conqueror, who had been
> disgraced and under arrest since 1082, but was still credited with his manors]
> there is one church and one hythe...

and

> Ralph, son of Thorold, holds of the Bishop, in the hundred of Toltingtrow,
> Meletune (Milton) ...There is a church and 1 mill of 49 pence, and a hythe
> of 20 shillings, and 3 servants...

As will have been realised, the Town Pier stands at the junction of the two parishes of Gravesend and Milton, and it has been thought by some that, there being no value set upon the Gravesend hythe in Domesday, Milton bore the assessment of what was a common hythe of the two parishes. There may, however, have been a hythe in Gravesend parish, possibly the old landing place for the Cross Ferry at the Three Crowns Causeway. This adjoins the present ferry landing place. The causeway beneath the old Town Pier may have been Milton's hythe.

What were the duties of the servants (the word used in Domesday is 'servi') can only be conjectured. That there was at that time a cross-river service to meet needs of the period can be taken as certain, and in all probability communication with London by river, later to be known as the 'Long Ferry' was already on a regularised footing. That a payment had to be made to the possessor of the manorial rights suggests that this was obtainable from the traffic charges made and the revenue earned by the transport service. From the amount set down as the value of the hythe - 20 shillings - some larger revenue than that arising from mere cross-river traffic may be assumed, and the Long Ferry would be likely to provide the bulk of the sum required.

Mention of the Long Ferry compels a brief treatment of the privileges which were conferred upon Gravesend watermen to whom were granted the sole right of conveying passengers by water between Gravesend and London. A royal grant of 1401 to this did not so much originate the privilege as confirm one that was already existent.

> We are informed that from time whereof the memory of man is not to
> the contrary, the Men of Gravesend ... have been accustomed,
> and were used, without any interruption, freely quietly and peacably
> to carry in their own vessels whatsoever persons coming to the town
> aforesaid, and willing to go thence by water to our city of London ...
> that they in their own vessels, may for ever freely ship such persons
> coming to the said town of Gravesend and willing to go thence to our
> said city of London by water, etc.

It is interesting that the rights under this Charter were granted to 'the men of the town', not the Lord of the Manor and seems to show that they had some sort of corporate existence long before the Charter of Elizabeth, as is also evidenced by the Petition relating to the building of the first St. George's Church or Chapel.

The Thames between the city of London and Gravesend was for centuries the highway taken by travellers proceeding farther into Kent, the roads out of London to the south-east being in bad condition and subjecting the traveller to robbery by highwaymen. Those intending to proceed farther into Kent before the coming of stage-coaches did so by hiring horses from hackneymen; these, having made their journeys, returned to Gravesend and delivered up their steeds, which were all distinctly branded as a proof of ownership. The profession of 'hacqueneyeman' appears in local church registers.

The earliest mention of the landing-place after that in Domesday is in 1286 when on 2 June a violent storm seriously damaged 'the causeway and landing place'; and in 1293 complaint was made to the Justice of the Assize of the dangerous condition of the 'bridge and chalk causeway leading to the water'. A decree was issued compelling the lord of the manor to repair the river moiety, and the men of Milton the land moiety. The term 'bridge and chalk causeway' suggests that the approach to the river was by a raised platform of timber and that the foundation was a built-up base of chalk, square blocks of which material were employed as 'footings' of later buildings in the vicinity.

It is to be noted also that the reference is made in the decree to the fact that, owing to the bad state of the bridge many 'both of our country and strangers are liable to suffer losses'.

From this may be gathered that trading vessels from other countries were even at that time accustomed to moor off the town, their seamen landing at the bridge.

At the same assize certain boatmen of Gravesend, Robert Gnoubal and Richard Dugil, were called to answer a charge that they had demanded double the fare allowed in the statute which was one halfpenny for conveying a passenger to London. They craved mercy and were placed under a bond of forty shillings. How serious a penalty this was Pocock points out by stating that a halfpenny in 1293 was the equivalent of a shilling in purchasing power 400 years later.

The upkeep of the landing place over the next 400 years probably devolved upon the holders of the manor of Gravesend and upon the inhabitants of the town, a manorial record in 1360 referring to '128 pieces of elm timber to make piles for the new wharf'. The term 'wharf' suggests a built-up structure rather than the bridge or causeway of a century before.

When the town's Third Charter was granted in 1632 an annual sum of £6 14s. 4d. was fixed as payable to the Duke of Lennox as lord of the manor for the better maintenance of 'Gravesend and Milton Bridge'. This sum was paid until 1677 when it fell into abeyance for 15 years, at the end of which time the Corporation of the Borough put before the representative of the possessor of the manor that a sum of £115 13s. 9d. had been expended upon repairs to the bridge, whereupon the further payment of 'pontage' as it was called was excused and the Corporation became sole owners.

Little more is forthcoming regarding the structure of the quay until, through the medium of Pocock's reporting, we learn that 'about 1765 the Town Stairs or Landing Place at the waterside were built of wood and often out of repair ... To remedy this evil the Corporation in 1767 erected a spacious wharf with a crane &c to land goods, and made a substantial stone bridge or causeway ... on this wharf are many sheds or shops which the Corporation let out mostly to gardeners, for the speedy supplying of ships'. In 1828, the Corporation built a new stone landing place (builder Mr McIntosh). It was opened by the Lord Mayor of London. Now that horses have all but disappeared from our streets, mention of the 'horse-wash' referred to in Corporation accounts, may require some explanation. It was the custom at the end of a day's work for draught horses to be ridden down into the river in the summer, where they refreshed themselves by splashing around: at the side of the quay a sloping descent was provided for this purpose. Another payment under date 7 January 1636 was made to porters of 'two shillings for ducking of Goodwife Campion', this being carried out by strapping the unfortunate misdemeanant into a 'ducking stoole' and immersing her in the river.

The Town Pier (which was closed in 1969 when the passenger ferry was transferred to West Street Pier and the car ferry discontinued) was built in 1834 (designed by Tierney Clark, engineer, builder William Wood, cost £8700) and opened by the Earl of Darnley. Its construction was vigorously opposed by watermen of the period whose living depended to a large extent upon landing passengers from the steam vessels plying between Gravesend and London, and damage was caused to the early work undertaken to prepare for the building of the pier. The first steamboat on the Long Ferry was the *Margery* built on the Clyde by Wm. Denny of Dumbarton, in 1815, and they soon replaced the tilt boats used on the ferry since the 17th century when they in turn replaced the traditional barge. Efforts in recent years to establish a boat service to London have all failed.

The pier was bought from the Corporation by the London, Tilbury and Southend Railway in 1885 and became their Gravesend station. It has now been restored by the Corporation. The pontoon was sold when it was closed in 1969 and for a few years the Pier was used as a restaurant.

The *Three Daws* on the east side of the Town Pier square is now the oldest public house in the town. Its many passages and stairs are said to have enabled sailors to escape the press gang and smugglers to ply their trade. By some miracle it escaped the many fires, in spite of its wooden construction. Its earlier name was the *Cornish Chough* (1488-1707), and later the *Three Cornish Choughs* (1707-1778). In 1582, the innkeeper was Ralph Wellett. It seems to have been associated with pilgrims crossing the river on their way to the shrine of St. Thomas, the three Cornish Choughs appearing in the arms of Canterbury City. A reference to it as the *Three Daws* appears in the Gravesend Register of 1667. Opposite, where now stands the *Pier* hotel, was the *Christopher,* referred to in the Close Roll of 10 March 1445. This public house or its successor was removed in 1828 when it was bought by the Corporation for £2300 and demolished and Town Pier Square was laid out. The *Pier* hotel was seriously damaged by the fire of 1846, when damage to the extent of £100,000 was done, and the Corporation at last established a proper fire brigade.

West Street on fire

Chapter 4

WEST STREET AND CLIFTON MARINE PARADE

WEST STREET has suffered from wholesale demolitions partly undertaken to widen the road to form the west-east route of the town's one-way system, and as a result of earlier slum clearance, the north side, between West Street and the river, being redeveloped in recent years and still continuing. There was a date stone '1887' on one of the shops near the Town Pier Square. It is now hard to picture the square as it was as late as 1900, when its many shops competed with those of High Street for the custom of 'carriage folk', whose pair-horse broughams with liveried coachmen and footmen were to be seen drawn up at the grocer, the butcher or the fishmonger, while the ladies from the large houses on. the outskirts of the town made choice of bacon cuts, joints or fish. In addition, on both sides of the street were shops with heaps of brown shrimps at twopence a pint, piled on clean white boards, the fruits of the labour of shrimpers, whose bawley-boats caught them and dispatched much of their catch to London shops and restaurants. Other shops specialised in herring, kippers and haddock smoked on the premises. Starbuck's, for 250 years, ships chandlers, slopssellers, wharfingers and barge masters, still remains, in new premises, on the old site.

One great drawback of the street was its narrowness, in places only a carriage-width, besides which, on its south side, were the packed courts and alleys, many of them with wooden or lath and plaster houses in which the working-class men lived. Cesspool drainage with shared w.c.s and water from stand-pipes made this a most unhealthy area, frequently subject to cholera outbreaks in the middle and early years of the 19th century. At the end of the 19th century and in the early 20th century the courts and alleys were regularly hosed down with disinfectant by the Council to keep disease at bay. A slum clearance scheme, strongly opposed by some of the inhabitants, was put into force in the 1920s and the area between West Street and Church Street completely cleared. Suttis Alley, St. John's Place, Pump Alley, Mermaid Court, Rawlinson's Place, Caroline Place Chapel Lane and Passenger's Court have all gone. It was in Chapel Lane that, Pocock informs us, stood 'the oldest building in Gravesend'. He did not, however, enlarge on this statement beyond giving an illustration of one of its door lintels. In 1948, however, a baker's shop (Jackson's) was demolished in West Street, and some 40ft of ragstone wall standing about 13ft high came to light parallel with Chapel Lane to the east and abutting to the south on the old Ragged School. Efforts by the local historical society to have this wall preserved were unsuccessful, but some photographs and a rough plan survive. There seems little doubt that this wall was the last remnant of the extensive manor house and chapel described in HM Stationery Office's *The History of the King's Works*. It was built by Edward III between 1362 and 1368, Bernard Cook being clerk of the works, at a cost of £1,350. Henry Yevele supplied materials. The old wall appeared to have some pieces of Reigate stone as well as rag, and there are references in the accounts to this stone as well as chalk and flint. There are also references to a hall, chapel, kitchen, great gate, little gate and park gate. In 1369-70 a new Wharf cost £39. In Buck's long view of the town (1738) there appears a small tower in this area which may well have been the remains of the 'great gate'. In 1376, Edward III transferred the manor to the Convent of St. Mary Graces, and they were authorised to use the materials from Gravesend for making a 'dormitory refectory cloister and other needfull buildings' for their convent, the 'East Minster', which stood on Tower Hill on the site lately occupied by The Mint. (For a detailed consideration of this building see my article in *Archaeologia Cantiana*, vol. CVII, 1980 p.193). In 1799, there was a theatre called the Playhouse in Chapel Lane.

West Street is probably nearly as old as High Street. It is mentioned as early as 1418 as 'West Street juxta Tamisam' and it may be that it was here that houses stood when in 1380 'certayn galeys of warre owt of France came to Gravvsende and brente a grate part of the towne'.

The river side of the street had until a few years ago the distinction of possessing more licensed houses in its 400 yards length than any other street in the town. Many of these were survivals from the time when large sailing vessels were moored off the town awaiting supplies, and intending passengers, officers and crews together with their friends required refreshment and lodging ashore before the final 'farewell'. Later, some of these catered for visitors during Gravesend's prosperous years as a holiday resort, and a reminder of these times could until 1972 be seen from the river in the derelict glass-fronted dining room of the *New Falcon* hotel, noted for its whitebait suppers and as the venue for mayoral banquets during the 19th century. It later became the New Falcon laundry, and was used for this purpose until about 1960. The last proprietor was a Mr Meggie, a character known locally as 'Mr. Pickwick'.

Midway along the north side is the landing stage for the cross ferry between Tilbury and Gravesend. Until 1965 this was the landing place for the car ferries. The last two boats were the *Mimie*, built in 1927, and the *Tessa*, in 1924. They were broken up in Belgium in 1965 when the car ferry ceased.The opening of the Dartford tunnel rendered them obsolete. They had for some time been inadequate to deal with the summer traffic, when long queues formed waiting to cross the river. Their predecessors were the *Edith*, built in 1911, and the *Gertrude* built in 1906. At this period they were usually known as the 'cattle boats', as large flocks of sheep used to cross the river from Essex to the Kent markets. The earliest steam ferry seems to have been a chain ferry, which started in 1824. This was followed by the *Earl of Essex*, *Earl of Leicester* and the first *Tilbury* owned by the London, Tilbury and Southend Railway, whose Act enabled them to run a ferry for railway passengers only. The present diesel passenger boats were introduced in 1960. Prior to that time the passenger service was operated by three steam boats, the *Rose*, built in 1901, the *Catherine*, in 1903, and the *Edith*, formerly used for cars and cattle. The *Rose* and the *Catherine* were the last passenger boats on the Board of Trade Register to be lit by oil lamps.

The beginnings of the cross ferry are difficult to determine. Pocock records (1797) that the Governor of Tilbury Fort 'claims the ferry from his premises to Gravesend on the same terms as the Corporation of Gravesend and Milton do theirs; and he built for the greater convenience of passengers a public house for his ferrymen to dwell on the spot'. This is the public house now known as *The World's End*. It may be assumed that led to a regular service between the *Three Crowns* landing stage (which was the Corporation ferry's landing place), as it came to be known, and the *World's End* causeway on the Tilbury side. By the early 19th century the Gravesend departure place was known as the Ferry House. The Corporation and Government ferries were usually let to the same ferryman, and both were purchased by the London, Tilbury and Southend Railway in 1886. The ferry was sold by British Rail in 1984 and is now owned by White Horse Ferries.

Where Bath Street on the left joins West Street, now a roundabout (now both part of the main traffic route), was a water gate or dock running into the land at this point. Cruden cites a deed of conveyance of 1567 whereby Robert Laiston, shipwright, acquires a property known as Spalding's Wharf in the west part of Gravesend (which abuts on the Thames to the north, on the water gate or dock on the east, on the Queen's Highway on the south, and on other property on the west). This would place the property just on the west side of Bath Street. Later, the dock and watercourse were covered in and known as Pipe Street.

At the foot of Bath Street was Metcalfe's wharf, where 100 years ago was Nettleingham's Steam Flour mills, burnt down in 1904. Later, when the property was taken over by Pattullo, Higgs and Co., it was the spot at which some thousands of tons of nitrates were landed, at a time when the use of nitrates for fertilising agricultural land was widespread. Farther westwards, Russell's Gravesend Brewery (one of four local breweries which have all disappeared) together with its wharf covered a large area. All of the area has been redeveloped for living accommodation. Some of the buildings still remain, the Maltings and proprietor's house having been converted to maisonettes. Trumans had their offices and bottling store and depot here from 1932 when they took over and closed Russells' Gravesend Brewery, which had carried on brewing here since 1858. Their symbol of a shrimp still remained in the brickwork until 2000 when the wall was demolished. The Shrimp brand symbol together with the 1926 tile have been restored to the wall of the flats on the northern side but in a higher position. They sold 'Shrimp Brand Beers'. A slipway on the right and Stuart Road on the left mark the end of West Street, and at this point Clifton Marine Parade is entered.

The viaduct overhead and the Pier and bridge are witness to hopes unrealised. West Street Station was built by the London, Chatham and Dover Railway in 1886 to compete with the

Top left: Chapel Lane, 1932

Top Right: *Three Crowns*, 82 West Street, circa 1912

Bottom picture: J.Lucas, Fish Curer, 23 West Street

Starbuck's, West Street, 1934

The *Three Crowns*, the Car Ferry, the *Privatee*r and the *New Falcon*, West Street, 1929

Top picture: West Street, 1929, looking west

Bottom picture: Russell's Brewery drays in West Street

Mermaid Court, West Side, northern end, off West Street, 1929.

'Bycliffes' the home of Alderman Ditchburn

South Eastern line to the Central station. It was originally intended to have a station nearer the High Street, but this was never built. It was closed for passenger traffic in 1953, although it continued to be used as the Gravesend goods depot until 1968, when it was closed completely. The pier was at one time used for a service to Clacton, and between 1916 and 1939 the Batavier service (from the Pool of London) to Rotterdam, called to pick up up passengers during which time the line had a 'boat train' from Victoria. The station has now been completely demolished and the site redeveloped. The Pier is used by the adjoining slipways.

About 70 feet to the west of the viaduct were discovered in 1910 the skeletons of two male persons in chains, and in 1957 further skeletons were found in the vicinity. It was probably in this area that a gibbet stood on which malefactors were hung, as Pocock also records in 1796 the finding of two men buried in chains at the west end of the Rope Walk which ran above the later Clifton Marine Parade on the north side. Iron manacles found near the site of the gibbet are now in the local museum.

In Gravesend's prosperous period as a health resort, the Clifton Marine Parade was a pleasant promenade, and except for a short length at its western end where waggons crossed the road to load chalk into waiting sailing ships, provided an undershore walk with open views of the river all along the way to Rosherville. This pleasant prospect was ended when the whole of the land upon its south side was acquired by the Imperial Paper Mills Ltd, in 1909, in order to erect huge mills and include storage room for pulp and other requirements of paper-making. On the river side the view of the river was obstructed by the construction of wharves and buildings thereon. One of the cranes was blown into the river in the first daylight air-raid in 1940. The Imperial Paper Mills were closed in June 1981, and the buildings and chimneys demolished, except the offices which remain as 'The White House' which seems to incorporate the porch and other features from 'Bycliffes'. This riverside walk has now been re-established along the north edge of the industrial estate.

In 1796, bathing-machines were first used upon the foreshore, with the Clifton baths at the rear, and in 1837 the baths were rebuilt in pseudo-Oriental architecture. They provided swimming facilities, separate for each sex, hot and tepid baths for the languid; while the New Thames Yacht Club (a break-away from the Royal Thames Yacht Club), formerly Pallister's hotel, and the Union Yacht Club with which the New Thames amalgamated, was the centre of considerable yachting activities: King Edward VII when Prince of Wales and Kaiser Wilhelm II were frequent visitors during the Gravesend Yacht weeks. The Royal Yacht *Britannia*, built by D.W. Henderson on the Clyde in 1893, was brought round to the Thames and was first raced at Gravesend in April of that year. Seats were provided for visitors in front of the baths where, to quote a chronicler of 1864, 'the convalescent may enjoy an animated view of the river and the scenery of the opposite coast', which was at that time open marshland, Tilbury Docks not being constructed until 1886. The New Thames Yacht Club was wound up in the early 1900s, Charles Arkel of Chatham was the last Commodore. The large yachts at one time used to anchor in the Tidal Basin when the docks were built at Tilbury.

Just within the Parade at its eastern end was an ascending road leading to a row of old wooden cottages and an extensive rope-walk, and some distance farther at its western end to the dwelling-house of its proprietor, Alderman Ditchburn, which could also be approached from the Parade by means of a stairway. Just beyond the stairway was the garden of the quaintly named *Hit or Miss*, whose name has provided a mass of conjectures. It certainly had this name in 1805. Rebuilt in 1929, it survived until the Imperial Paper works closed. Hereabouts in the 17th century was a municipal bowling-green held in the name of the Corporation of the time, and here later, when the ground had been excavated for chalk, was a rifle range for Volunteer regiments in the 1860s. Either of these uses may have provided the inn with its name.

Near the Gravesend boundary, where pulp ships later unloaded at a pier, there were from 1780 the shipbuilding yards and slips of William Cleverly, who built there a number of warships, the first being the *Zebra* (320 tons 18 guns) and merchant vessels, up to nearly 2,000 tons, these, of course, being sailing ships. Shipbuilding was continued here by William's son Henry, who subsequently found a better source of profit in lime-burning and providing chalk ballast (also used for 'marling' heavy clay lands) for coasting ships bringing coal from northern ports into London river.

Lime-burning provided a return to an activity which existed in Gravesend from at least 1168 when it was supplied for work at Dover Castle under Henry II. Cruden cites a document in 1696, which gives details of profits of lime-burning, with the note that, when Mr Etkins had these cliffs, Mr Stanbrook had three kilns going and Mr Marshall two. Entries of deaths of chalk-diggers and lime-burners are in local church registers.

The business of chalk-shipping and lime-burning was later carried on by Lieut.-Col. Gladdish, connected with the Cleverlys by marriage, and later still by William Fletcher, both of whom resided in a house, 'Bycliffes', near the wharves, which was built by William Cleverly. Beneath the cliffs was a row of cottages, known as Slaves Alley, in which the 'chalkies' lived after they gave up living in caves in the cliffs. The Imperial Business and Retail Park has developed the area, the first stores, Asda, being opened on 7 November, 1988. At the same time a new road was opened from this area to Snaggs Bottom, Northfleet, where it joins Springhead Road, making use of the tunnel under the Overcliffe formerly used by the Gravesend West line.

The building of the Yacht Club (used as a V.A.D. Hospital in the First World War) survived until 1938, when it was demolished and the last of the chalk cliffs were dug away and dumped on the foreshore to provide additional wharfage. The offices of the Imperial Paper Mills were built on the riverside using in part materials from Bycliffes which were demolished including interior fittings. The columned porch may be that from Bycliffes. although no photographs of the front of Bycliffes appear to have survived. This building with an extra storey still survives as 'the White House' part of Thames Shipping Services; the memorials to the employees of the Imperial Paper Mills killed in the First World War and to the first Lord Northcliffe (1922) are still on the front of the building.

The Northfleet boundary adjoins Gravesend at the point (running along the bottom of the cliff at the rear of Pier Road) where the road rises. Just beyond the old Borough boundary in Northfleet was a row of cottages called Teapot Row, the inhabitants of which provided teas with watercress from Springhead for visitors landing at Rosherville Pier. The roofs formed the carriageway for the houses in Rosherville Place and their chimney flues ran up through the houses above. They had a small area for a drying ground below the cliffs where their washing was hung out. So closes this chapter on West Street and its continuation, Clifton Marine Parade, now the area of the Imperial Business Park.

From this point we return to visit St. George's church.

The Clifton Hotel (Thames Yacht Club) and the Clifton Baths in the distance, looking west.

The *Hit or Miss* public house.
In the distance can be seen the towers of the Clifton Baths.

Tea Pot Row, June 1954, awaiting demolition.
The site is now occupied by Warren Hastings House.

The interior of St George's Church before the removal of the galleries in 1897.

Chapter 5

ST. GEORGE'S CHURCH

THE CHURCH of St. George was visible from West Street and, as we return from the journey described in the last chapter, we will turn into Church Street at the roundabout to make our way to the church. The first 'board school' to be built in the town, in 1876, was on the south side of Church Street, to the west of the church. Known as 'Church Street Schools', it was closed in 1975, and after being used as a temporary Magistrates' Court it was demolished in 1979. The present church was built in 1731 on the site of an earlier church, built about 1480, and destroyed by fire in 1727 (see Chapter 2, p.16). The pre-Conquest parish church of Gravesend is presumed to have stood, as did its successor, on a piece of ground between half and three-quarters of a mile to the south-west (see Chapter 13). St. George's was licensed for saying Mass on 22 April 1497, and consecrated on 2 April 1510 by Bishop Fisher. On the same day he rededicated the church of St. Mary after its destruction or damage by fire.

The chapel of ease or oratory, dedicated to St. George, was constituted the parish church in 1544: the reasons set out in the Letters Patent were that the church of St. Mary was at so great a distance from the town that infirm people, pregnant women, and others, found great inconvenience in attending. From contemporary records it would seem that St. Mary's church had already fallen into decay, and the last burial in its graveyard was in 1598. The first St. George's was apparently built by a body of trustees who raised the money and who intended it to be 'one day our Parish Church' i.e. for the town of Gravesend of which part was in Milton Parish but this did not happen, St. George's merely replacing St. Mary's as Gravesend's Parish Church.

What the first St. George's church looked like is unknown as no illustration survives. We can, however, gather from vestry notes that it had a wooden steeple which was in poor condition in 1719, being just a case of boards. This can be seen in a view of the town from the river in 1662, and from Thorpe we know that it contained a number of memorials, including a rhymed inscription in memory of James Bere, the navigator of Frobisher's ships, and consisted of a chancel, nave, north aisle and 'handsome' vestry room. There was also a brass sconce left by David Varchell. All the church furniture, including this memorial, were destroyed in the fire of 1727. Thorpe's list of the inscriptions on these memorials appears in Pocock, p.67.

Faced with the need to build a new church the Corporation, supported by the local vestry, sought the aid of Parliament under the Act of 1714 of Queen Anne for building 50 new churches by means of a grant out of accumulated funds produced by a tax on coal entering the Port of London. This was more successful than an earlier application for a grant under the Act to effect repairs to the earlier church and rebuild its steeple in brick and stone.

A grant of £5,000 was obtained through a Private Act of Parliament from the source above mentioned. This enabled work to be put in hand under the direction of Charles Sloane, a local architect, a tablet to whose memory is still to be seen on the west wall of the church. The foundation stone was laid on 3 June 1731, and the church was opened on 11 February 1733. In the interim Divine Services were held in the Town Hall.

The fact that the church was built from the coal tax was commemorated in the following verse:

> This Fabrick which at first was built To be God's House of Pray'r
> And not to pamper Priests of Guilt Or hold a sleeping Mayor
> Once perish'd by the vengeful Flame Which all its beauties raz'd
> Nor could the awful Patron's name Protect the Pile it graced
> But as it fell before the Fire
> Which then destroyed it whole
> So how to Heav'n its heights aspire And rise again by Coal.

The Corporation of Gravesend organised a scheme for providing a peal of bells by private subscription. Eight bells were hung, inscribed with the names of those subscribing, and during the next 100 years or so they were rung on every possible occasion, not only on national days of importance, but whenever important personalities, English or foreign, passed down the river aboard ship. The payments to the ringers varying from 5s. plus 1s. for 'beare' in 1660 to £3 13s. 6d. for two days' ringing in 1805 for the victory of Trafalgar. A dumb peal rung when Lord Nelson's body passed by water on 23 December was not charged, the ringers giving their services.

The church today contains a number of wall memorials and stained glass windows in honour of local 19th-century celebrities. There is also in the churchyard a bronze statue of Princess Pocahontas, by William Ordway Partridge, presented by the people of Virginia and unveiled by the Governor of Virginia on 5 October 1958. Pocahontas (Matoaka) was the daughter of the Red Indian chief, Powhattan, whose courage was said to have saved the life of the English captain, John Smith, when her father planned to kill him. She probably died on board a ship in the river in 1616 and was buried beneath the chancel of the older church, and in 1914 two windows were inserted at the east end of the nave on either side of the chancel and filled with stained glass by the Colonial Dames of Virginia. United States visitors come to the church during the summer months to inspect the windows, which have in addition to the large figures of Rebecca (Pocahontas's Christian name) and Ruth (the biblical personality who left her Moabite home to dwell in Israel), small representations of Pocahontas from contemporary sources. On the west wall is a framed facsimile of the entry in the burial register of 1616, reading:

> May 1616.
> Rebecca Wrothe, wyffe of Thomas Wrothe, gent. a Virginia Lady borne, was buried in ye Chauncell.

Her husband was in fact 'John' Rolfe, not 'Thomas'.

Among other memorials is one to General Gordon, who was a resident of Gravesend while he was Commanding Royal Engineer in the district.

When the church was built a gallery ran along the north side, the pulpit being opposite where the war memorial is now. The west gallery and organ were purchased in 1764 by a legacy of £400, left by John Ison, who owned the *Catherine Wheel* in High Street. In 1818 a south gallery was added and the pulpit moved into the centre of the church and, in 1833, upper galleries were added at the west end, the outlines of which can be seen on either side of the old organ. In 1892, the chancel was extended and, in 1897, the north aisle built by Basset-Smith, and all the galleries removed except the west one. When the church was closed in 1952 and St. James became the parish church, the north side was converted into a flat by Mr G. Tatchell, the honorary custodian, and the church used as a Chapel of Unity and Mayor's Chapel. In 1962, it was reopened as a church to replace Holy Trinity, and in 1968 became the parish church once more. In 1970, the north aisle was again reopened and a new organ - in part from St. James' Church - built, and the church restored chairs, replacing the open sittings (installed in 1872 to replace the original pews). When the work was carried out four column bases were found which had been used for the north gallery supports, apparently from the old church. St. George's churchyard was closed for new graves in 1854. The last burial there was that of Maria Cruden in 1909. The Cruden tomb was a fine altar-type tomb near the west door. It was dismantled when the churchyard was cleared to make 'Pocahontas Gardens' in 1957 (see *Gravesend and Northfleet Revisited*, p.43, for illustration).

In Church Street, the thoroughfare north of the church, there stood for many years the Ragged School, built in 1862 to replace the original Ragged School, started in a wooden shed in the Old Main (Clifton Road) in 1851. In course of time a Penny Bank, a Free Day school, Mother's Meeting, shoeblack brigade and soup kitchen (1864) were carried on for the benefit of the dwellers in the courts and alleys in the neighbourhood. In 1914, a crèche was added and it was renamed the Gordon Mission (in memory of General Gordon, who was one of the many voluntary helpers in the Church Street premises and who presented his Chinese flags to the Mission). In 1932, its activities were transferred to a new housing estate at Dickens Road, Denton, where, under the title of the Gordon Mission it carries on religious and social work

St. George's Church from an old engraving
showing how the church looked before the Victorian alterations

St. George's communion plate and register opened at the page
of the Pocahontas entry. Picture date June, 1966.

St. George's from the south-east, circa 1900.
Picture taken from the back window of a house in Wakefield Street.

in more encouraging circumstances. The Gordon Mission moved to Valley Drive in 1934. The Princes Street building was demolished in 1955.

Although it has disappeared as a public thoroughfare, Chapel Lane calls for mention here. It was a wide-paved footway with dwelling-houses on both sides, leading from West Street to Church Street, where it issued nearly opposite the churchyard gates. There is reason to suspect that Chapel Lane was originally church property as several entries in the Vestry accounts in the 18th and 19th centuries record payments for repair made out of church rates. The name is thought to go back to the end of the 15th century when St. George's was built as a chapel of ease. A house on the south-west corner was for some years after 1800 the post office of the town. Chapel Lane remained as a flagged path across the car park to West Street until the area was redeveloped in 1982.

Along Church Street on Friday, 16 June 1797, the body of William Wallace, one of the mutineers who had taken a leading part in the Mutiny of the Nore, and had shot himself upon its failure, was taken from the belfry of the church where it had lain for inquest, exposed to the view of the populace at the church gate, and then taken on a low carriage via Bath Street, West Street, High Street, to cross roads near the junction of Darnley Road and Old Road, where it was buried with a stake driven between the thighs according to the custom of the time.

In 1881, there was the Invicta Steam Brewery in Church Street which became Isidore Baron Berkowitz and Co. in 1884 and disappeared from the directories in 1885.

Built as the Ragged School, Princes Street, in 1862
renamed in 1914, the Gordon Mission pictured here just prior to demolition in 1955.

Chapter 6

BATH STREET, STUART ROAD AND PRINCES STREET

RETURNING ALONG Church Street westwards, we pass the site of Kempthorne Street, demolished in 1964 and now devoid of houses except for the rectory and church hall opened in 1970. It owed its name to a lady who became the wife of John Wakefield, and to whose memory a table tomb with an epitaph in verse once stood at the south-west corner of the churchyard. Her father, Thomas Kempthorne, was a Commissioner of the Navy, and was stationed at Chatham. Her husband, whose name is perpetuated in Wakefield Street, was earlier a waiter at the *King's Head*, Gloucester. Mrs Wakefield died in 1772. The whole of this area up to the rear of the shops on the north side of the New Road has now been developed as the St. George's Centre.

Bath Street was the road which led to the Clifton baths, hence the name - previously Fairfield Road - and before turning southwards the last remaining portion of the former highway, to Northfleet, must be noted opposite. Clifton Road was the main road to Northfleet, cut in 1716 to replace an earlier road nearer the river.

It became dangerous by being cut into for chalk needed for ballast for ships, and for lime-burning, and was replaced by the present New Road/Overcliffe/London Road, in 1802. It was still known as the Old Main (Road) in 1900, although its official name was changed to Clifton Road. A small cottage which stood on the south-east corner of this road until 1950 was used for the first Ragged School and was the last thatched house in the town. There is an illustration of it in the Library Collection and an illustration on p.43 of *Gravesend and Northfleet Revisited*.

The first gas works, established in 1824, was on the west side of Bath Street, just south of the Old Main until 1843, in which year they were removed to the banks of the Thames and Medway Canal at the east end of the town, where, extended and improved, the plant was operated by the South Eastern Gas Board until 1958. The town was first lighted by gas on 9 December 1824.

Stuart Road embodies one of the names of the Darnley family, and when the railway to West Street was opened in 1856 the road was claimed as a private road and barred under his lordship's orders. The barriers were broken down by employees of the company, and legal steps threatened, but the differences between the parties were settled without resort to law.

Between Bath Street and Stuart Road is the Gravesend and North Kent hospital which, since 1948, has been administered by the National Health Service. This hospital, opened in 1854, had its origin in the gift of a site by the Earl of Darnley in 1853. The first dispensary in the town was opened on 2 December 1850 at 89 (later 133) Milton Road, at the corner of Wellington Street, its object being 'to assist the really destitute poor of Gravesend and Milton and vicinities, unable to pay for medical aid'. Until 1948 the hospital was conducted on a voluntary basis. The well-known hospital fetes at Rosherville Gardens and elsewhere, the annual gala week and carnival, the hospital ball at the old Drill Hall, as well as industries, private individuals and friendly societies provided financial support.

A description of the hospital in Jottings of Kent, 1864, under the title of 'Gravesend Dispensary and Infirmary' is given here to provide a contrast with the hospital as it is today.

> This substantial building of brick approached by a flight of stone steps under a
> near portico, is divided in two parts, the front portion being the Dispensary,
> comprising waiting and consulting rooms, the surgery and the private residence
> of the indefatigable house surgeon; here sick poor, not receiving parish relief,
> have medical aid and medicines for one penny . . . The Dispensary has beds for
> twenty patients; on an average there are from six to ten under treatment in the
> Infirmary, and upwards of one hundred weekly in the Dispensary.

N.C.H. Nisbett was the architect of the new building of 1895. The hospital was greatly extended over the years and the new block was opened in 1971. The opening of the new Darent Valley Hospital in 2000 had put its future in question. It is to be a district hospital. The

The first gas works, west side of Bath Street.

Wakefield Street, 1962

Top picture:
Pleasant Row

Bottom picture:
The Ship, 20 and
21 Bath Street.

last of the original Bath Street buildings have just been demolished to make way for new buildings (2005).

About 50 yards down Bath Street from New Road on its eastern side there stood until 1834 a small National School, but in that year it joined forces with the Free School in King Street (see Chapter 8) under a scheme for joint management.

At the eastern side of the square formed by Church Street, Bath Street and New Road (see Chapter 8) is Princes Street, known earlier as Princess Street, and earlier still as Bread Street and Gravesend Backside.

Princes Street was associated for many years with Congregational or Independent worship. The chapel was closed in 1953 and its congregation moved to Old Road East in what was formerly a large private house known as 'Glendillon'. This has now gone and the congregation has moved to the United Reformed Church in Singlewell Road. A meeting-house and burial ground and minister's house were built in Princes Street in 1717, with help from London Dissenters. This was enlarged in 1797 and rebuilt in 1838. John Gould, a well-known local architect-builder, who lived in Princes Street, was clerk of works of the 1838 Princes Street chapel. Extensions in 1860 and 1879 included a lecture hall, schoolroom and library. The Princes Street Schools were started by the British and Foreign Schools Society c.1845. The first Sunday School in the town was started by this church in 1801 in a room in Swan Yard. The building was finally demolished in 1961, the site now being occupied by Marks and Spencers and the St. George's Centre, Wakefield Street, Kempthorne Street and Bath Street had been developed by a local builder, Robert Smith, in the 1830s. There was a small street (Robert Street) on the estate leading to Moscow Road named after him. Evidence of a small Roman settlement with a road leading to the river was found in 1979 when the area was being redeveloped.

Princes Street Congregational Chapel

41

Chapter 7

OVERCLIFFE AND ROADS ON ITS SOUTH SIDE

CHAPTER FOUR of this guide brought our peregrinations at its close to the Northfleet boundary by the riverside. Our starting point now is directly south of the riverside boundary where Gravesend joins Northfleet on the road cut by the Turnpike Commissioners in 1801, mentioned in Chapter 6. This section of the road between Northfleet and New Road is known as Overcliffe, formerly spelt without the final 'e'. The first houses, built about 1835, were those on the north side, identified for many years as Darnley Terrace. They were demolished about 1953 and the site is now occupied by a garage (Cliffords). At the time they were built the surrounding ground had not been cut away, and there was pastureland on both sides and at the rear, level with the gardens. This formed part of the old Fairfield which stretched to Bath Street, and where the annual Gravesend Fair was held. This was excavated during the years which followed, and by late in the 19th century almost all the old Fairfield had disappeared. Until the acquisition of the quarry in 1909 by the Imperial Paper Mills, two lime kilns stood in the quarry at the back of Darnley Terrace, their glow when lime-burning was being conducted lighting up the foliage of trees around with an 'Inferno' glare. In spite of the commercialisation of the quarry, nightingales sang there until just before the end of the 19th century.

The residences on the south side of Overcliffe were built at varying times from 1864 onwards until 1870 and were provided with deep gardens behind which was pastureland extending back to Pelham Road and cut only by the railway which runs obliquely in a north easterly direction to Gravesend Central station. This land was known as Mr Cove's field in the early 19th century, a cottage with an orchard towards the eastern end of Overcliffe, between St. James's Street and St. James's Avenue, being known as 'Cove's Cottage'.

Upon part of the pastureland, Gravesend Cattle Fair was held in the early 1890s when the old Fairfield had been so reduced as to make it too small for that purpose. In 1893 the northern part, where now is Lennox Avenue, was fenced in with corrugated iron sheeting set vertically to provide an enclosure for the newly-formed Gravesend United Football Club, itself the result of the joining of forces and interests by the Gravesend Football Club and Gravesend Ormonde, the latter largely composed of Gravesend watermen. The ground was entered from Overcliffe over a semi-public cart-track from Overcliffe to Pelham Road, which was closed during football matches despite public objection. Just to the north of the railway bridge were cowhouses and milking sheds of a dairyman and cowkeeper named Cackett, whose name still adheres to the bridge leading to Grange Road, which figures as Cackett's Bridge in local minds. At one time he seems to have lived at the Manor Farm House, Pelham Road. The site of St. James's Avenue was Cackett's Meadow. The houses in Lennox Avenue and St. James's Avenue were erected between 1910 and 1919.

Lennox Road was cut in 1877: before that time there was no road for vehicles between Darnley Road and Dover Road, Northfleet, except for the above-mentioned cart-track. For some years, Lennox Road was popularly known as the 'New Cut', and was much used by persons learning the popular new art of 'bicycling'.

The larger houses in Overcliffe, east of St. James's Avenue, all had long gardens opening upon what is now St. James's Road (many of these have now been shortened and houses built, which front on to the latter road). At its western end, St. James's Road petered out into a nursery with large glasshouses, the proprietor being one named Spicer. All this area was formerly included in the 40-acre Fairfield.

The three houses in a block Nos. 6, 7 and 8 Overcliffe, now an accountants and formerly the Gravesend Art School, were earlier private houses.

The Overcliffe on its north side, with its wide flagged pavement, was an attractive promenade: before the last century it had only an asphalt patched footway bordered by a broken quick hedge. Until 1978, buses of the Maidstone and District Company, with services to large areas of Kent and Sussex, occupied much of the roadway at busy times; the company's booking offices and garages built in 1923 stood upon the last remaining patch of the old cattle fairground, at the corner of Stuart Road with the bus garage at the rear now the site of Iceland supermarket. This site gave much trouble due to cliff falls, until a concrete retaining wall was built.

The first Maidstone and District bus service to Chatham started in 1911. In 1923, the company took over the services which the Tramway Company had started in 1913. They were both members of the British Electric Traction Company's group. The first motor buses in the town were two small 12-seaters operated by Messrs Smith and Day between Gravesend and Northfleet between July 1901 and August 1902, while the tramway was being relayed for electric operation. Mr Smith had a cycle shop at 60 and 61 New Road with a large Penny-Farthing cycle wheel above as a sign.

Maidstone and District Bus Depot, 1962

Chapter 8

NEW ROAD AND KING STREET

NEW ROAD is that section of the main thoroughfare which extends from Stuart Road to the top of High Street. The first building on the north side, proceeding from Overcliffe (now a furniture shop run by the Pounce family) was from 1855 to 1937 St. James's Church day school, having a stone wall adjoining the path enclosing the open square as a forecourt. The southern part was burnt down in 1976 and the present shop built on the site. The shops adjoining which belonged to the Gravesend Public Halls Company were demolished in 1989 and a new block of shops built on the site of the previous ones. They having been built as dwelling-houses in the early years of the 19th century. The large building now used for Youth Employment, lately used as a shop and formerly the Super cinema, was built in 1880 as the Borough of Gravesend British Workman's Halls. It then became the Gravesend Public Halls and was used for meetings, lectures, concerts and entertainments. An upper hall, smaller in size, was used for social functions. It was here that films were first regularly shown, first in the small upper hall in 1910, moved to the two larger lower halls in 1911. The hall was given the name of the Popular Picture Palace in 1912, and after various names became the Super with 954 seats in September 1933. It was opened by Anna Neagle with *Cavalcade*. It was equipped with the first cinema organ in the town. It, like the other cinemas in the town, became part of the A.B.C. Group in November 1958. The building was refronted in 1992 as part of the Public Halls redevelopment scheme.

From 1852 to 1968, there stood at the corner of Darnley Road the church of St. James. It was the first building to be erected on the land south of the New Road and west of Darnley Road. It was built at a cost of £3,400 under the Church Building Act of 1818 with a small grant of £300. S.W. Dawkes was the architect, and the style was decorated Gothic. It was built of Kentish ragstone (which stood up to the weather better than the rag at either Holy Trinity or Rosherville) and slated. It was cruciform and had a very large square central tower which gave it somewhat the effect of a toy fort. The nave was not much larger than the transepts. The church was said to have been modelled on Poynings in Sussex. When it was demolished in 1968 the very fine stained glass east window of the crucifixion, by Williment, went to the Victoria and Albert Museum, and the oak altar (which dated from 1953) went to Cobham. The site was presented by the Earl of Darnley, and the church's first incumbent was the Rev. John Joynes, whose brothers and father had been, or were, incumbents of local churches. It originally had galleries in both transepts, but these darkened the church so much that they were removed. The clock in the tower was presented in memory of Captain Marsden, a former harbour-master and a worshipper at the church. Between 1952 and 1968, it was the parish church of Gravesend.

The site of St. James' Church was developed by Blue Circle Industries and their offices were called 'Blue Circle House'. In 1988, when they ceased to occupy them, it became Joynes House, after the Rev. John Joynes, the first vicar. There is a stall in memory of his descendant Spencer Joynes, for many years Church Warden of St. James', in St. George's.

Irregular roofs and upper storeys still existing in a few of the shops at the western end of New Road serve to remind us that when the road was first constructed it was largely a road of small cottage dwellings, some of which on the southern side stood behind iron railings which remained until the closing years of the 19th century, when the houses were converted into shops. The north side facing south was always considered the better side for trade by the local business community. The *Sun* public house stood until 1970 at the corner of Bath Street, and until 1928 The *New Prince of Orange*, built in a similar style stood at the corner of High Street. They may be compared with the chemist's shop formerly at the top of Princes Street. They were all of the same style of architecture, built of local stock bricks and slated with mansard roofs and dated from the early 19th century, when New Road was cut; local 'grey' (i.e. yellow) stock bricks, Welsh slate brought by water from North Wales and baltic timber were all readily available.

Next to the *Sun* was Moore's Boot and Shoe shop later Jack's Store, fruit and greengrocers, a little further along, no.39, in 1909, became the Penny Bazaar, the original Marks and

Top picture:
St. James' Church,
1962

Bottom picture:
New Road looking
eastwards, 1960

Salvation Army Citadel, New Road, just prior to demolition.

Anglesea Place

Spencer's and continued as such until they erected a new store in 1927, on part of the present site. To the west of this was Missing's, a large drapers and toystore which became the British Home Stores, rebuilt soon after Marks and Spencer's built their new premises in 1960.The rebuilt shop of Boorman's, nos 17 and 18 (now Samuel's) was the first shop to have a roller blind (1880) instead of a blind supported by two iron rods in the gutter. The next was E.C. Paine's at nos 22 and 23.

Between Darnley Road and Garrick Street, on the south side of the road, is a building which was erected and opened in 1910 as the Gem Picture Theatre with 750 seats in the auditorium and 330 in the balcony and two boxes. It had a stage for plays and an orchestra pit. In earlier times it had a rather splendid art-deco entrance and stairs. The architect was Charles Lovell, son of the solicitor, Edward. It became the Regal, part of the A.B.C. group in 1934, and a bingo hall in 1965. Garrick Street has been widened and in 2000 become part of the circulatory road system for buses, now being developed.

At the east corner of Garrick Street stood the Theatre Royal, later the Salvation Army citadel. The Theatre Royal was opened for the presentation of plays in 1807 by Mr J. Trotter. It suffered many fluctuations of fortune, being closed and then reopened in 1822. Another period of varying fortune followed, and it appears to have reached its greatest height of popularity in the 1870s, but it declined again in public favour and it was given to the Salvation Army, by Mr Ruddell, the then owner, in 1883. Its new owners removed the two-tier balcony and made other alterations to fit it for its new role. On 20 October 1883, there was rioting in the New Road, after the Salvation Army sought to hold a meeting in the town. A strong contingent of 'roughs' calling themselves the Skeleton Army, gathered outside the railway station and pelted members of the Salvation Army coming by train to Gravesend with 'rotten eggs, mud and other unpleasant missiles'. The troubles lasted for some days and a mob of 4000 gathered outside the Salvation Army premises in New Road and threatened to burn it down. There was great opposition to the Salvation Army because of their 'anti-drink campaign'. The Salvation Army Citadel was demolished in 1969, and at the same time the *Eagle* public house and a builder's merchant's yard adjoining, which was formerly the Royal mews; one of the leading livery and bait stables in the town was also demolished. In the 1980s a leading seed-merchants (Simes) premises on the west side of Garrick Street was demolished and the site together with the site of the cottages in Garrick Street at the rear became a car park and taxi-rank, now incorporated in the highway.

Further east two private houses (75 and 76 New Road) standing back from the road with long gardens in front were demolished in 1958 to provide a site for the Co-operative store now replaced by Debenhams and Barclays Bank, built in 1987. These two houses were formerly occupied by Dr Charles Pinching, the third and last generation of a family of Gravesend doctors who had originally lived on the Terrace. The western one of this pair of houses was at one time the offices and printing works of the *Gravesend and Northfleet Standard*. It was taken over by the *Kent Messenger*, who for many years printed a 'Gravesend' edition. It was also at one time the residence of F.B. Nettleingham, the owner of the Steam Flour Mills in West Street and Mayor in 1878–9.

The premises demolished in 1973, occupied by Lloyds Bank, were built in 1906 by Alfred Tolhurst as offices for his firm and as a branch of the Capital and Counties Bank (architect, George E. Clay, builders Beal and Hubbard). They occupied the site of earlier offices built in 1867 and a small public house. Behind it was an oblique path which at the beginning of the 19th century led to a nursery garden which gave the name to Garden Row next to the offices just mentioned and Garden Back Row or Pinching's Row to the parallel row adjoining Pinching's garden. The nurseryman's residence, a wooden building, was later the stationmaster's house, and then used as a builders' office, pulled down in 1971.

The whole of the area to the south of the New Road and west of Stone Street was redeveloped (1974–6), as the Anglesea Centre by Lloyd's Bank property company architects, Peter Beake, Buckles and Partners, only the Midland (now HSBC) Bank on the corner of Stone Street being left. Lloyds TSB have a new bank here and Barclay's in the adjoining development of the Co-operative premises. On the opposite side of New Road, a large development has taken place between the back of New Road, St. George's Church and Princes Street, known as the St. George's Centre. Two of the walkways preserve the names of

Wakefield Street and Kempthorne Street. The centre was opened by Princess Michael of Kent on 5 July 1983, developers Gravesham Borough Council and CIN Properties company.

The former Midland Bank branch stands on ground that for many years was a stonemason's yard, first in the occupation of one Brisley, but from 1830 until 1900 the business was conducted by Charles Steel and his son, who died in that year. At one time negotiations were afoot for building a cinema on the site, but these fell through, and the bank bought the area and erected the present dignified building. The architect was T.B. Whinney.

In the 1830s, no.81 was the post office of the town, but in 1842 the office was removed to the corner of Edwin Street. In 1882, no.82 became the Colonial Meat Company when refrigerated ships were introduced and opposite, at no.3 was Nelson James and Sons, their rivals.

The section of New Road between Princes Street and High Street and between Stone Street and Windmill Street was from 1801 until the coming of the railway in 1849 the most lively in the town. Here the coaches plying between Faversham, Canterbury, Dover and London halted to pick up and set down passengers, and to change horses. Pocock speaks of 17 coaches each way each day, and a 'Gazeteer of Gravesend' (1840) lists the names of at least 15 coaches and omnibuses serving the town and their times and destinations, on pp.14-15. In 1847, Bagshawe wrote: 'There is now only one coach remaining compared with 70 a few years ago from London to Dover', so there must have been almost continuous traffic at this point. One report talks of a coach every hour. The *New Prince of Orange* with its 'tap', on the corner of Princes Street, occupied the whole of the road on the north side, the *Nelson* with its 'tap' on the corner of Stone Street, that same length on the south side. Each had their stables in the middle opening on to New Road.

An omnibus ran from the *Nelson* daily to Meopham, Wrotham and Ightham, and a coach arrived from Maidstone every morning in time to catch the 8 a.m.boat to London in the years following 1815, when the first steamboat undertook regular services to London. It also waited to pick up passengers from the boat when they returned from London in the evening.

The *Nelson* hotel in the days of the coaches and, indeed, until as late as 1876, had a balcony overlooking the street from which departing passengers could be waved 'farewell'. The hotel front was reconstructed in the year mentioned and the balcony and the stables removed and the road widened. Its predecessor was the *Flower de Luce*, dated back to 1528, later the *Granby*, from 1783 to 1805, when it became the *Nelson*. Next door, to the north, was the *Carpenters' Arms*, demolished when New Road was cut. New Road and King Street were pedestrianised (except for buses) during most of the day in September 1990. The *Nelson* is now MacDonalds.

Readers who have followed the preceding chapters will realise that our steps have now led us around the outside of a square (with an excursion along the former Clifton Marine Parade) since we began in Chapter 2 our entry into High Street. Proceeding eastwards we now enter King Street.

King Street was known until the late 18th century as St. Thomas's Street (see above, Chapter 2), and on a site now occupied by the Woolwich and Abbey National building societies there stood until 1928 the King Street school, and its predecessor, the old Free school. In his *St. George's School, Gravesend, 1580–1955* the late Mr D.W. Jenkins describes the school thus:

> The school itself was a wooden building, about 60 feet long which faced south.
> There was a gable at one end and a dormer window at the other. The second
> storey overhung the ground floor and was lighted by a window which ran
> the whole length of the building. Very possibly the schoolroom was on
> this floor, while the schoolmaster lived on the ground floor.

It seems to have been an example of an upstairs timber frame hall, like Faversham Grammar School. The school seems to have always occupied this site until 1928 (see Cruden, p.223).

When, in 1835, it was decided to join forces with the National school, which had been started in 1817, a grant of £490 was obtained from the government and the old building was demolished and a new school erected with a 'front owing something to the design of one of the wings of Cobham Hall', whose owner, Lord Darnley, was Hereditary High Steward until

75 and 76 New Road, Gravesend and Northfleet Standard,
newspaper offices, and the surgery of Dr. C. J. W. Pinching.

Circa 1920s King Street looking westwards into New Road
not as the postcard proclaims New Street

The Free School is the timber jettied building in this view of King Street looking east circa 1835. On the right hand side are the weatherboarded St. Thomas' Almshouses.

The shop that was next door to the National School. A. Tulk & Son, Merchant Tailors, 5 and 6 King Street, circa 1925. The shop continued to trade until about 1950. Mr. A. Tulk, died in 1940 and his son, Mr. L. Tulk, was killed during WWII while serving in the Royal Navy.

1974 and Lord of the Manor of Gravesend until 1989. The architect was William Tierney Clark. The boys' department was on the ground floor, and the girls' school above. This seems to have been an unusual case where the church took over a free school which had been maintained by the Corporation.

This school remained in being as a church school until 1928, and in February 1939 a new St. George's secondary church school was opened off Upper Wrotham Road (see Chapter 14), and the premises were sold for commercial purposes to provide funds for it. Barclays Bank built new premises on part of the site with living accommodation for its manager over (now Woolwich building society) and Williamson's built a cafe on the eastern part of the site, the original home of the Gravesend Rotary Club (now Abbey National building society).

At the corner of Queen Street there stood until 1971 *The Mitre* which was at one time known as the *Duke of York* and previously the *Pelican*: what influenced the change in name is not clear. With the cottage adjoining it was a pleasant red brick building with a dentil cornice and the last remaining building of this period in King Street.

The south side of the street was of later development. Until well into the 19th century the wall of a garden of a house whose entrance was in Parrock Street (now the Conservative Club) ran along a length of the street on that side. Nearer Windmill Street on the same side are the County Court offices; built in 1878, for a time used as a Crown Court in 1974 and now restored to its original use as a County Court. The National Westminster Bank (1898) and David Greig's (1903) now part of the National Westminster Bank, were built on the site of the almshouses. In front of these almshouses was the cab rank in the 19th century; in the late 19th and early 20th centuries it was customary to station a long-extending fire-ladder on two large wheels outside the bank in King Street each night in case of emergency. The architect of the National Westminster Bank (then the London County Bank Co.) was Alfred Williams. It was built in the Arts and Crafts style of red bricks with Ancaster stone dressings and with columnated porch and two cupolas.

National School, King Street

Chapter 9

QUEEN STREET, EAST STREET AND HARMER STREET

IT IS PROPOSED in the first part of this chapter to complete the square of which Chapters 2 and 8 on High Street and King Street cover the west and south sides. Our starting-point is where King Street (dealt with in the last chapter) leads into Milton Road and is crossed by Parrock Street and Queen Street. Turning to the left we descend Queen Street towards the river.

This street was known in the early 18th century as Milton Backside, as Princes Street was Gravesend Backside, the street backing upon the High Street. It is probable that from early times a trackway or bridle path led from the Town Quay along the present line of the street. When an Act for paving streets in Gravesend was passed in 1773, Queen Street was not among those named, but in the Milton Highway Surveyors' Accounts for 1806 there are payments for 'paviors' work in Queen Street' and a bill for 36 tons of pebbles laid down there.

On the right as we descend the street there was a space at the rear of the *New Inn* (which is dealt with in the chapter on Milton Road), now occupied as a yard and garage for Royal Mail which was in the latter part of the 19th century a busy livery and bait stable conducted by Richard Turner. In addition to the provision of hack horses, carriages and three-and four-horse waggonettes for hire, the proprietor had at one time available for emergencies horses to be harnessed into the town's fire brigade vehicles upon an alarm being sounded.

Adjoining the stables was one of the half-dozen or so blacksmith's forges of the town, the chief business of which was the shoeing of the numerous horses employed in various forms of transport. This forge was carried on by one Vaughan. It may be noted here that the last farrier to carry on business in the town, and who devoted himself in the intervals of shoeing and wheelwright's work to the production of artistic ornamental scroll work in metal was Wm. Harpum. His forge was on the opposite side of the street a few yards lower down and closed in 1960. It had been in his family since 1906. Some of his ornamental ironwork can be seen in Milton church.

Some newly erected shops on the left-hand side of the street including Bayldon's the butcher, about 40 yards down, stand upon the site of a house demolished in 1951, which was believed by many to be the residence of George Etkins, Sheriff of Kent in 1681, and owner of the Manor of Parrock until he disposed of it to the Corporation of Gravesend in 1694. Cruden speaks of Etkins's house as being on the west side of Queen Street and identifies the site more closely as being on the south side of *Anchor and Crown* Yard. The *Anchor and Crown* public house was in a direct line with the house. Before its demolition the upper storey had been altered, but experts declared it to be about 300 years old, and the demolition revealed that it was erected upon oak posts nearly a foot square and 20 feet or so in length, with the bark still adhering on the unworked side, and with the butts of the posts at the upper end. Cruden gives an illustration of the north end of this house. David Goodsall the grandfather of the Kentish historian Robert Harold Goodsall was a herbalist in Queen Street and R.H. Goodsall's father was born at 35 Queen Street and served as Third and Navigating Officer on the *Great Eastern* when laying the Atlantic cable.

About 70 yards lower down is the east end of the market (see Chapter 2) and opposite it on the right side is Terrace Street, at the corner of which is the *George Inn*, the only one now left of four – the *Rose of Denmark*, the *Roebuck* and the *Ordnance Arms* having gone. Demolition and the construction of the new ring road have completely altered the appearance of the lower part of the street known as Crooked Lane. It was a narrow, short street of sharp turns, where common lodging houses were situated. The *Ordnance Arms* on the right which was behind a cobbled space derived its name from the time when the land around belonged to the War Department, Henry VIII having built a blockhouse by the waterside below this point. Behind the *Ordnance Arms* was Sussex Place, a pleasant row of cottages largely inhabited by waterside workers, with gardens in front, reminiscent of the time when it was imperative for water-men to live near their work. Thames House at the end of Sussex Place still survives, now used as an annexe to the *Clarendon* hotel.

The opportunity has been taken since the removal of the old houses to open up this part of

Buildings in Crooked Lane, May, 1932.

The riverside looking east towards Terrace Pier circa 1908.
Steps leading to the *Old Falcon, King of the Belgians* and *The Old Amsterdam*, plus the barrels in the yard of Woods Brewery can be seen.

Top picture:
*Old Falcon
Hotel,* East
Street,
circa 1909

Bottom picture:
from an old
engraving
dated 1819
showing the
Blockhouse
from the east.

the riverside and plant it with shrubs so as to make it a smaller promenade. Turning towards the former Town Pier, dealt with in Chapter 3, we cross what was known for centuries as East Street. Prior to a fire in 1857, East Street was barely more than carriage width, and the destruction of houses at the bottom of High Street enabled the Commissioners to widen it somewhat by taking the old Star steamship building site into the roadway.

Like West Street, East Street had its share of licensed houses. In addition to the *Three Daws* there was the *Old Falcon* rebuilt in 1882 with a glass studio on the roof used by William Wylie, well-known for his maritime pictures, the *King of Prussia* (whose title was changed to the *King of the Belgians* soon after the outbreak of the 1914–18 war), and the *Old Amsterdam* (where the Corporation banquets were held, and which is referred to in the well-known sea shanty 'A Roving'), while a few yards farther on a site now occupied by the former St. Andrew's Waterside church, was the *Spread Eagle*, part of the old house still remaining. This building was used for the Mission to Seamen before it moved to Tilbury when the docks were opened in 1886.

Set between them, in East Street, there was for many years during the latter part of the 19th century, the boat-building premises of Bill Warner, where during slack times watermen gathered to converse with the builder on football and politics, upon both of which subjects he held strong opinions. Mr. Warner senior had served his time with Corbett's boat-building yard at Greenwich and started the business at Gravesend in what had been a fish shop in 1864. He built a boat with seven planks a side instead of the usual six. The business was continued later by his son, until just after the 1939–45 war. Wood's brewery (taken over by Russell's in 1911) formerly Beckett's, occupied a site on the riverside here. There was also the dwelling-house of the owner of the brewery. The Woods lived here until George Wood built Woodlands for his home in Wrotham Road. Beyond these was a coalyard owned for many years by Edward Bannister and Co. The site, which included a number of old weather-boarded buildings, was cleared in 1954. The area is now covered by the pleasant enclosed green, provided with seats for residents and visitors.

The foreshore around St. Andrew's Waterside Mission church is generally known as Bawley Bay, this being formerly the moorings of the boats used for shrimping called 'bawleys', of which there were large numbers during the 19th century. *Thistle* was the last of the traditional Bawley Boats which belonged to Bill Sutherland (died 1972) mentioned in 1982 as being at Gravesend again. From about 1920 motor-boats were used, and the last shrimper to use this mooring belonged to Ted Burbury, who retired in 1965. The bay on the west side of the church is Blockhouse dock: the whole area came within the blockhouse property before it was disposed of in 1835. The actual blockhouse building, erected in the reign of Henry VIII, occupied a site on the east side of the *Clarendon* lawn, now occupied by the car park. The Gravesend blockhouse was excavated by the Thameside Archaeological Group in 1975 and the foundations of a brick with ashlar trimmed bastion found.

Opposite the church there was until shortly after the Second World War a row of fishermen's cottages, known officially as Thames Terrace, but colloquially as Bawley Row. A boatbuilder, Waters's, was at the western end.

St. Andrew's Waterside Mission church was built in 1870 as a place of worship for the waterside fraternity. The architect was G.E. Street. It was a daughter church of Holy Trinity, Milton (see Chapter 11) and its registers contain records of the baptisms by the clergy of the church, of emigrants awaiting departure to Australia and New Zealand in the 1860s and 1870s, when the voyages were attended by the dangers which sailing-ships were exposed to in those southern seas.

St. Andrew's Church had its origin in the devotion of the Rev. C.E. Robinson, a vicar of Holy Trinity, 1861–71, who made it part of his duties to visit emigrant ships lying in the river and which needed a shore headquarters. He and members of his congregation took over a closed public house, the *Spread Eagle*, and converted it into a rest and recreation centre, providing educational opportunities and services. General Gordon, who died at Khartoum in 1885, was one of the workers.

The Rev. C.E. Robinson wrote a letter to a leading church journal in 1868 suggesting that anyone who had lost a loved one should help to build a mission hall instead of a costly marble memorial. Miss Beaufort, daughter of Admiral Sir Francis Beaufort, replied, and promised to meet the cost of erection if the foundations were built up to the level of the road. This challenge was met by willing workers, and the foundation stone was laid on St. Peter's Day, 1870, the church being consecrated on St. Andrew's Day, 1871, 'To the Glory of God and in memory of Admiral Sir Francis Beaufort, K.C.B.'

The interior of the roof of pitch pine is like the inside of an upturned boat, with the beams as thwarts, and the mosaic above the altar depicts 'The Stilling of the Tempest'. The windows also depict religious subjects.

In order to find space for the church on the quay, part of the old public house was pulled down, the remaining portion being known as the Mission House. One of the gifts to the church was a set of gold communion plate used for many years by the church. It has the arms of the Bishop of Augsberg and may have been Napoleonic 'loot'.

The church was closed in 1970 and has now been acquired by the Corporation for an arts centre. At Harvest Festivals it was decorated with fish nets and gear from the boats and celebrated the harvest of the deep.

Just beyond the church there is an attractive view of the river across a pleasant riverside lawn, the property of the owners of the *Clarendon Royal* hotel, which dominates the southern side of the road. The title of 'Royal' and of 'Clarendon' have full justification in history, part of the hotel standing upon the site of the residence built for James II when, as Duke of York, he was appointed Lord High Admiral. As he married Anne, daughter of Edward, Earl of Clarendon, the selection of the name of his spouse was a natural one. It was first let by the War Department to William Eagle in 1830 and then sold to John Chaplin, of Rochester, who converted it to a hotel. He was the son-in-law of Alderman Harmer. The dance hall to the east was built circa 1905 and was the first such hall in Gravesend to have a sprung floor.

The extreme west end of the *Clarendon*, formerly the *Clarendon Shades*, was for some years until 1952 in the occupation of a Mr Sydney Cumbers, who rejoiced in the literary appellation of Captain Silver. Here he accumulated a large and varied collection of ships' figureheads, models and nautical gear, fitting up the upper floor overlooking the river as a steamship's bridge. A small riding-light hung over the doorway, and adjacent to the *Clarendon* lawns anchors of vessels that have long passed into the breaker's yards found a resting-place. The whole collection is now in the National Maritime Museum at Greenwich, the figureheads being in the Cutty Sark.

Almost opposite the alley at the eastern end of the *Clarendon* on the north side of the road was the Associated Lead Manufacturers Ltd., red lead factory on Milton Wharf, and on the east a slipway and shipbuilder's yard of John Ratzen.

At the rear of the *Clarendon*, set back from the Terrace, was a long building known as 'Clarendon Cottage'. It was once known as 'Grape Vine Cottage', and in the last quarter of the 18th century was the Milton parish workhouse. Nearby on the north side of the Terrace was a large double-fronted house demolished about 1950, which was the last common lodging house in the town. In the 19th century it was the residence of the Pinchings, who for three generations were doctors in the town (see New Road, Chapter 8). The first one who lived here had been a medical orderly in the navy and set up as a doctor when he retired, no qualifications being required for a medical practitioner at that time. He became one of the leading doctors in the town.

The area now occupied by houses and the Thames Navigation and former boat repair yard was occupied by the Terrace Gardens (which extended from the rear of the *Clarendon* hotel under the north–south Royal Pier Road as far as the Customs House property and from the river to the Terrace) and was laid out in 1833, by J.C. Loudon. With pleasant landscape-gardens, flower beds and shrubs and winding walks, it was the rendezvous of both residents and visitors who obtained admission by ticket or payment at toll-offices, which were situated on each side of the Harmer Street entrance on the north side of the Terrace. There was also an entrance next to no.9 The Terrace. After being semi-derelict for a number of years, the gardens were closed, and houses were built in the early years of this century after the receiver sold the Terrace Pier and Gardens to a local company, The Royal Pier Estate Limited formed by the Pilots in 1893.

The pier, designed by J.B. Redman, is now the headquarters of the pilots formerly organised by Trinity House but now, since 1998, the Port of London Authority. In Gravesend's palmy

St. Andrew's 'Napoleonic loot'.

The Terrace Pier with, in the foreground, a wheelbarrow from the Terrace Gardens.

Clarendon Cottages, 1926, once known as Grape Vine Cottages.
In the 18th century used as Milton Parish Workhouse.

The Grand Theatre, Harmer Street.

days it was a busy landing and embarkation point for visitors brought by paddle-steamer in thousands in the summer season. A temporary pier was first erected in 1835 slightly to the west of the present pier, which was opened in 1842. It was from this pier that the Princess Royal of England, daughter of Queen Victoria, left the shores of England on 2 February 1858 as the bride of Prince William of Prussia. It was bitterly cold and snowed all day. Here, too, in 1863, Princess Alexandra of Denmark first set foot on English soil when she came to this country to wed Edward, Prince of Wales, later King Edward VII. In 1874, the Duke and Duchess of Edinburgh landed here after their marriage. The Duchess was the only daughter of Tsar Alexander II of Russia. The Duke was Earl of Kent and later Duke of Saxe-Coburg Gotha. The pier was on occasions the place of departure of Queen Victoria when she made her voyages to the Continent in the earlier part of her reign, before Port Victoria Pier was built. The new pilot station was opened by the Duke of Edinburgh on 1 June 1976.

The Terrace Pier was restored in 1893 by the new company. It had been unsafe and when the pilots had given notice of this to the receiver he in turn gave them notice to quit and they bought the Pier from him. The new pontoon and bridge were built by E.A. and H. Sandford, engineers, at the Canal Basin, the repairs and alterations to the Pier itself were carried out by Messrs Goose and Son. I do not know this firm but there was a W.P. Goose, Government Contractor, at 124 Milton Road, which was the house in Cumberland Terrace next to the old Barracks entrance. The engineer in charge was a Gravesender, J.J. Robson, M.I.C.E., who was the engineer for the 1914 Rochester Bridge.

Harmer Street, built in 1836, was part of a design by Amon Henry Wilds for the Milton Park Estate Company. It was originally intended to have a second crescent opposite Berkley Crescent with a road (now The Grove, but then called Upper Harmer Street) leading to Windmill Hill. A.H. Wilds exhibited a plan for this showing the crescents and bathing establishment at the Royal Academy in 1830 (see Gravesend Historical Society's Transactions no.13, 1967 and A.J. Philip p.150). Only the northern part of the scheme consisting of Berkley Crescent and Harmer Street was carried out. This road is now a conservation area and still has an air of faded dignity. Harmer Street owes its name to the fact that James Harmer, an alderman of the City of London, who resided at Ingress Abbey, Greenhithe, played an important part in the development of the scheme, both financially and administratively. There is a large painting of him in the former no.2. Magistrates' Court.

In 1887, the clock tower was erected to commemorate the Golden Jubilee of Queen Victoria. The total cost was £1,097 – £756 19s. for the tower, £66 17s. 6d. for the architect, £225 for the clock and £48 for sundries. The architect was John Johnson, who with Alfred Messon was the architect of Alexander Palace, and who was also responsible for some of the buildings in The Grove, including the former butcher's shop now a motor cycle shop, at the junction with Parrock Street. The foundation stone was laid on 10 September 1887, and the Clock Tower was completed on 9 November 1889, although the chimes presented by Alfred Tolhurst were not completed until February 1890. It is usually stated that the clock and chimes came from the London Road tower at Rosherville Gardens, and certainly the clock was removed from the tower at about this time, but no mention of this appears in the contemporary reports in the papers which give the clockmakers as Smith and Son of Derby, and the bells cast by Warner and Co. of Cripple-gate. It was restored in 1977 by the Corporation in spite of objections by some members who wanted to pull it down. E.A. Mole, the proprietor of Nottons the tailors in Berkley Crescent, paid for the restoration of the metalwork at the top as the Council were not willing to restore this. In addition to a plaque of Queen Victoria, one of Edward VII was added in 1912 by Alderman H.E. Davis, who held the office of Mayor six times. A new plaque was added to the west side of the tower, of Elizabeth II, in Portland Stone by local sculptors Stephen and Catherine Lonsdale. It was unveiled by Lord Montague of Beaulieu, Chairman of English Heritage, in the presence of the Mayor, Peter Hart and Frank Gibson, Chairman of Impact. There were previously shrubs enclosed within artistic iron railings on the north side of Milton Road, filling in the arcs of the Crescent. The last of the acacia trees round Berkley Crescent survived until 1968, and the colonnade was complete until about 1920. It was restored in 2000 under the Impact scheme.

At the north end of Harmer Street on its eastern side there stood until 1955 a stucco-covered building with an ionic portico which had been built in 1842 as The Literary Institution. The architects were Messrs Cobham and Wright, a local firm, and it cost £3000. It originally contained a reading room and lending library, a lounge and promenade, a billiards room and an assembly room for concerts, recitals, lectures and balls: furnished with a very fine organ presented by Alderman Harmer, it was much patronised by visitors to the town until the 1840s–1850s. It was also known as 'The Assembly Rooms'. As the fortunes of Gravesend as a holiday centre decreased, its fortunes, too, diminished, and for some seasons it was known as 'Kelner's Bazaar' after its proprietor. In the 1890s, an extensive reconstruction took place: the broad gallery which stretched along its northern side was taken down, galleries at the west end constructed, and the building reoriented to conform to the required shape of a theatre, becoming first The Prince of Wales Theatre of Varieties in 1884 and The Grand Theatre of Varieties in 1900. The coming of cinema to the town from 1910 onwards introduced competition which the Grand was unable to stand against, and after being sold in 1927 it closed in 1933, although the bar remained open. In 1952, the roof fell in, and in 1955 it was rebuilt as a public-house, and because of its former function, was given the name of *The Call-Boy*.

Alderman James Harmer (c.1777-1853) of Ingress Abbey, Greenhithe.
From the portrait in the redundant courts, High Street, Gravesend.

Chapter 10

MILTON ROAD

THE END of the previous chapter brought us to the Jubilee clock tower. A turn to the right leads after about 100 yards to the cross roads of Parrock Street, Queen Street, King Street, and Milton Road, the point from which the previous chapter started. It is worth noting that the west–east road from the Northfleet boundary (Chapter 7) has changed its name four times in not much more than a half-mile. From London Road it has become Overcliffe, New Road, King Street, and now is Milton Road, and a mile farther east is Rochester Road.

The land between Parrock Street and Love Lane was laid out with streets and developed by the Gravesend Freehold Investment Company as part of the Milton Park Estate in 1836. This included the Pound Field. In 1775, it was described as containing hops, cherries and apples with farm buildings and two cottages. In 1830, it was still possible to stand at the corner of what is now Parrock Street and Milton Road and look over open fields to Milton Church and the higher ground towards Cobham. The streets that now occupy the triangle formed by Parrock Street, Wellington Street and Milton Road will be dealt with in a later chapter.

On the left hand, at the corner of Queen Street is the *New Inn*, a house with several interesting associations. Originally the place of residence of Lord Paston, it later became the property of Dr Holker, who, in April 1734, entertained there the Prince and Princess of Orange, the latter the daughter of George II, when they were weather-bound on their return to Holland after their marriage.

The property being available for purchase in 1780 when the *New Tavern* (Chapter 11) had to be vacated on its requisition by the War Department for construction of waterside defences, the licensee, named Ward, removed to Dr Holker's house, for which he obtained a licence, and gave it the title of the *New Inn*. At that time the grounds attached to the house were extensive, reaching nearly as far as the western side of where Harmer Street is now, and covering the area upon which Berkley Road, Wilfred Street and Bernard Street were built in the 1880s. Part of this ground was made into a bowling green, and thus the *New Tavern* green habitués were able to indulge in their favourite pastime in fresh surroundings. From the former bowling green was brought a memorial stone to one of the former bowlers, Alderman Nynn of the Gravesend Corporation, upon which was inscribed a verse extolling his skill at bowls. In the 19th century this was later removed to the bowling green of the *Prince of Wales* inn, near Milton church. It is now broken into four pieces but can be viewed at the Chantry Heritage Centre.When the road through Gravesend in the early years of the 19th century allowed stagecoaches to pass along this main street of Gravesend, the *New Inn* became one of the halts for such vehicles. The building included the present shops adjoining the *New Inn*, the extent of which can be clearly seen from the roof-line.

The church on the south side of the road at the corner of Parrock Street has a curious history. In the 1830s, when the population of Gravesend and Milton had become double that of 30 years previous (9,445 against 4,539) and the town was a holiday resort as well as a residential and business district, the two parish churches of Gravesend and Milton were unable to accommodate the Church of England worshippers of that time, and after considering an application for a grant under the Church Building Acts of 1815 and 1825, a scheme to build a 'proprietary chapel' by a group of local residents and businessmen was launched at a meeting in the Town Hall, a company being formed having a capital of £5,000 in £50 shares. The church was built in 1834, the architect being a Mr William Jenkins (Junior). The builder was George Cobham, a local man. It cost £7,200, which greatly exceeded the estimate of £3,950, and the shares declined in value, being advertised within a year at a 20 per cent reduction.

The church was put up for auction at the London Auction Mart on 21 July 1842, but although the particulars stated that 'the purchaser was not restrained as to use' and that 'a residence or several houses might be built on the ornamental gardens which surrounded it' no purchaser was found. In 1843, it was bought for £4,000 by the Rev. W.J. Blew, curate of St. Anne's, Westminster. Previously it had been offered to the Rochester diocesan authorities, but the Archdeacon of Rochester was only prepared to pay £3,500.

The Rev. Blew ministered here until 1851, the year of the so called 'Papal Aggression' (when the Roman Catholic Church established their Hierarchy in this country) when he and other High Church members of the Church of England wrote to Cardinal Wiseman regretting the way he had been received in England. This led to a complaint to the Bishop of Rochester, who inhibited the Rev. Blew from performing service for six months. In July 1851, Mr Blew sold the church to Cardinal Wiseman for £4,000, the Raphael family of Parrock Manor contributing a large part of the purchase price, and the chapel became a Roman Catholic church. The Roman Catholics had formerly, from 1849, worshipped in a 'small brick edifice' in Milton Road near the site of Peacock Street, under the Rev. Riort. Roman Catholicism was introduced into Gravesend by a Polish Franciscan priest, Fr. Gregory Stazievitch, who with a handful of men of his persuasion met in 1842 in a room situated in a court on The Terrace, later at 149 Windmill Street before building the small chapel in Milton Road dedicated to St. Gregory. The Church of England church was dedicated (although not officially) to 'St. John the Baptist' but the Roman Catholic Church is dedicated to 'St. John the Evangelist'.

A new steeple with saddleback roof was added to the church in 1873 by Goldie and Child, and, in 1840, adjoining premises were secured as a convent and school run by the Sisters of Mercy. In 1955, the convent was removed to more extensive premises at Hillside in Old Road East. Alongside the church an organisation called the Mechanics Institute had its library and lecture-room in the early 19th century, but this failed for lack of support.

The next building calling for notice in this road is the handsome Methodist church (architect Derek Buckler and Partners) on the north side of the road, which was erected in 1906 on the site of the first Wesleyan chapel, whose foundation stone was laid in 1819 by the Rev. Joseph Benson, a close friend of John Wesley, whose evangelistic zeal led to the world-wide extension of the Methodist movement. The old building was very plain of structure, but in 1841 it was enlarged and a new front designed, having arched windows and a pediment above in the classical style, within which the words 'Wesleyan Chapel' were incised. Iron railings enclosed a narrow space in which bodies of deceased members of the church were interred. The architect and builder of this building was John Gould.

Opportunity was taken both in 1906 and in 1956 to extend the site and provide space for the many activities connected with the church. Here were held the concerts of the Pleasant Sunday Afternoon Association, which catered for both men and women, usually known as the P.S.A., and later the Gravesend Philharmonic Society gave choral concerts here.

Crossing to the south side of the road and viewing the clock tower and Berkley Crescent with its restored colonade as one, it is possible to visualise the style intended for this part of the town in the 1830s. On the south-west corner of the Grove and Milton Road was Messrs Woodford and Co., who were an important off-licence with extensive cellars. Later the National Provincial Bank occupied the site. The upper floors were for many years until 1953 occupied by the North Kent Club, founded as the North Kent Cycle Club in 1877, which met at first at the *Mitre*. Woodford's off-licence later moved to Parrock Street.

The post office, on the south-east corner of The Grove since 1869, has occupied premises in Milton since 1842. Previously it was in New Road for a few years after its removal from Church Street (Chapter 5). With the expansion of post office functions and payment of pensions, it has outgrown the premises of the 1890s, ousted the postmaster from his apartments and absorbed a dwelling-house and former offices in The Grove. The conveyance of letters and parcels for many years performed mainly by rail had one lingering connection with pre-rail days when, in the closing years of the 19th century, a four-horse coach drew up just before midnight at the post office from Rochester, unloaded bags of mail and loaded others before departing for Dartford, where horses were changed and the coach proceeded to London, the London coach returning to Rochester with its load drawn by the changed horses. This coach service was the result of a dispute between the post office and the railways when the former began to carry parcels, and to protect their own parcel services the railways charged the post office a high price for this traffic. In 1887, the post office started running coaches to Brighton, and a number of other services followed, including one to Chatham which served Gravesend. The last of these coaches finished running in 1909.

Separated from the post office by a private house there was at the same period a wheelwright's yard and shop. Here iron tyres were shrunk on to wooden cart wheels by placing the red-hot tyre around the wheel and binding it on by applications of a quantity of

St. John's Roman Catholic Church prior to 1873

Milton Road and Clock Tower. Note the Wesleyan Chapel which dates the picture to
before 1906 when the present Methodist Church was erected.

Top picture: Park Place, Gravesend.

Middle picture: St Peter's and St. Paul's, the parish church of Milton.

Bottom picture: Milton Church of England School ('Duck Pond' School), 1962, far left can just be seen Milton Road Board School.

cold water poured from spouted cans. Adjoining this yard at a slightly earlier date was a corn, hay and straw dealer (Boorman's), in the days when feed and bedding for horses were essentials as important as the petrol supply of the present day. Between Wellington Street and Peacock Street (now a garage) were a row of houses demolished in 1961. The corner house at the Wellington Street end, no.133, was from 1850 to 1854 the first dispensary and hospital to assist the really destitute poor of Gravesend and Milton and vicinities unable to pay for medical aid. At no.137 lived George Newman, mentioned below, whose shop was opposite (for an illustration and further details see *Gravesend and Northfleet Revisited,* p.76).

On the opposite side of the road between the *British Tar* and the *Globe* was a row of shops, intersected by Bentley Street. No.25, now only a one-storey building, was, before rebuilding, in 1894 a grocer's shop, kept by George Newman, who also aspired to poetry, he having had conferred upon him the bardic title of Lloegryn. The *British Tar* is, as far as I know, the only building surviving in Gravesend with Mathematical Tiles (front upper storey only); the ground floor has bricks with weather boarding at the rear: perhaps 'job lots' or they fell off the back of three carts!

Adjoining Love Lane, the narrow pathway at the back of Wellington Street, where now is a row of shops, and yard in part belonging to the Cooperative, there was in the years between the two world wars a large timber yard which was engulfed in a huge fire in 1928. Before that time there stood on the site Cumberland House, a day and boarding school for boys, kept by James Mallinson, who had removed the school from Park House opposite in 1893. Cumberland Avenue was built in 1899, but Cumberland Terrace, the row of tall buildings farther east, dates back to the very early years of the 19th century, and was in 1830 the only building on the south side of this part of Milton Road. Just beyond is the Milton Road entrance to the former barracks. Within this roadway, just outside the barrack gates, was a small conventicle of a group of Baptists. In 1962, when Trinity schools were burnt down, the school was moved to a site just inside this entrance to the barracks and has now been rebuilt on the barracks site.

Park Place, laid out in 1834, which occupied the north side of Milton Road at this point, was in the 19th century an impressive row of detached and semi-detached houses with stucco fronts by Amon Henry Wilds, with its own accommodation road behind a park-fence and shrubbery. With a clear view of the Thames and its shipping at the rear of the houses, it was a popular place of residence for the gentry, including the Channel Pilots of the town. It also attracted a number of proprietors of private schools, at one of which, Park House, known as Queen's College, the boys wore mortar boards and gowns. It was built in 1835 and became Queen's College in 1842. In 1900, it became the offices of the Associated Portland Cement Co., Ltd., and later still the headquarters of the Gravesend Conservative party, and Park House Club. The houses were pulled down at the end of 1957 and flats built on part of the site. The remaining part was used for the new telephone exchange. One house at the extreme east end of Park Place survived until 1971.

It will be noted that Milton Road a little farther on veers to the right over a railway bridge before turning back in the former direction towards Milton church, seen about 200 yards beyond. This deviation was made in the late 1860s. Before this time the road continued to the north of the railway (the road here still bears the name 'Milton Road') to a level crossing. The old crossing-keeper's cottage was pulled down in 1975, when the new mock Georgian houses were built. There was also a halt here known as Milton Road between 1906 and 1915. On the right-hand side of the present road on the brow of the hill just beyond the bridge was a building largely of corrugated iron used as a recruiting centre and drill hall. Prior to 1890, this building stood in Wrotham Road near the junction with Essex Road, where it was The Pavilion, a theatre of Gravesend's holiday resort days. It was pulled down circa 1976. The large house next to it was built by George Butchard, engineer, in 1872. He died in 1901 and from 1911 it belonged to William James Champion, the Denton farmer and organist at Milton Church. In 1982, it was converted into flats and the grounds were developed. It has now been demolished and purpose-built flats occupy the site. The very pleasantly laid out gardens bordering the road next to it are a great improvement upon the ugly advertisement hoardings which formerly occupied the site. The former Imperial Paper Mills bowling green with its clubhouse set off the aspect. The playing fields are now occupied by the Gravesend Rugby

Club and the Hockey Club astra turf pitch.

Although not in Milton Road, with which this chapter deals, the Gravesend Grammar School for Boys (prior to 1944 the County School) comes more conveniently under this heading than under any other. It lies beyond the new Milton rectory, and access is reached from Church Walk, which leads southward on the Gravesend side of the old rectory, the present rectory having been built in the back garden.

The school is a modern building, the first block, now known as 'the workshop block' being erected in 1931. The land had been acquired from Bernard Arnold, the son of George Matthews Arnold, in 1924, for use as a playing field for the school. A pavilion was erected on the playing field and between 1931 and 1938 work proceeded on additional buildings, the school moving into the new buildings in the latter year. The official opening took place on 12 October 1938, the then chairman of the Kent County Council, Edward Hardy, Esq., performing the opening ceremony.

Seventeen classrooms are provided, an assembly hall, with stage (upon which school plays are presented at regular intervals), laboratories and workshops, headmaster's and staff rooms, offices, and so on. There are also hutments to provide room for activities for which convenient rooms in the main building are not available. Extensive playing fields stretch eastwards towards Denton. A heated swimming bath was also added but is not now used. The east building was badly damaged by a bomb in 1940, but has been fully restored and extended.

At the top of the hill, at one time the 480 bus terminus, and once the terminus of the Gravesend tramway, is the eastern limit of Milton parish, which was for many years the boundary of the borough of Gravesend and the limit of the built-up area. Beyond are Denton and Chalk parishes, formerly separated from the municipal area, but included within the borough from 1935. This portion of the Gravesend administrative district will be surveyed in a later chapter.

Milton church, dedicated to St. Peter and St. Paul, approached from the west by a long flagstone pathway with lych gate, dates back to the 14th century, but earlier than this a church stood in Milton, at least from Saxon times. What antiquarians regard as a surviving remnant of an earlier church on this site is to be seen low down at the south-west corner, where a filled-in arch is part of the present structure: but this cannot confidently be regarded as part of the church existing here in 1086 and noted in Domesday Book.

If, instead of entering by the war memorial lych-gate at the west end of the paved pathway, we walk a few yards up the hill, a wrought iron gate of handsome design which was cast by Robert L. Priestley Limited of Albion Parade, bearing a replica of Gravesend's first coat of arms of date 1568, is seen at a point where the churchyard wall is observed to be of different construction than that farther westward. This wall is in the process of being rebuilt. The reason for the difference is that until the early 19th century the churchyard terminated here. In 1805, a piece of manorial waste ground was taken into the churchyard, and in the following year some more land was added on the north side. Both the lych-gate and the iron gate were erected in 1951.

As we enter by this gateway, the sundial over what was from the 16th century until 1819 the south porch of the church claims notice with its motto, 'Trifle not, your time's but short'. This remarkable sundial deserves close attention for its many interesting features. It was restored by the then rector, the Rev. Hilary Day, in 1972. It was designed by James Giles, master of the Free school in King Street (noticed in Chapter 8) and bears witness to his scientific knowledge and attainments. The method of telling the time by it is explained in Pocock, p.142 and *The Kentish Traveller's Companion*, 1779, p.87. The porch was used as a vestry from 1819 until 1950 and is now a small chapel or shrine fitted out by the Rev. Day.

The tower, under which we enter through the west doorway, is probably of a little later date than the body of the church. It contains a peal of eight bells and is topped by a crown and formerly, the Prince of Wales's feathers (which were lost in a storm in 1986). When this vane was restored in 1954 by Mr W.G. Harpum, a strip of metal inside was found which had the words 'G. Thomas 1842' on it, and Mr Harpum added his own name and the date. There is a story that, when the work was being done in 1842, Queen Victoria passed in her carriage with the infant Prince of Wales en route for London and, hearing the bells being tolled in her honour, authorised the addition of the Prince of Wales feathers. Five of the bells were hung in

1656, one in 1810 and the other two in 1930. The clock was added in 1875.

The base of the tower acts as porch and in the left corner is the stairway to the ringing chamber and the belfry, while the doorway ahead leads into the rather narrow interior, there being no side aisles, with a gallery on the north side and a west gallery largely occupied by the organ. This was installed in 1829 as a barrel organ, was rebuilt in 1887, and renovated in 1936. A door on the left, formerly the north door, leads to the vestries, built and furnished in 1950 and also the Parish Centre, added in 1992, at a cost of £240,000. The architect was David Croydon, the builders Constant and Durling. The interior of the church is an interesting example of 18th-century plastering and ceiling and dates from 1790, when the old lead roof was removed, the walls were increased by two feet, and the present slated roof put on. The work was done by Thos. Hall of Dartford, and the addition to the walls can clearly be traced on the outside.

The east window, the only stained glass in the church, was given in memory of Dr C.J. Pinching in 1852. The two outer panels were blown out by enemy action on Tuesday 2 September 1940.

There is no physical chancel, but there is a sedila on the south side under the south-east nave window. The corbels of a previous roof still exist, with grotesque heads and other carving.The plaque in memory of General Gordon on the south wall of the interior was originally in Trinity Church and when this was pulled down it was rescued by a Mrs F.M. Garrett of Milton Place. She presented it to Milton Church in 1985 and it was unveiled by the Mayor, Councillor F. Gibson and dedicated by the Rector Rev. Hilary Day on 26 January 1986. On the eastern wall of the church is to be seen the outline of what seems to have been a very large window or, as has been suggested, a former chancel arch, but no evidence of this could be found from a small excavation by the Gravesend Historical Society in 1976.

It only remains now in this chapter to note the former rectory on the south side of the road, built in 1860, replaced by a modern building in Church Walk and the *Prince of Wales* public house. The *Prince of Wales* was built in 1792 by Michael Beddell, then Lord of the Manor and obtained its licence that year. The farm buildings were at the rear. The Alderman Nynn stone was moved to the bowling green here when that at the *New Inn* was built on. It is now in the Chantry Heritage Centre.

The field to the north of the church, where Raphael Road and the railway now lie, was called Miller's field, and it is probable that the mill mentioned in the Domesday Survey was a tide-mill near here. The river would have flowed up to this area before the river walls were built, and the marshes drained. It was for this mill that William Morton paid 19 shillings and 2 pence rent in 1393, and from which 'Milton' probably obtained its name.

Milton Road Primary School (now a car sales store) was opened on 18 October 1884 by the Mayor, George Hubert Edmonds (W.F. Gosling was the architect and W.J. Nightingale the builder) and closed at the end of the Summer term 1976. It was the second Board School in the town. Milton Church School which stood on the corner of Raphael Road opened in 1860 and closed in 1938. It was used as the Parish Hall until 1990, when it was demolished, and the site is now a car sales business. The new hall to the north of the church was built partly with the proceeds and opened by Leonard Jones, the senior lay reader, in November 1992. The church schools were always known as 'The Duck Pond School' from the pond which adjoined the site to the north and which may have been the remains of the mill pond.

Chapter 11

MILTON PLACE, WHITEHALL PLACE AND HOLY TRINITY CHURCH

WE HAVE NOW COVERED the whole of that part of Gravesend north of the main road, with the exception of that portion lying east of Harmer Street. A convenient starting-point for this section is the junction of Milton Place and Ordnance Road with Milton Road. In the angle of these two roads until 1963 stood Holy Trinity church, a cruciform building in the decorated style with a tower forming the porch at the south-west end of the nave. The architect was J.Wilson, and the church, built of Kentish rag and slated, had a series of carved heads round the cornice, and an elaborate hammer-beam roof. It was originally intended to have a spire, but this was never built, and the tower was finished with an open-work parapet and four pinnacles at the corners. It cost £4,300 to build and received a grant of £600 under the Church Building Act. When built in 1844 it seated 1,000.

The scheme for the erection of a new church had the approval of the diocesan authorities after the archdeacon's failure to purchase St. John's. The site for Holy Trinity was given by the Board of Ordnance, who owned the land northwards to the river on condition that seats were made available for customs officers. The corner-stone was laid in May 1844 by the then Countess of Darnley. The consecration took place on 21 August 1845, and the first incumbent was the Rev. Richard Joynes. It was stated to have been built with only one gangway or aisle so that they should not be able to have 'Popish' procession (as was the case at St. John's) and was intended to be low church. It later became somewhat high church with Choral Communion instead of matins at an early date.

The church became within a very short time the 'fashionable' church in the town. The provision of a very fine organ fostered the musical side of the services, and the congregation included a large proportion of the more prosperous waterside community – pilots, customs officers and watermen, with their families. The congregation, however, dwindled as the residential area moved to the south of the town after the Second World War. The ragstone deteriorated very badly, and although some work of restoration was done and a new east window inserted in place of one damaged by bombing, the church became unsafe and was demolished in 1963. It was here that the Trinity Sunday Pilots' Service was first held in 1908, a senior representative of Trinity House (the then governing body of the pilot service) usually attending. When the church was demolished the service was transferred to St. George's, where it continued to attract a large congregation until Trinity House ceased to be responsible for the pilots in 1988.

A project for building a school adjacent to the church was launched in 1865 and a building in ragstone with decorated Gothic windows was erected. The architect was G.E. Sweet. This building was destroyed by fire in 1962, when the school was moved to Milton barracks. It is the last Church of England primary school in the town.

Milton Place, the road leading directly north to the riverside was, when it was first built in the early years of the 19th century a very desirable place of residence as it commanded a prospect over meadows to the lower part of Gravesend Reach and the Lower Hope in which could be seen, either at anchor or under sail, the great three-masters bringing overseas produce from the Far East and the southern seas and pilots who lived here could watch for their ships and were within easy distance of the Terrace Pier. Here, too, at no. 10, was the double-fronted Penny's Library, established in 1826, where visitors and residents foregathered to exchange gossip and indulge in leisurely reading. A memory of this period was enshrined in the name Library Place, a turning on the left which led to Bentley Street.

Opposite the point where East Terrace joins Milton Place are the handsome gates of Fort Gardens. These lead into New Tavern Fort, built in 1779/80, and now laid out as public gardens. The fort was re-modelled in 1868–72 to take ten heavy guns, mostly 9-inch 12-ton rifled muzzle loaders. Some of the emplacements for these guns still exist and the magazines underneath are virtually intact with their special arrangements for lighting. In 1905, two 6-inch converted breech-loading guns were installed in separate emplacements overlooking the promenade. There is a separate magazine for these two guns which survives complete with shell and cartridge hoists. It was garrisoned until the end of the First World War. The

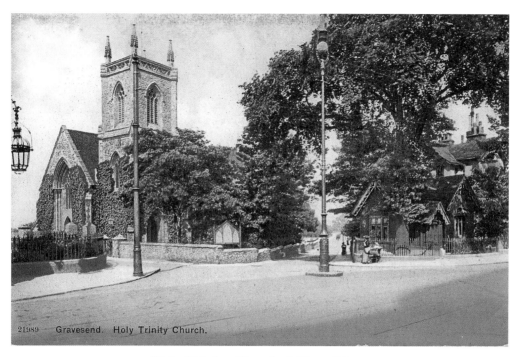

Holy Trinity Church, Milton Place

Fort House, Gravesend

Opening of the Fort Gardens, 1932, for the Mayoral Tercentenary.

THE NATIONAL SEA TRAINING SCHOOL, GRAVESEND   M 277

The National Sea Training School, Commercial Place, pictured from the river.

commander during that period was a Major Crookshank, who carried out a historical survey of the Chantry. Between the wars a 6-inch coast defence gun was kept in one of the emplacements and was used by 167 Heavy Battery Royal Artillery T.A. (Thames and Medway) for training during long summer evenings. In 1930, the Corporation acquired the site from the government (having previously bought the moat and land adjoining the promenade in 1910) and laid out the gardens which were opened in 1932 by the Earl of Darnley as part of the celebration of the Mayoral Tercentenary. The beauty and arrangement of these gardens are striking testimony to the aim of successive councillors and aldermen of the borough to provide for both residents and visitors a restful recreational centre sheltered on the north and east from chill winds, and in which concerts and other entertainments are held. The Fort has been largely restored and opened to the public by the combined efforts of the Council and Thames Defence Heritage (New Tavern Fort Project) led by Victor T.C. Smith.

An earlier generation only knew of this area as a mysterious enclosure behind unclimbable walls and embankments with a formidable spiked iron railing protecting a moat. Stores and married quarters of a detachment of Royal Engineers occupied buildings fronting the site. Abutting upon the roadway a little farther south stood Fort House, the residence of the Commanding Royal Engineer, who from 1865 to 1871 was General Gordon, known as 'Chinese Gordon', who met his death at Khartoum in 1885. In the 1830s, it was a private school and later a private dwelling-house, at one time the residence of the town clerk, Coombs.

It was in Fort House that Gordon entertained the lads from the poorer parts of Gravesend, seeing that they were well fed on their visits, teaching them the rudiments of reading and writing and arithmetic at a time when there were very few facilities for education, giving them instruction in Christian belief and behaviour, and finding the most worthy of them employment. His interest in their physical well-being and growth was evidenced for many years after his death by a scale in feet and inches scored upon one of the door frames which was used to measure the growth in height of boys from the time of their first becoming his 'kings' for entry in a logbook kept for that purpose. Opportunities for recreation were provided by permission to play cricket and other games in the 'Captain's Field', now part of the recreation ground adjoining the promenade.

Unfortunately, Fort House was reduced to a heap of ruins by the explosion of the warhead of one of the two V2 rocket missiles reaching Gravesend during the Second World War. (This projectile, or what remained of it, could be seen for many years afterwards within the fort grounds.) This event took place in 1944. The V2 also demolished houses on the west side of Milton Place, together with the former Milton tithe barn which had for many years been leased by the Corporation as a yard where the dust carts were kept. During the war Fort House was used as the food office. The site of Fort House is now a rose garden, with bricks marking the foundations.

Just before reaching the promenade on the right is Milton chantry, Gravesend's earliest existing building, still with its original timber roof of common rafters with simple collars and ashlar pieces on the wall plates, of the late 13th century. This chantry chapel was re-founded about 1321 by Aymer de Valence, Earl of Pembroke, on the site of a hospital founded in 1189. An outline of its history is given at the end of this chapter.

The roadway at this point comes to an end with only a footway to the Gordon promenade to the right: this will be considered later. Straight ahead lies the causeway known as the New Bridge, built upon piles which terminate with a wooden staircase at low tide point. It is impossible not to feel that there is here a great deal of history of which no record remains. When Aymer de Valence endowed the chantry in the 14th century, certain lands in Essex were charged with its support. These were in Nevendon and South Benfleet, and it is reasonable to suppose contributions in kind were brought across the river and landed at a spot near to the chantry, rather than land them at the Town Quay to be brought down over rough roads and paths to their destination. If so, it is possible that a landing-place existed here six centuries ago, and that this became in time a public landing-place. In the 19th century the causeway and bridge were repairable by the Vestry of Milton, items such as 'to planking and repairing rails on causeway, New Tavern, 16s' (1809)' and, in the same year, 'drawing 45 feet of plank round the causeway, £1 2s.6d' entries that suggest that the parish was responsible for the upkeep of a public way to the river.

Later, it became known as Wates's Bridge, the hotel upon its western side being kept by a licensee of that name from 1813–1883. It was a hotel where Charles Dickens occasionally resided: part of it became known later as the *Commercial hotel*. It had an outlet from its riverside to the New Bridge as well as possessing a quay of its own. In 1886, it became the Sailors' Home and in 1918 it was taken over by the Sea School authorities, the old building was demolished and the Sea School itself extended to provide facilities for training of youth for the Merchant Navy.

The main Sea School building on the landward side was, from 1886 onwards until its acquisition for youth training purposes in 1918, the Sailor's Home, where sailors of all nations could procure lodgings between discharge from one voyage to signing on for another. The Sea School was moved to new premises on Chalk Marshes in 1967 and the building was demolished in 1975. In 2003, the premises on Chalk marshes became a Metropolitan College for crime-fighting and a 'riot-town'.

Outside the main gates of the Sea School was the garage of the St. John Ambulance Association, and near by up a short flight of steps an office occupied in the late 19th century as a Royal Engineers' office.

The large Customs House which adjoins was erected in 1816 to house the Excise authorities on a site formerly occupied by the *Fountain Inn*, which was transferred to the south side of the highway and remained there until 1914. In 1836, the Board of Customs removed from its earlier offices in Whitehall Place, as the line of houses between Milton Place and East Terrace is named, into the Excise building, with direct access to the river. The end house in Whitehall Place from which the Board removed was destroyed as a result of the enemy action mentioned earlier in this chapter. It had on top a look-out with glass front from which vessels coming up the river might be seen at a great distance. Offices in Whitehall Place, now occupied by commercial firms, were until just before the Second World War in the occupation of other waterside authorities. In one of the houses Robert Pierce Cruden, author of *A History of Gravesend* (1843), resided for a time.

With the *Terrace hotel*, the Terrace proper begins, the roadway on the left, probably following a very old footway, being known as East Terrace. The Terrace was built in 1791 by James Leigh Joynes, the first row of houses to be constructed in the town as a private venture. He also paved the footway at his own expense. The ground upon which the southern side of the Terrace was built was known in the 17th century as 'The Camps'. It was also known as the Sconce lands, a sconce being a small fort. Pocock records the existence of earthworks here and that the debris resulting from the disastrous fire of 1727 (Chapter Three) was used to level this area. Further east nearer *New Tavern* a fort was erected in 1667, known as Trinity Fort, with an earthen bank thrown up in three weeks as a defence against the Dutch who were blockading the Thames and had sailed up the Medway and burnt the ships of the fleet at Chatham. This thoroughfare issued at its western end into Queen Street (Chapter 9). The western part of The Terrace is now part of the west–east ringroad.

Having now covered the whole of the area east of Harmer Street we may now return to a brief history of the chantry. From the 14th century onwards there seem to have been difficulties, partly due to the insufficiency of the endowment provided, and the advowson of Milton church was added to the chantry which was 'in honour of the Virgin Mary. and the Apostles Peter and Paul', which latter saints, it will be noted, are those whose names are borne by Milton church. The chantry priests celebrated offices in Milton church and some of them were rectors of Milton.

A number of disputes between the diocesan authorities and the patrons of the chantry occurred from time to time, and the building suffered decay. In 1524, Sir Thomas Wyatt was given a licence to found a chantry in the old chapel of St. Mary in Milton, but it is doubtful if this was ever done. It was eventually let to William Wylde of Milton, when the property, now lost to ecclesiastical purposes, was described as 'all that chapel in Melton, called Melton Chapel, together with the hall, pantry, kitchen, storehouse, chambers, &c. with their appurtenances belonging to it, and also one wharf, one orchard, a pond, two gardens, and two closes of land lying on the south and east sides of the said chapel, containing 13 acres. . .' Pocock adds to the above quoted description that all that remained of it in 1778 was the chapel, part of which was built chiefly of flints and rag stones, and that it was cased over with brick in 1781. This brick casing has since been removed in places to reveal some of the flint construction. The brick structure at the east end was demolished and a new gothic window was constructed in the old wall in 1946.

In 1697, the chantry had become an alehouse, and it remained so, its title being changed from the *Zoar alehouse* to the *New Tavern* in the following century. It so remained until 1781, when the Board of Ordnance acquired the property and demolished ten houses on the northern side in preparation for the erecting of the bastions of the fort. As stated in Chapter 10 the landlord of the *New Tavern* removed to Dr Holker's house in Milton Road, which he named the *New Inn*.

A newspaper of 1846 records that, while foundations for a magazine were being dug, many skeletons of former occupants were found.

The existing building which is of flint, ragstone and rubble construction, with some of the interior lined with chalk blocks, seems to have been the cross-wing of a timber-framed building which abutted on its south side, probably the Hall referred to. It is not mentioned by Pocock but by this time was probably used as, or as part of, the alehouse. This building, together with the chantry, was encased in bricks at the end of the 18th century, and, after being used at one time as the residence of the rector of Milton, whose rectory was next door until 1860, became a row of cottages which were demolished in 1969. In 1972, after protracted negotiations, the Ministry of the Environment agreed to restore the chantry with the assistance of grants from the Pilgrim Trust and other bodies, and to take the building into guardianship. It is of interest to note that from 1938 until 1945 it was used as a centre for Air Raid Precautions, and fitted up with showers for gas decontamination. In the First World War troops used it as barracks. More recently it has been used by the Borough band, the Scouts and for a time as a local museum, maintained by the Gravesend Historical Society. The late, Mr E.W. Tilley acting as honorary curator. The Kent County Council and Gravesend Borough Council took over the Chantry Management on 7 September 1995, for use as a Heritage Centre.

Chapter 12

THE PROMENADE AND CANAL AREA

FROM THE ROADWAY at the head of the New Bridge where our last chapter closed, a turn to the right leads to the Gordon Promenade. The promenade is of comparatively recent construction and until the late 1880s was largely a stretch of saltings covered by high Spring tides nearly up to the wall surrounding the fort, and at other times a repository of seaweed and flotsam of all kinds. Advantage was taken of the sinking of a schooner called the *Spring*, loaded with bags of cement, to purchase the damaged cargo and use it to face an embankment, the ground behind being levelled to the required height. Some of the built-up cement bags remained visible until 1978, when work to strengthen the sea wall was undertaken in connection with the Thames Barrage. The western section of the Promenade was opened by the Countess of Darnley in August, 1886. The *Spring* was repaired, refloated and renamed the *Gravesend*. Later it was demasted and became a coal hulk moored midstream for unloading coal into lighters, between the Canal Basin and Denton. A bandstand was built in 1890 at a cost of £100 (demolished 1933) and further land was bought from the railway in 1902, and in 1906 shelters were built.

Just on the left as the promenade is entered from what was once known as Commercial Place are the boat-sheds and clubhouse of Gravesend Rowing Club, established in 1878.

For many years there stood at a point near the north-west corner of the present canal basin what was known as the Round Tree. This was regarded as marking the seaward limit of the Port of London, beyond which the duty on coal entering the port was not chargeable. This was a convenient, rather than an exact landmark, as the eastward end of the parish of Milton is some distance farther east. The tree was damaged by gun practice from the fort towards the end of the 18th century, and early in the 19th century was mischievously set on fire, sailors from a collier lying in the Canal Basin extinguishing the flames. Its end came when it was blown down during a violent storm, with strong winds from the south-south-west on the night of 5 August 1825.

After the destruction of the tree, an obelisk was set up in its place in 1826 and when excavations were made for its foundation bricks were found similar to those used in the Gravesend blockhouse, from which it seemed that this was the site of the Milton blockhouse. Excavation on the spot by a small group of the Gravesend Historical Society in February 1973 confirmed the existence of these foundations. From early maps earthworks are known to have existed here. The use of this stone as a landmark being no longer needed, it was taken down and lay for many years on the edge of the Canal Basin. In 1892, it was re-erected at the entrance to the Gordon Memorial Gardens, but with no mention of its former function.

The playing ground on the south side of the promenade was part of the fort grounds until late in the 19th century, being known as 'The Captain's Field'. It was in 1886 that it was leased to the Corporation and became the first public recreation field, with the familiar name of 'The Rec', and was purchased in 1910. Here, in 1911, Gravesend's first municipal swimming bath was built, to be filled in when the larger swimming bath in Ordnance Road was opened in 1938. The ornamental water on the western side of this ground was originally the moat surrounding the fort, and together with the Glen was laid out in 1911.

Adjoining 'The Captain's Field' on the east are the Gordon Memorial Gardens and the ground itself their original lay-out being due to the munificence in 1890 and 1892 of George Mathews Arnold, J.P., eight times mayor of Gravesend. A metal plate on the plinth of the before-mentioned obelisk records the circumstances of the gift of the gardens and the eastern part of the foreshore. The statue of General Gordon was sculptured by John Broad and made by Doulton of Lambeth.

Across Ordnance Road or, as it was earlier known, Coal Road or Free Coal Road owing to its leading to wharfs outside the coal due area (because much of the coal landed in the Canal Basin was transported along this road to the town), the large red brick building was the Gordon Secondary School, completed in 1932, now the Chantry School. The triangular ground upon which it is placed was formerly a grass field affording pasture for cows, kept by a dairyman of Queen Street, 'Joble' King. Until the 1920s, he or his sons used to drive these

The Promenade and river circa 1930

The Canal Basin in the 1950s

Top picture:
Gravesend Canal
Basin and first
railway station

Bottom picture:
The *Brunswick
Arms* public house.

cows up Milton Road and down Queen Street to be milked each day at his dairy. After milking they found their own way back down Milton Road to his field. At other times it was used as a football field. Opposite were the municipal swimming baths mentioned earlier in this chapter which were closed and demolished when the new baths at Cascades were opened.

The road in front of the Gordon School forks to become Albion Terrace on the right branch (later Norfolk Road). The first three turnings, Albion, Augustine and Brunswick Roads, were built upon what was known in the 18th century as East India Field, the chartered company of that name using it as a site for a hospital and camp for its soldiers when their ships were moored in the river off Gravesend. The three roads used to form thoroughfares to Milton Road, as do Prospect Place and St. John's Road farther on. Part of this area was cleared for redevelopment in 1972. On the corner of Norfolk Road and St. John's Road is one of the earliest pillar boxes in the country, dating from 1855.

By taking the left fork towards the river and skirting the Gordon Memorial Gardens, the Canal Basin is reached, and nearer the riverside the road over the canal entrance which leasd to engineering and other works now being redeveloped. By the side of the canal entrance is the clubhouse of the Gravesend Sailing Club (founded in 1894, at the Rosherville Hotel and moving here in 1905) whose members use the Canal Basin for laying up and fitting out their craft. At the western end of the Canal, now filled in beyond the Basin, there stood until 1942 a small cottage, the roof of which was an upturned hull of a boat, with a window in one side. This is held by some to have been the inspiration which led Dickens to invent the house of Peggotty in David Copperfield. (Peggoty's house, however, is described as being constructed of a vessel in an upright position.) A little farther on between the Basin and the Albion Parade there was constructed in the early 1800s the Albion swimming baths, circular in shape, a rival to the Clifton. baths at the west end of the riverside (Chapter 4). These failed to succeed as the Clifton baths did, and for many years lay as a muddy pool.

The Thames and Medway Canal, to give it its correct title, was a project which also failed. Its sponsors conceived of it as a means of transporting barges from the Thames to the Medway without the inconvenience and danger of sailing round the Isle of Grain, so saving time and expense. An Act of Parliament was passed in 1800, giving powers to cut the canal across marshland to the high ground at Higham and thence by the tunnel two miles in length to the Medway at Strood. The first engineer in charge was Ralph Dodd who was also the engineer for the proposed Thames Tunnel. An Act was obtained and some £57,000 raised and four miles cut from Gravesend to Higham. An alteration was then made in the course which resulted in a two and a half mile tunnel instead of an open cutting. Fresh capital was raised under a new engineer, Ralph Walker, and on 27 November 1809, the first stone of the entrance lock was laid at Gravesend; in 1810, a new Act including the shortened course and tunnel was obtained. In 1817, William Tierney Clark was appointed engineer and an Act of 1818 provided for a further £100,000 capital. Finally it was opened throughout, at the Gravesend end, on 14 October 1824. The Port of London refused to allow a lock to project into the river, so that it was only possible to leave and enter the canal when the tide was high, which delayed traffic. Finally, in 1845, a single line of railway was laid from a station at the Canal Basin to Strood, running through the tunnel on stilts in the water. This was taken over by the North Kent line of the South Eastern Railway in 1849, who filled in the tunnel and doubled the track. The canal continued to be used as far as Higham, where there was a small basin with a wharf until 1935, when it was finally abandoned, and has since been gradually filled up (although an effort has been made to re-open a section) with the exception of the basin which was acquired by the Corporation in 1972 to lay out as a marina and pleasure gardens, with a block of offices on the south side.

On the south side of the canal stood the former gas and electricity works. The older works, formerly the Gravesend and Milton Gas Light and Coke Company's works, were transferred to this part of the town from earlier premises in Bath Street in 1843. The manufacture of gas at Gravesend ceased in 1958, and the works were demolished; only the gas-holders remain. The electricity undertaking was launched in 1900 as a municipal venture, current being first provided for the opening of the electric tramway in August 1902, and for general consumption in 1903. The builders were the local firm of Wallis and Moulton of Stone Street. The surplus profits of the undertaking were applied to reduction of the rates. The undertaking was nationalised in 1948 and is under the control of the South Eastern Electricity Board. For some years the station continued to act as an auxiliary station for the national grid, but was finally closed in 1970 and has since been demolished. The first electric street lighting was provided in 1903 when the Corporation installed 12 arc lights in the main road. These were invented by Jablochkov circa 1876, consisted of two carbon tubes with a current forming an arc between; when the carbons burnt too far apart they ceased to arc and had to be let down on a wire controlled by a winding handle in the post's skirt and adjusted.The changeover from gas followed rapidly in Gravesend but Northfleet continued to use gas for street lighting until after the Second World War, no doubt owing to the fact that the current was supplied by the Gravesend Corporation, who extended their supplies into Northfleet from 1905.

Adjoining the above undertakings there stood in the early years of the 19th century the Gravesend station of the Gravesend and Rochester railway mentioned above. It was on the length of canal between this point and the bridge at Denton that rowing boats could be hired and on which skating took place in the winter. It was also used in the 1900s for the Gravesend Model Yacht Club's Regatta.

The Boat House and
Thames and Medway Canal

PART TWO

Chapter 13

BETWEEN NEW ROAD AND OLD ROAD: THE WESTERN SECTION

IT IS PROPOSED in the present section to deal with the district lying between the main road and the other west–east road, Old Road, which runs at a distance of about half a mile south of the main road.

A convenient starting-point for this section of the guide is that part of the old municipal boundary in Old Road West near the top of Victoria Road, Northfleet, where the dividing line between the two parishes runs roughly north and south, and, as this line is somewhat difficult to follow without some guidance, a brief note of its course may be given here. Near the top of Victoria Road there is on the north side of the Old Road a passageway which may be followed across Havelock Road and at the back of Mayfield Road, Northfleet, towards the railway line. From here the boundary between Northfleet and Gravesend which was the setting-out point of Chapter 7, which dealt with Overcliffe, may be seen across the edge of excavated ground. Returning then to Old Road at the top of Victoria Road, the pedestrian may trace the boundary southward down Victoria Road (marking a stone in the eastern wall) thence across Pelham Road South and along Five Feet Lane on the east side of the *Rose* inn (the first house in Perry Street) as far as and along the back of the houses on the south side of Salisbury Road to Bedford Road until the boundary crosses into municipal property at Dashwood. The line can be picked up again at the boundary stone in Dashwood Road where, after a triangular venture into Woodlands Park, it included the south-east corner of the gardens of New House and then across New House Lane, through the middle of the flank wall of two cottages in which there is a stone as well as in the wall of New House, along the rear of Lane's Avenue, Northfleet, and sharp left to Claphall, Wrotham Road (an old boundary stone stands here) and continues across the golf links to Singlewell Road, where there is, or was, another stone in the lane just north-west of Gypsy Corner. (The above is the old Gravesend boundary: the district added to it will come within the next Part.) The possible Saxon 'banks and baulks' of the old boundary can be traced in the fields to the west of Wrotham Road and across the golf links, and there is a ditch marking the boundary in Woodlands Park.

Returning again to the original starting-point in Old Road West – described at the beginning of the second paragraph – we may observe that, with the exception of a few older houses on the north side, the houses on both sides of the road are comparatively modern, having been built in the years following the 1890s. The ground between Pelham Road South, Old Road and Victoria Road, upon which many of them stand, was originally glebe land, i.e., land belonging to Gravesend church (the income of which was payable to the incumbent, the upkeep of the church being payable by the Vestry out of the church rate, which ceased to be compulsory in 1868 by an Act of W.E. Gladstone). Until the Glebe land was built on in 1890 it was a triangular orchard. (A road leading out of Pelham Road South has been named Glebe Road in commemoration of this fact.)

Along this same Old Road there rattled during the 18th century the stage-coaches conveying passengers between London and Dover, the name of Dover Road, Northfleet, bearing witness to this traffic. In some documents of the period the road is referred to as the London–Paris road. It ceased to be so regarded when soon after 1801, the newer road through the town was followed by the coaches. Dover Road – Old Road was maintained by the Turnpike Trustees from 1711 to 1801, when the New Road was opened and the Trustees moved the milestones to this road. In the early 20th century a loop of the electric tramway ran south up Pelham Road to the *Pelham Arms* and then went along Old Road West and Dover Road to the *Leather Bottle* and a small one man tram rattled from the *Pelham Arms* (later cutback to Dover Road Schools to the *Leather Bottle*). Double-deck open-top cars running from the town to the *Pelham Arms*, were later extended to Dover Road Schools when competition from the single-deck Gravesend and District buses to Perry Street started.(See Chapter 8.)

Arrived at this junction of Pelham Road with Old Road, a choice has to be made of the road to be followed in embracing the triangular area enclosed within Pelham Road, Darnley Road and Old Road, to which the rest of this chapter is devoted. At these crossroads there may have been a settlement in the Saxon period. The famous Domesday Book in 1086 makes reference to a church as existing in Gravesend, and we are justified in believing that it stood hereabouts, possibly upon the site of the rear of the *White Post* public house, occupied by later churches until the early 16th century.

Additional evidence of the antiquity of this area was discovered in 1838, at a spot between Salisbury Road and Cecil Road on the south, near where the Co-operative dairy premises stood, of a hoard of 552 coins, mainly Saxon, bearing evidence of having been struck between 814 and 878 AD, which had lain buried for nearly 1,000 years. These may have belonged to an ecclesiastic who, when a Danish invasion was imminent, buried them, and did not live to retrieve them, as buried with them was a silver cross about two inches each way with its decoration unfinished, illustrated in the *Numismatic Chronicle,* IX, p.14.

Proceeding along Pelham Road we reach a row of houses, called Wolselly Terrace in 1885, Havelock Road and Granville Road being part of the same estate. We then arrive at the *White Post* public house. It was here in the back gardens of a row of cottages now called Pelham Terrace, and formerly Whitepost Terrace, that the first parish church of Gravesend, dedicated to St. Mary, stood. It was rebuilt in 1510 after a fire but ceased to be the parish church in 1544, although it seems to have been derelict or in a state of bad repair for some years prior to this date. What the appearance of this church was is not known. William Crafter, a friend of Robert Pocock, Gravesend's first historian, in his inter-leaved copy of Pocock, inserts a plan made on 26 November 1822, of the church and churchyard as he conceived it to be from examination of the site, giving a length of 325 feet and a breadth of 100 feet, with marked in heavy lines the few remains of stone foundations existing at that time. Gravestones, including one carved as though covering the grave of an ecclesiastic, and bones of interred persons have also been found on or near this site. The hedge bordering the road, and some of the foundations, were grubbed up in the 1820s, the latter being used for road material. A red floor tile with green glaze dug up at this time is now in the local museum. The site was sold for building in 1844 when the *White Post* and cottages at the rear were built. In front was St. Mary's (sometimes called 'Queen Mary's') Green. To the north of the *White Post* was the Gravesend Rifle Club, a 2.2 range. It was used by the Home Guard for shooting practice during the 1939-45 War.

Pelham Road did not receive its present name until the middle of the 19th century. Up to that time – and afterward in common speech – the narrow roadway was known as Manor Lane, from the Manor Farm extending along its southeast side, Style's Lane, from the name of the farmer who tilled the ground, and later White Post Lane. At the junction of Pelham Road and Darnley Road was a pond which in 1823 was the subject of threatened litigation between the representatives of the rector of Gravesend and the Vestry, because the latter body had removed soil from the pond. A reference to this pond is to be found also in the burial registers of Northfleet for 1833. For many years the *White Post* inn retained its dwelling-house aspect with a croquet lawn at the side.

The *White Post* was not always a fully licensed house. It became so in 1846 when an extensive fire in High Street necessitated the hurried removal of the licensee of the Black Horse, W. King, who successfully applied for the transfer of his licence to the *White Post.*

The name of the *White Post* inn may be attributed to its proximity to the before-mentioned glebe land. A writer in the early years of the 19th century mentioned the glebe land as being distinguished by white posts set along its borders, and it is thus easy to see the transference of these features to provide the newly-built house with a name.

Opposite the inn is the entrance to the Gravesend Grammar School for Girls, erected in 1926, and then known as the Girls' County School, and, from 1944, the Grammar School and Gravesend School for Girls. For many years the land upon which it is built was part of a large stretch of pastureland which extended until the early 20th century as far east as the roadway now known as Arthur Street West and out to the Old Road on the south. Part of this was used during its latter period as a sports field before the school was erected, and today the school's playing field extends as far as The Avenue, which will be mentioned later.

The school was officially opened on 20 October 1926 by the Duchess of Atholl, who was at that time Parliamentary Secretary to the Board of Education. The architect was W.H. Robinson of the County Council.

Junction of Pelham Road (Styles Lane) and Darnley Road.
Oil painting in Gravesend Library, Gravesend Farm.

Clifton Grove, 1969

Bomb damage 16 Pelham Road, September 5, 1940

The *Somerset Arms* and Barrack Row.

Proceeding along Pelham Road on the north-western side of flint-built Bycliffe Terrace, with nearby a pair of semi-detached villas, a field extended as far back as Campbell Road, where in the early 1890s Gravesend Ormonde football club played. This club was amalgamated with the Gravesend town club to become Gravesend United and for some time played on the girls' school site where it had a large stand (see Chapter 7). After passing Lennox Road the next turning on the left is Grange Road, just within which until 1943 stood a large drill hall used by the Territorials, and in the 1939–45 war as the headquarters of the Home Guard. It was also available for meetings, dances and fetes. It was built to profit by the roller-skating craze of the turn of the century and opened in 1910 as The Pavilion Skating Rink. It was destroyed by enemy action, when a bomb struck the Home Guard ammunition dump in October 1942, and most of the men on guard duty that night were killed. They are buried in Gravesend Cemetery. Grange Road opens out at its western end into Lennox Road, and behind it on the southern side is a diverted path which was until the 1890s a favourite pathway to Southfleet across fields. It continued along Campbell Road and then via a present alley to Park Avenue which was part of the path.

The first houses on the west of Pelham Road were built about 1870. One of these calls for notice: 'Mayfield', which before the erection of the Grammar School for Girls was the County School for Girls (from 1914 to 1926). It later became the Technical School and then again part of the Girls' Grammar School and, in 2000, become Bronte School, which moved from Parrock Road. 'Mayfield' was built in 1875 as a residence by Mr. I.C. Johnson, claimed as the first developer of Portland cement, who died in 1911 aged 101. It was one of the earliest concrete houses. Next to Mayfield House was Adisham House, at one time the home of H.H. Stephenson and his family, after whom Stephenson House in The Grove is named. In the 19th century this was the residence of Alexander Walker, one of the brewers of Wellington Street and the Chalk Maltings. After being used for educational purposes it was demolished and a church of Jesus Christ and the Latter Day Saints has been erected on the site (architects Messrs Butter and Robinson, builders Tendrig).

The Grange on the corner of Grange Road, architect John Sulman, was built in 1876, and was for many years the residence of the Commanding Officer of the regiment at the Barracks.

We have now all but arrived at the junction of Pelham Road with Darnley Road which, until the late 18th century, was a roadway within a field closed by gates at both ends. In 1797, the Vestry ordered the gates to be taken away. The northern gate was a few yards south of the present junction.

At the point where Darnley Road and Pelham Road meet there was in the early 19th century a pond, and behind it the homestead of Manor Farm. This was the farmhouse for the Gravesend Manor Farm which belonged to the Earl of Darnley, and his tenant farmed the land from the Northfleet boundary to Windmill Street at one time. The house was demolished about 1890, a granary remaining until it was destroyed by fire in 1911. The pond was filled in, and the pleasant triangular open garden occupies its site and part of the homestead garden. For many years the site was occupied by large hoardings for billposting. The farm was known as 'Styles', later on 'Elliott's', from the name of the tenants.

It will be necessary now to turn in a northward direction, first in order to begin the description of Darnley Road at a point where it makes a junction with New Road (see Chapter 8). The northern part of Darnley Road was known until the late 19th century as Somerset Street, the shops adjoining the Somerset Arms public house being at that time private houses. Barrack Row is so-called from a row of very small dwelling-houses which occupied the site of the shops and the rear of the former cinema. These dwellings were for a time the married quarters of army personnel.

Dominating Darnley Road opposite Barrack Row and the railway station is the Victoria Building. It was built in 1893 (architect Lieut.-Col. C.T. Plunkett) and was opened by Princess Beatrice on 19 July 1893. It was at one time the Municipal Day School, and had mixed classes of boys and girls. They sat on separate sides of the class and had their own separate playgrounds, entrances and stairs on each side of the building. It was a punishable offence for any of the boys to speak to any of the girls outside school, even though they were in the same class. Later it was known as the School of Science and Art, the art rooms in the north wing having north-facing skylights and there being sufficient spare room to house the Gravesend

Free Library in two of its rooms. It then became the County School for Higher Education when this was taken over by the Kent C.C. The extension at the rear was opened in 1901 (architect E.J. Bennett, builder Messrs Multon and Wallis). In 1931, part of the school was moved to Milton (see Chapter 10); in 1939, it was taken over by the Technical School. The Girls' School had earlier outgrown its allotted space within the school in Pelham Road, described earlier in this chapter. It is now the Adult Education Centre.

The demand for increased space for scientific education soon caused the eviction of the art side of the college to premises in Overcliffe (see Chapter 7). In order to cope with this growth of demand for space for the technical and engineering side of the college and for evening classes, new buildings were erected in Pelham Road, later used by the Girls' Grammar School.

A statue in terra-cotta of Queen Victoria, presented by G.M Arnold to the town to commemorate the Diamond Jubilee of Her Late Majesty Queen Victoria, stood before the college, now moved to the corner of St. James Road.

Opposite, and approached by Barrack Row (the western end of which is Clive Road) and Rathmore Road, is the railway station (formerly Gravesend Central), connecting the town with London to the west and the Kent coast and Maidstone and the Medway towns to the east. The station was opened in 1849, by the South Eastern Railway, the architect being Samuel Beazley, and until 1971 it had a rather pleasant Tuscan portico, the columns of which were boxed in by British Railways in an effort to 'modernise' it. It has since been restored to its former splendour with Tuscan columns and balustrade of fibre glass at roof level and has become a feature of the town. Canterbury West, also built by Samuel Beazley, was restored at the same time. The original North Kent line to London Bridge ran via Woolwich and Blackheath, and there was one train every two hours, with one extra train up in the morning, and one extra one down at night. After the Dartford loop was built in 1866, most of the fast London trains ran via Sidcup, until the line was electrified to Gillingham in 1939, when they ran via Woolwich, stopping there and at Dartford. In 1930, the line to Gravesend was electrified but the fast train from Gillingham and the coast continued to be steam hauled as did the through coast train until the electrification to the coast was completed in 1959.

A park for motor cars was constructed by the Corporation in 1957 on land used hitherto as allotment gardens at the rear of Cobham Street, and this is accessible from Rathmore Road, entering upon it from Darnley Road with exit at Wrotham Road end (Stone Street). The site of the old turntable (removed about 1930) and later bay platform have also become a car park for railway workers, as has the old goods depot for commuters on the down side. The old stable, however, remains now used for car sales.

The streets leading out of Darnley Road on the eastern side, Cobham, Darnley (named as a compliment to the Darnley family), Spencer (from a well-known chemist tradesman who lived at Ruckland House, now Masonic Hall) and Arthur Streets, with Trafalgar Road, were built largely between 1840 and 1860, as were other small streets to which they lead. Cutmore and Brandon Streets were so named from owners of the land, Clifton Grove (another Darnley complimentary name) and Nine Elms Grove (stated to be so named because of Nine Elms station in London at a time when it was believed the railway station would be sited in that vicinity. A row of cheaply constructed houses was erected on the site in the hope of obtaining higher compensation from the railway company if the line was built). Brandon Street was originally called Station Street when it was intended to build the station at the southern end.

South of Trafalgar Road until the late 1890s there was open ground, with the exception of Lynton House (demolished in 1970). At the beginning of the last century, this house was the home of Samuel Macartney, a local solicitor. It is reported that he insisted on having a pint of Gravesend shrimps for tea or an evening starter every day which his wife had to peel for him. Shrimps could at that time be bought peeled for 2d. per pint as opposed to the usual 1d. per pint unpeeled.

In the early years of the 20th century the house was a kindergarten school for boys and girls run by the Misses Kennedy, who later moved to 'Little Lynton' in Wrotham Road opposite Kent Road when Lynton House was taken over by the Kent County Council and which between 1918 and 1926 housed the juniors of the County School for Girls with some boys. Later still Lynton House became the Income Tax office. Beside it was a nursery garden with glass houses. Essex Road and Kent Road belong to the late 1890s. The site of Lynton House is now Weavers Close.

At the junction with Old Road a right turn brings us to the corner which we left to explore Pelham Road. On the left, opposite The Avenue, which connects Old Road with Pelham Road, is the sombre front of Gravesend cemetery. It is, perhaps, a grim comment upon life as a whole to reflect that this was the entrance to scenes of gaiety in the 1830s when the place was known as Victoria Pleasure Gardens, and visitors to Gravesend attended concerts and balls in what is now the cemetery chapel, partook breakfasts and suppers amid scenes of jollity, and practised archery or played bowls where now stand the headstones of graves. The decline of visitors to Gravesend as a result of competing pleasure resorts by the sea brought about a severe diminution in patronage and the proprietors disposed of the gardens to others who there established the cemetery by Private Act of Parliament in 1838. It was taken over in 1905 by the Gravesend Corporation. Since then the area of the cemetery has been extended on more than one occasion and now reaches out to more than double the depth of the earlier site. The entrance lodges and gate with Grecian Doric columns were built c. 1840 by Mr Geary, the cemetery architect. The cemetery gates have now in part been restored by the Corporation. Next to the Gardens was a small public house, *The Victoria Tavern,* from 1843 to 1846. The building was for many years used as a Polling Station at election times, but has now been demolished and houses built.

The next turning on the left, Cecil Road, leads to Cecil Road Primary School which, when it was built in 1909, was known as Cecil Road Board School, and catered for a wide range of pupils, from infants to those aged 14, the school leaving age. Prior to the erection of the Gordon School in Ordnance Road it was the most modern of the elementary schools in the town.

Gravesend Cemetery
On the right hand side just in front of the gateway building
can be seen the tomb of William Wood the builder
whose grave was said to be topped by a piece of old London Bridge
and which appeared to be a baluster

Chapter 14

BETWEEN DARNLEY ROAD AND WROTHAM ROAD

THIS CHAPTER TAKES in a square on the south side of Old Road. Starting at the corner of Dashwood Road and Old Road we proceed down Dashwood Road (formerly Dashwood Lane) in a southerly direction, noting on the left Bartlett Road and Lynton Road South, roads constructed in the early 1890s. At the corner of the latter road stood until 1972 a corrugated iron building erected in 1904 and then known as St. Mary's Mission church. After the new church was built in Wrotham Road in 1938, it was used for Sunday school activities a branch library and other organisations, but has now been replaced by modern town houses. (The new church and parish will receive attention later.)

Farther on, Woodlands Park, a public recreation meadow stretching to Wrotham Road on the east, is not entirely in Gravesend parish, a wedge-shaped area of Northfleet encroaching upon it and retreating to continue its boundary southward leaving the west side of Dashwood Road within Northfleet borders. On the right stood until 1971 Dashwood House, at one time the house of the Coopers, the house furnishers, and later of C. Percy Taylor, the Chief Engineer of the Associated Portland Cement Manufacturers when it was formed in 1900. C. Percy Taylor married a daughter of George Wood, the brewer who lived at Woodlands. Dashwood House was later used as Town Planning and other offices and the grounds as nurseries by the local council. The site has now been developed as Barnfield. Next door is New House Farm, a pleasant late 18th-century former farmhouse, and on the corner stands New House (now maisonettes), both in Northfleet parish. The land on which the farm buildings stood has now been developed for houses with a new road, Farm Croft.

The roadway at right angles fronting us is New House Lane, and Northfleet parish is to the right. The boundary between the two parishes proceeds southward across fields, so we turn left along New House Lane and then Cross Lane, known at one time as Cutthroat Lane. At the junction with Meadow Road was a pond. The road now leads to St. George's School, the senior Church of England school of the district, built to meet the need when the older church schools became obsolete. It was opened in February 1939 by the then Bishop of Rochester, the Right Rev. Martin Linton Smith. A plaque at the entrance to the school contains these words:

> This school has its origins in the old Gravesend Free School in King Street,
> founded about 1580 and amalgamated with the National School founded
> in 1816. In 1932 the site of the combined school in King Street was sold,
> and out of the public funds provided under the Education Act, 1936,
> supplemented by the proceeds of the sale of the King Street site the present
> building was erected.

At the junction of Cross Lane with Upper Wrotham Road we turn to the right in order to bring into this chapter the modern St. Mary's church. The district served by the mission church mentioned above had increased in population since 1904. The roads facing the church, Hillingdon Road, The Fairway and Dennis Road, were built in the 1930s, and a need was felt for St. Mary's to become a parish in its own right. The new St. Mary's church was consecrated on All Saints Day, 1938, by Dr. Linton-Smith. It cost £6,190 and remained a daughter church of St. George until 1951, when an Order in Council created a separate parish with St. Mary's as the parish church. The new church hall was opened in 1971, but seriously damaged by fire in 1972, and was rebuilt.

Retracing our steps to the corner of Cross Lane and wending north, we may remind ourselves that the road we are following was constructed between Gravesend and Borough Green as a turnpike road with toll-gates at intervals in 1825, thus linking Gravesend and Tonbridge via Ightham.

After passing Woodlands Park (the main gates to which are a memorial to George V's Silver Jubilee in 1935) we reach Woodlands hotel, which was built in 1896 as a private residence by Mr George Wood, alderman of the town, when he removed from his residence in East Street,

Top picture: New House,
July, 1998.

Bottom picture:
Pinnocks Alms Houses, 1993

87

Top picture:
The old Fire Station,
1963, built by Hopkins

Middle picture:
Woodville Terrace

Bottom picture:
Stone Street, 1959

beside the brewery which bore his name. The road upon the right slightly farther on, St. Thomas' Avenue, leads to Trosley Avenue, Pinnocks Avenue and Woodfield Avenue. This last name is derived from the fact that the land between Wrotham Road and the back gardens of the houses in Singlewell Road was until the close of the 19th century a brickfield owned by a Mr John Wood, and later his son George, who was not related to the gentleman who built Woodlands, but who lived at 'Westfield', Singlewell. The site of the brickfield was owned by the Raphael Trustees as part of Parrock Farm and, in 1922, they sold it to Mr James R. Pettman, a builder and brickmaker who, after making a large batch of bricks, developed the site for housing. He was the last private resident of Dashwood House.

At the junction of Wrotham Road and Old Road stand the almshouses connected with the name of Henry Pinnock. They were built on this site in 1898 to replace those at the corner of King Street and Windmill Street (see Chapter 2), and with funds collected in memory of Prince Albert and for Victoria's Diamond Jubilee. A plaque on the corner front gives particulars of the charity. Extensions were built in 1937, 1951 and 1960. They have been rebuilt since 12 August 1992, when Mrs Cynthia G. Sparrow, the longest-serving trustee, laid a foundation stone for the first new block of 20 flats or bungalows, her father, Alderman P.E. Lines, had been responsible for an earlier block. The architects for the new block were a local firm, Cavell and Mallock (contractors Ian G. Post). The rebuilding of the whole almshouses was completed in 2000, only the hall remaining from the original series. Subsidence from a dene hole and possibly old clay diggings caused the trouble with the original blocks here.The architects for the original block were F.R. Farrow and B.C.H. Nisbett, and, for the extensions, Thorold Bennett.

Previously, there stood here for many years a couple of one-storey thatched dwellings known as 'Reed's Cottages', of late 18th-century date. They belonged to the parish at one time and were used to house cholera victims in the 19th century.

Crossing Old Road, we enter Wrotham Road as distinguished from Upper Wrotham Road, although the former name is now used for both lengths. Prior to the road to Wrotham being turnpiked in 1825, the road from Gravesend made a 'T' junction with Old Road West. The line is made quite clear by projecting the frontage of the houses on the east side of Wrotham Road which coincides with the flank wall of Oban Lodge, where the junction must have been. The road south made a further 'T' junction with Old Road West to the west of the present road junction and can again be ascertained by inspecting the houses in Old Road and the line of those in Upper Wrotham Road. Until the 1950s, a ladies' bowling green occupied the north-west corner. Adjoining this and continuing northward are dwelling houses built in the late 19th century at the time that Kent and Essex Roads were cut and the development laid out by the Kent and Essex House Land and General Investment Company Limited, who bought the land in 1884.

Where Essex Road opens upon Wrotham Road there stood until the 1880s The Pavilion theatre and its grounds where, during the summer season, and occasionally during the winter, plays, operas and concerts of a high order were staged. Tragedy overtook its proprietor, Thomas Eves, in 1884, when in the Pavilion grounds he was robbed by two of his youthful employees and beaten with sticks until he died. The enterprise which he had carried on with such success fell into decay and the building in which the entertainments were presented was sold, and rebuilt in Milton Road as a volunteer drill hall (see Chapter 10).

Portland Road, which rises steeply opposite Essex Road, connects at its eastern end with what was formerly known as West Hill but now is considered part of Windmill Street. The next chapter will include reference to this southern slope of the hill.

A hundred yards or so farther north along Wrotham Road there stood until 1964 St. Luke's hall. It was built as a 'mission' church of St. James's district in 1890 (architect, Basset-Smith), and served the neighbourhood until the Second World War, after which it found occasional use for meetings connected with the church, and was used for Church Lads' Brigade, Sunday school and similar meetings. The site is now occupied by a Welfare clinic. On its southern side there was erected in 1956 a hut as the training centre and headquarters of the 402 (Gravesend) Squadron Air Training Corps.

Wingfield Road, which dates from the 1880s, recalls the name of Gravesend's first member of parliament, Sir Charles Wingfield, when the town received its separate borough franchise in 1868. The site was before that time known as 'Sandybanks', and was an area of derelict land where youth found amusement in leisure hours. It had previously formed part of Clark's nursery gardens. It and the frontages to Wrotham Road and Windmill Street were laid out for development by Alfred Tolhurst, when the proprietor of the nurseries went bankrupt. Near the *Bat and Ball* in Wrotham Road lived in 1851, 'J. Russell Town Scavenger'.

Nearly opposite Wingfield Road the Bat and Ball cricket ground was for many years used for county cricket. It seems to have started about 1845 as a private cricket ground for Ruckland House, and in 1853–4 the Earl of Darnley and others formed the North Kent Cricket Club with the Bat and Ball as its home ground. Here the giants of the game have registered some of their great personal successes: Dr W.G. Grace, Frank Woolley, Kenneth Hutchings, G. Jessop, to name but a few. Lionel Troughton, Kent's Gravesend captain, was also among them. Great consternation was expressed when, after a long history of cricket, the ground was bought in the first decade of the last century by a local builder for building, but a determined effort by individual enthusiasts raised the money for its repurchase, and the builder, also a Gravesend man, agreed to relinquish it. In 1960, Mr R.J. Billings bought the land and gave the Club a 999-year lease at a peppercorn rent. In 1976, a pair of iron gates were erected at the Wrotham Road entrance in memory of Sydney Croft, a leading Club member, who had first played for Gravesend when he was 12. They were stolen one night in 1979 but were replaced in 1980 as part of the Club's centenary celebrations. Not only cricket, but bowls, tennis and, more recently, hockey, are played upon its well-kept green. The Gravesend Cricket Week, when the County matches were played here, was long a feature of the summer season. The Mayor had a tent and enclosure in which he entertained the favoured few to tea. In 1970, one final County Championship match was played, this being against Warwickshire, while in the following year, a full County side played the Pakistan touring team. This all ceased after 1971, when the state of the pitch and the lack of parking facilities caused the County to stop playing here.

Trafalgar Road, which borders the cricket ground on its northern side, had, halfway down, standing back within its own grounds, St. James's hospital, which, before the passing of the National Health Act, was the Gravesend and Milton Workhouse, built in 1847 by a Board of Guardians under the Poor Law Act of 1831. The Casual Ward had a door onto Trafalgar Road where at about 6 o'clock in the evening, a small group of travellers could be seen waiting for supper, bed and bath. They had to work in the House chopping wood and so on the following day and, after another night, were released to continue on their way, often in search of work. In 1908, Sarah Hall died, an inmate of the main workhouse since it opened in 1848. The office of the Receiving Officer was in Arthur Street. It was replanned and renovated in 1948, largely as a residence for aged and infirm people. It was closed in 1985 and the patients moved to Joyce Green. The site has been redeveloped as sheltered housing accommodation, known as St. James Oaks.

In Wrotham Road, set high up on the eastern side, is Wrotham Road Junior School, built in 1894 as Wrotham Road Board School (architect George Cobham), the third of such schools built in Gravesend. It was seriously damaged by fire on 3 April 1977. An arsonist was later charged who had also caused fires at St. Joseph's and Lawn Road, Northfleet. From this point northwards the houses belong to an earlier date than those to the south, dating from the opening years of the 19th century. Before the erection of the houses between Wrotham Road and Darnley Road, much of the ground was known as 'Man of Kent Fields', named after the licensed house on the corner of Arthur Street.

The next house to call for notice is the Masonic Hall, which was Ruckland House for many years until it was taken over by the Masonic Order in 1906. Its name recalls its first owner, Lawrence Ruck, a Gravesend grocer and provision merchant of the late 18th century who, with his brother, owned land upon which Ruckland House stands. It had previously belonged to Benjamin Brandon, who used it for a market garden. After his death it was bought by Charles Spencer, a local chemist in High Street. Until the close of the 19th century it was the residence of Mrs Spencer, his widow. The area containing Darnley Street and Cobham Street was laid out in the 1840s by Messrs Pillow & Pollock. On the north side of Darnley Street a group of Primitive Methodists erected a Chapel in 1863, with a school room. They had previously worshipped in the building in Stone Street. Closed just after the Second World War the building is now used for industrial purposes. In the 1890s, there lived at no.20 Darnley Street, Mr F.J. Ebdon, a medical electrician. The Victorians considered being treated with electricity improved one's health and John Russell the Mayor, amongst others, was charged with electricity every morning on his way to work at the Brewery.

Zion Place opposite the Masonic Hall, was so named because it lead to the Baptist Zion chapel in Windmill Street, which was built in 1843 (see Chapter 2). It is called 'Woodville Street' on the 1863 Ordnance sheet.

Woodville Terrace has been swept away to make room for the Civic Centre and the police station, mentioned in Chapter 2. These houses, built in the 1840s by William Wood, a builder and brickmaker, stood within their own private road bordered by trees within a low wall mounted by iron railings. Latterly they were used by various departments of the Gravesend council as offices. Albert Place which curved from Wrotham Road into Windmill Street, was named after the Prince Consort, and the public house on the corner of Windmill Street was called the Queen's Arms (1836-1963, not demolished until 1968). All this has now vanished to make way for the Civic Centre forecourt.

It is at this point in our perambulation that Wrotham Road becomes Stone Street. Wrotham Road, constructed in 1825 as a turnpike highway, was stated to have its beginning in Windmill Street. Before the construction of New Road in 1801, what is now Stone Street was regarded as part of Gravesend Backside (now Princes Street). In 1761, the state of the old main road across the chalk cliff was so dangerous owing to quarrying, that the Turnpike Trustees decided to take over the road from Queen Mary's Green by John Goldsmith's farmhouse to the Manor Road (now Pelham Road), and to construct a new road, known as Blackberry Lane, along what are now the back gardens on the north side of Cobham Street into Windmill Street. The curved front of the Gravesend Rubber Company's shop, and the curved wall beside their office (both demolished 1973) marked the line of this turnpike road which was abandoned, and the site of Blackberry Lane sold, when the New Road was built by the Trustees in 1801. The stucco-fronted buildings occupied as offices and shops, and now nos. 21, 22 and 23 Stone Street, were built in 1789 as Gravesend and Milton's workhouse. Before that year, the housing of indigent people was undertaken separately by the respective vestries. The two end buildings were added later and are not part of the workhouse, which can still be clearly identified by the roofs at the rear.

The open square known as Railway Place was in Gravesend's holiday resort period covered by stables for the horses of stage-coaches, and here were also stabled donkeys and goat chaises for the children of visitors. All these were swept away by the coming of the railway in 1849.

On the western side of Stone Street, north of Clive Road, were until comparatively recent years a row of small weatherboard cottages with their own trim-kept gardens enclosed within low wooden palings. Later, they were converted to shops, but one cottage at the northern end remained until 1953, its last inhabitant, a Mrs H. Stone, having lived there for 40 years. Beyond was P.E. Lines and Co.'s (later Olby's) builders' merchants yard. Previously the site was a stable-and-cart yard for tip-carts, and next to 'Shades the baker', later occupied by the Gravesend Co-operative Society's undertaking department before they moved to Milton Road, was a livery and bait stable yard, occupied and run first by Mrs Houghton in the early 1890 period, and later, at the beginning of the 19th century, by J.C. Aylen, a well-known cyclist and founder of the North Kent Cycling Club. It was known as the Borough Mews and from here Alfred Joseph Clark ran his horse-bus to Meopham, and on certain days via Singlewell Road to Cobham, prior to 1914. A second multi-storey car park, opened in 1976, now dominates the west side of Stone Street.

Just before New Road is reached there was a store for builders' merchants small goods (also P.E. Lines Company, later Olby's). Previously there was an open space before a building set back somewhat where a hay, straw and fodder merchant carried on business. The building was originally built about 1800 as a hall for the Oddfellows Friendly Society. Later it was the Baptist church until their church was built in Windmill Street in 1843; then it became a Primitive Methodist Church and as late as 1912, there was still a total immersion font in the building. All this area has now been redeveloped as part of the Anglesea Centre. The corner bank premises are dealt with in the New Road section (see Chapter 8).

Chapter 15

PARROCK STREET, PARROCK ROAD AND OLD ROAD

FROM THE BOTTOM of Stone Street, with which the last chapter closes, we proceed to the northern end of Parrock Street where, it will be remembered, Chapter 9, which dealt with Queen Street, started. Instead of turning left, as in that chapter, we turn right, our aim being to include in the present chapter Parrock Street and Parrock Road as far as the Old Road, with reference to the streets lying to the westward of the two former and north of the latter thoroughfare.

First to note upon the right is the low-built house lying back from the road which for many years has been the home of the Conservative Club. It was previously the residence of Evan Lake, Esq., solicitor and member of the Gravesend Corporation. In the early years of the 19th century its walled garden ran along the south side of King Street (Chapter 8) for some distance.

Bordering the roadway here and nearer Manor Road there was until the early part of the 19th century, Glover's Pond, so named because a man of that name ended his life by drowning there. It was guarded from the roadway by posts and rails, and details of repair to these are to be found in vouchers of Milton Vestry for the first two decades of the 19th century.

Cromer House, next to the Conservative club, was used by the Rev. Haslam as his residence when he was Rector of Gravesend, the Parish having no rectory at that time and until the Rev. Mitchell was appointed Rector in 1925, when the Parish bought a house in Pelham Road. During the 1939-45 war, Cromer House became a Y.M.C.A. club for service men stationed in the Gravesend area. Next door was the residence of Dr Firth, who was the first medical man in Gravesend to cover his rounds in a motor-car. He had previously ridden a bicycle of an unusual type, built at a cycle works at Northfleet, which was propelled by an up-and-down movement of the feet, and included one of the first freewheel devices.

Manor Road was noticed in Chapter 2 as a turning out of Windmill Street. The houses beyond, interrupted by the railway, were known before its coming to Gravesend as Parrock Place, and in one of these houses there died in September 1833, at the age of 76, Jeremiah Lear, the ne'er-do-well father of Edward Lear of Nonsense Book fame.

Parallel with Parrock Street to the west and connecting Manor Road with Lord Street was Eden Place (now the site of the multi-storey car park opened in 1972) which in Gravesend's short-lived pleasure resort period was a favourite place of temporary residence for visitors. Lord Street also connects Parrock Street with Windmill Street: its name preserves that of its builder. It is now part of the town's circulatory one-way system and has been doubled in width by setting back the north side. Leading out of Lord Street to the south was a cul-de-sac, Peppercroft Street, so named from a parcel of land bearing the title of the Peppercrofts. This area was developed by a Mr. Lord. In the early 19th century this site was occupied by a brickfield, at one time belonging to William Wood.

The whole of the area between Parrock Street and the backs of the houses in Windmill Street has been cleared and part is now used as a car park and part has been developed with blocks of flats known as Gravesham Court and Home Mead. There are now plans to develop the car park which was once intended as a site for new Courts and a Library.

Clarence Street, formerly called Star Street, from the Star hotel, which stood on the corner ran south in a straight line with the lower part of Parrock Street across the car park..

Other streets in the area were Union Street, with its extension leading into Windmill Street, bearing the name of South Street. The next upon the right, now the entrance to Gravesham Court, was Russell Street, in which was established in 1851 a day school which served on Sundays as a mission church until 1856, when, Christ Church having been built, it was used as a Sunday school. It continued its day school functions as a Church school and after the passing of the 1902 Education Act was enlarged and improved. It ceased to function as a day school upon the rearrangement of schools in the area in 1936. Clarence Row, its continuation, links up with Windmill Street and still exists, the Minister having decided that the houses on its north side built in 1906 in the grounds of Clarence House school should remain when the area was cleared in 1965. On the south side of Clarence Row is the Day Centre.

Parrock Street, June 1965

Druids Arms, 17 Lord Street,
public house dates 1870-1914

Clarence Street and corner of South Street, 1966

Remains of the rustic brick building, South Hill Road, 1962,
once part of 'The Shrubbery Tea Gardens', Windmill Hill.

Still farther south were John Street, Peter Street and William Street, commemorating members of the family of Mr L.P. Staff, mayor of the town in 1843, who was interested in the erection of the houses there. Opposite the junction of William Street and Parrock Street is an open space enclosed within the 'close' of Christ Church Crescent with Christ Church Road nearby. In the centre, some blocks of masonry remain as a reminder that here stood for 80 years from 1856 the former Christ Church, which was built to replace St. John's when this was sold to the Roman Catholics and at a time when the population of Gravesend was extending southward in this direction. The architect was R.C. Carpenter, who died while it was being built, and it was completed by William Slater. The church was for many years the 'parade' church for troops occupying Milton barracks nearby and was lengthened to the west to accommodate the troops, c.1867. Deterioration of structure necessitated the closing of the church on 3 December 1932. The church was taken down and rebuilt in Old Road East (see Chapter 17).

It is at this point that Parrock Street becomes Parrock Road, but before making our way along it, we cross Clarence Place (see Chapter 1) and ascend the somewhat steeper incline of Shrubbery Road which leads to the east side of Windmill Hill (see Chapter 1). A little distance along this road on the right are two public houses. The first, now called *The Windmill Tavern,* was originally a farmhouse dating from the 18th century. One of the King family was tenant in the early 19th century and the cottages at one time on top of the hill were known as 'King's Cottages'. King's Farm (estate) was named after another member of the family called Joble King. It is mentioned in Pocock's History as 'the farm to the north of Windmill Hill'. The second, called *The Miller's Cottage,* was once the residence of the miller when milling activities were conducted at the mill. It was considerably extended in 1973.

Nearly opposite the *Windmill Tavern* is the romantically named Primrose Terrace, a footway set high on the side of the hill, the back entrances to these houses being in Southill Road, which descends into Parrock Road. At a still higher level at the very top of the hill is Constitution Crescent, a row of four stucco-fronted houses, some of which have recently been restored and which form a landmark visible for many miles. Where the ground falls away to the east the road becomes Southill Road and in the triangle now occupied by modern town houses were at one time a number of buildings in 'rustic' brick, 'The Shrubbery' tea gardens. The house known as 'The Shrubbery' was in the early years of the 20th century occupied by Charles Cobham, a local architect and collector of local histories and guide-books. He was also one of Gravesend's pioneer motorists. He had an open Daimler in 1899. E. Chapman mentioned helping him at an election, taking voters to the poll (at the Town Hall) from Clap Hall and other outlying areas. Chapman's job was putting sand on the belt drive to make it grip whenever the car came to a hill.This area, before the erection of houses, was rough ground with sand and gravel pits, and in a hovel composed of boughs and odd timber dwelt an old fortune teller, whose clients were visitors to the hill. A footway from the east side of Constitution Crescent leads to Constitution Hill, which also opens out onto Parrock Road.

We retrace our steps again now to the point at which the deviation from Parrock Road began. In the triangle between Parrock Road and Shrubbery Road stands the South Hill Bank Club, formerly a private house in which lived Charles Chadwick, a solicitor, partner and son-in-law of G.M. Arnold, who at one time lived at Milton Lodge, opposite in Clarence Place. His son Bernard Arnold, lived here after his father built Milton Hall. South Hill Bank was built for Jacob Seater in c.1875 but rebuilt by Charles Chadwick in 1880 in a very short time in the Norman Shaw 'Arts and Craft' style of architecture. The first-floor glass is said to be Ipswich glazing. There are a pair of Arnold Lions on the gate posts.

We proceed along Parrock Road in order that we may observe the open view to the north-east over Harmsworth's sports ground, with Milton church in the middle distance (Chapter 10), to the lower part of Gravesend Reach, the Lower Hope and the head of Sea Reach. Attractive and stimulating at all times except when weather conditions limit vision, this wide scene is at its best in the evening of a summer day when it is bathed in sunshine and the long shadows of houses in the background fall across the nearer ground. Part of the field has now been built on with Bronte View. Those who built the houses set high above the road saw the great advantage of their site at a time when in the early and mid 19th century fleets of sailing ships filled the river's tideway. Some of these houses built about 1840 were named Bronte

Villas, probably from Nelson, who was Viscount Nelson and Brontë. A semi-detached pair were long used as a preparatory school by the Misses Vine, later taken over by a company and now moved to 'Mayfield', Pelham Road.

As we proceed southward passing Constitution Hill, it may be noted that it was at the point where it joins Parrock Road that the first pumping works of the Gravesend and Milton waterworks, built in 1833, stood, before their removal to the site on the south of Windmill Hill. This is now Rowland Lodge. On the opposite corner is 'Echo Cottage', where it is said that Louis Napoleon stayed under the name of 'Mr Smith' when he was in living in England prior to the revolution of 1848. According to a Mr Walter confirmed by Eddie Chapman, who lived in Parrock Avenue, you could about 1900 hear the famous 'echo' in Parrock Road near the junction with Constitution Hill, hence the name 'Echo Cottage'. Apparently one had to stand facing Parrock Manor. This was before much building altered the acoustic response.

The next turning upon the right is Leith Park Road, named after the builder and one-time Mayor, which led to the Gravesend pumping station of the waterworks, built in 1846 to replace the original pumping station in Parrock Road, and demolished in 1973. The square chimney was a well-known landmark. Until about 1890, water was only pumped at certain hours of the day and most of the older houses in the town had large storage tanks which were a source of trouble in frosty weather. Running south from this road opposite the waterworks was a cul-de-sac, Glen View, which commands a view over the western countryside towards Swanscombe Woods and beyond. The end of this road now leads to the new estate on the site of Milton Mount college, and town houses and the new houses of the Southwark Rescue Society now cover much of the east side of the hill with entrances from Parrock Road. At the end of the original Glen View on Three Tree Hill stood a brick-built tower windmill, which was pulled down at the end of the 18th century for the bricks.

Formerly, Parrock Road was narrow with barely two carriage-widths between Southill Road and Old Road East, large elm trees bordering it on the eastern side. These were left in the centre when a second roadway was constructed about 1910, but they were all felled in the 1930s and flowering trees planted. Near the junction with Echo Square there stood until 1972 on a high bank a building known for many years as Milton Mount college. It was founded as an educational institution for the daughters of Congregational ministers, although other pupils were accepted from an early date. The foundation stone was laid in 1871. The architect was C.E. Robins of Southampton (cost £9750). The college owed its existence to the Rev. William Guest, Minister of Princes Street Congregational Church. The first Headmistress was Miss Selina Hadland, a pioneer of girls' education associated with Miss Beale and Miss Buss said to be the first school in the country to teach domestic science. It remained as such until the 1914-18 war when, after the first air-raid it moved first to Cirencester and then to Crawley, where it continued until after the 1939-45 war. When the school left, the building was used first as a hostel for Vickers' munition workers, and later for a time as a hospital for invalid soldiers. Its use for V.D. cases was the reason for the school refusing to return. In 1921, it was sold for an orphan school run by Roman Catholic educational authorities and opened by the Roman Catholic Bishop of Southwark in 1926 and continued as part of the Southwark Rescue Society. In 1940, the home was evacuated to Ugbrooke Park, Chudleigh, Devon, the home of Lord and Lady Clifford. It returned to Milton Mount in September 1945 and closed in 1951, after which a number of new homes and buildings were erected on the Parrock Road and Glen View frontages as St. Mary's Homes. During the 1939-45 war it was occupied by the Auxiliary (later National) Fire Service and the Women's Voluntary Service as a canteen. After remaining empty for some time and a proposal to erect a new Civic Centre it was demolished in 1972 and the site developed for housing.

At Echo Square we turn to the right along Old Road in order that the stretch of road between Parrock Road and Windmill Street may be covered. (The south side of the road will be dealt with in a later chapter.) On the right is the remains of a high wall built with a type of hexagonal artificial brick made up of granite chippings set in a brick surround with cement. They were known as Parr and Strong's cellular bricks (see John Emmerson, *The Unromantic Castle*, p.162). In its centre was the front door at pavement level and a long flight of stone steps leading to Milton Court (now demolished; the site was excavated 1974/75), built of the same cellular bricks high on the south slope of the hill. This house, known for many years as

Top picture: Waterworks chimney, April, 1972.

Bottom picture: Bronte Villas

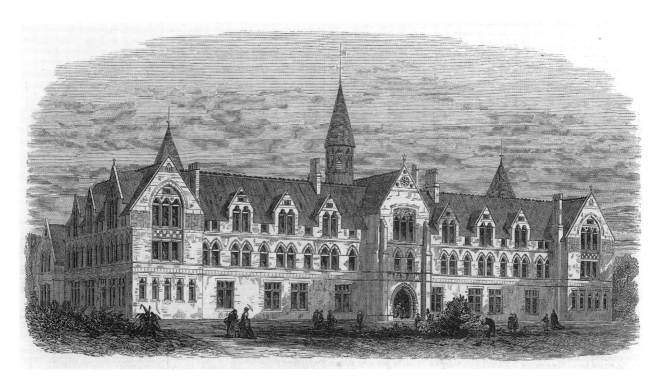

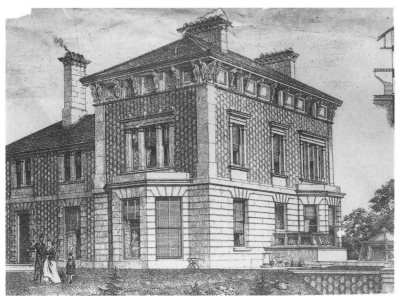

Top picture: Milton Mount
College later "St. Mary's"

Middle picture: Milton Court

Bottom picture: the *Old Prince
of Orange,* circa 1925

Tram Terminus, Windmill St, Gravesend.

'Simpson's Folly', was built by William Simpson after he had vacated a house at Rosherville, known as 'Chiltern Lodge', following a dispute with the Gardens authorities whose London Road tower, so he alleged, invaded the privacy of his garden. Later it was occupied by George J. Lucas a local dentist. From 1955 to 1967, it was a Preparatory School run by Captain H. True and his wife. The architects were Parr and Strong. The Coach House built in part with similar material still remains in Spring Grove. Some of the bricks here are filled with flint chippings.

At the junction of Spring Grove with Old Road East there stood until 1971 a house known as 'Glenthorne', latterly used as the Convent Grammar school. It was at one time the residence of John Russell, alderman and brewer of the town, and had a tunnel under Old Road which connected with extensive gardens running down to Cross Lane. A later owner, George Daniel Humphreys, who with his wife Catherine had 16 children, eight boys and eight girls, built a new house, 'Glendillon', on this garden, and this was for some years used as Milton Mount United Reformed Church. It was opened as a Congregational church in 1953, when Princes Street and Clarence Place churches closed. It joined with St. Paul's in Singlewell Road and the house was demolished. A block of flats, Wycliffe House, named after Wycliffe Church, which was united with Milton Mount United Reformed Church at the end of 1979, was built on the site. The Church Hall on the adjoining land still remains. Milton Court also had a garden on the south side of Old Road enclosed with a wall of similar material to that on the north side.

On the corner of Old Road East and Windmill Street is the *Prince of Orange* inn, rebuilt in 1932 on the site of an old coaching house of the 18th century, with a history going back into the 17th century. It was the coaching inn for London to Dover coaches which used the old road prior to the cutting of New Road in 1801 (see Chapter 8), after which all coaches passed through the centre of the town. When these changes took place, an inn at the top of High Street became known as the *'New' Prince of Orange* and the Old Road inn became the *'Old' Prince of Orange*, the licensee moving from one to the other. Adjoining the *Old Prince of Orange* was at one time a cricket ground. Before 1914, Stanley Bardoe the licensee installed a petrol pump near the side door in Windmill Street with tanks and a wood shed for the sale of oil and accessories for the benefit of motorists using Old Road as a by-pass for the town. On bank holidays and weekends his son used to stand on the pavement with a row of full petrol cans to catch passing motorists who wanted a fill-up.

Opposite the Old Road East side of the *Old Prince of Orange* were the glebe lands of Denton Parish, although in Milton Parish. They stretch from Singlewell Road to a point opposite Sandy Bank Road with a break in the middle of the rear boundary which ran south for a distance about half way along and ending at the east end in a point because the rear boundaries were not parallel with Old Road. This land was sold in 1870 to the Raphael family, who owned the surrounding land.

The area bounded by Parrock Street, King Street and Old Road East has now been surveyed, with the exception of the south part of Windmill Street, known for many years as West Hill. It is necessary, therefore, to turn north and deal briefly with this length of thoroughfare. On the right is the western end of Leith Park Road, spoken of earlier in this chapter, and just beyond, within its own grounds, stood until 1967 a residence which was witness to an ambitious scheme of building never completed. It was the dream of William Aspdin, who claimed to be the inventor of Portland cement (see Northfleet). He enclosed a large area between Windmill Street, Leith Park Road and Sandybank Road with a high concrete wall with large gate towers and entrances, a small part of which still exists, and started to build an extensive country house, to be known as 'Portland House', of which plans and illustrations exist. It was unfinished when he went bankrupt. 'West Hill House' (demolished in 1967) was the only fragment of this completed. The rest was demolished. Aspdin got into financial difficulties and the remaining part of the estate was developed with houses now known as Portland Villas, West Hill and Sunnyside, and the eastern part was bought by the Water Company. Town houses now occupy the site of 'West Hill House'. On the opposite side of Windmill Street is a nursing home known as 'Thorndykes'. This was formerly 'Rosemount', built c.1872 as the home of Charles Hatton, the solicitor and last part-time Town Clerk, later owned by Dr R.A. Freeman, the doctor/writer and creator of Dr Thorndyke, the detective.

As we pass Portland Road (see Chapter 14) we see 'Berkley House' on the left, formerly a High School for Ladies, and part of Milton Mount College at one time. It is faced with Suffolk bricks with red dressings but the sides and rear are local stock brick. Opposite it, set high on the slope of the hill, are houses erected during the 1930s, where once were the gardens of the popular *Tivoli* hotel (see Chapter 1). A plan for the layout of the Tivoli site may be seen in the Gravesend Reference Library. Before the various buildings were erected on this side of the hill and until the first decade of the 19th century there was a building known as '*The Blew House*,' partly farm and partly refreshment and public house, used by the visitors to Windmill Hill.

It was here that in our first chapter we moved northwards.

Surviving part of Aspdin's Portland Hall

Chapter Sixteen

BETWEEN PARROCK STREET AND WELLINGTON STREET

BEFORE 1840 THE TRIANGLE comprising Parrock Street, Milton Road and Wellington Street was open farming or market garden ground. In 1775, the junction of Milton Road and Parrock Street was known as Wheeler's Corner. Hops, apples and cherries were grown in these fields and there was a farm house, originally two houses under one roof, with a barn and farm buildings all part of Pound Field. The remarkable growth of population in Milton, which rose from 2769 in 1821 to 9927 in 1851, caused speculators in real estate to cast covetous eyes on the area with a consequence that the roads within the triangle, Edwin Street, The Grove, Peacock Street and Wellington Street, were cut and houses erected. The Milton Park Estate Company which had developed Harmer Street had as its directors members of the City of London Corporation, and these extended their efforts south of Milton Road, giving their names to some of the streets.

If we take as our starting-point the junction of Milton Road and Parrock Street as we did in our last chapter, and, crossing to the east side, walk up Parrock Street, we shall pass the Roman Catholic church mentioned in Chapter 10, and after a few yards reach the wall which guards the length of line laid down in the mid-19th century to connect the systems of the Gravesend and Rochester railway and the North Kent railway (see Chapter 12). Bordering this railway cutting on its southern side is Saddington Street, a name which was not given to it until late in the 19th century. Before this it was Farringdon Street, and was so named because James Harmer, a leading figure in the development of Gravesend (see Chapter 10) was Alderman of Farringdon Ward in the City of London. Its later name connects it with another City Alderman, a clothier named Saddington. It was in this area that the South Eastern Railway intended to have their Gravesend Station but the Council objected as it was in Milton Parish!

If we turn along this street we arrive at the first intersection, Edwin Street, another commemoration of City of London association, Alderman Edwin, who was interred in St. George's churchyard (see Chapter 5), having been also a City Corporation member. At a little distance up Edwin Street on the right the roadway opens into Parrock Street and makes with that street a smaller triangle at the apex of which stands a public house, the *Forester's Arms*, more colloquially known as 'the flat iron' because of its wedge shape.

We turn to the left over the railway bridge and note on the east side of' Edwin Street, near Milton Road, a low-built structure which has been in the course of years the town's post office, a Y.M.C.A. club, the offices of the Gravesend and Dartford Reporter and the 'Medical Hall', so-called from its being part of a chemist's premises in Milton Road used as a hall for meetings, concerts, parties, etc.

From this point we walk the few yards to The Grove along Milton Road. The Grove was first called Harmer Street South, or Upper Harmer Street, it being the original intention of its planners to continue the architectural treatment of Harmer Street to the south of Milton Road (see Chapter 10). When it was replanned as a series of semi-detached villas, it was for a time a private road with gates at each end. Changes which have taken place since their erection have introduced office and business premises to The Grove, the post office having brought within its area the lower houses on the east side. Two large office blocks, one on each side of the road, now occupy most of the remaining frontage between the post office and the railway. The block on the east, Stephenson House, built in 1965, now houses the Inspector of Taxes office (moved from Lynton House in 1969) and the offices of the Department of National Health and Social Security (moved from Ravenscourt in Pelham Road at the end of 1972) on the opposite side. Between these and the railway is a large double fronted house with two large stone eagles, now The Grove Club. A large house just beyond Saddington Street, called Harmer House, was built c.1842 by Richard Eves for Tobias Peffer who started a day and boarding school for boys. This was later taken over by a Mr Hedger and was known locally as 'Hedgers'. About 1894, he seems to have moved to The Pines, 107 Darnley Road. After remaining empty for some years Harmer House was taken over in 1900 by Mr T. Shaw and became Shaw's Laundry, continuing as such until c.1940, when it took over the Model

Laundry at the top of Whitehill Road and moved there. The site in The Grove and Saddington Street has now been redeveloped. At the junction of Saddington Street and Peacock Street is a building erected in 1846 by I.C. Johnson, the cement manufacturer, as a Zoar Chapel for Strict Baptists. The chapel was built before the railway and the level of Saddington Street was raised beside it. Now the chapel is an independent Hope Church.

On the left-hand side near the top of The Grove on a site immediately to the south of St. Andrew's Road, at one time occupied by a garage, stood St. Andrew's Presbyterian Church of England, established in 1870 by a congregation which worshipped for a time in the town hall. It was built at a cost of £5000; Edward Bedborough of Southampton was the architect, Messrs Ball and South the builder; and it had twin spires at the west end when built. It was demolished in 1965, but some of the stained glass was removed to St. Paul's church, its successor in Singlewell Road. S. Hopkins, Ornamental Plasterer to Gravesend Town Hall, lived in the road in 1884.

Opposite are the new premises of the Salvation Army, opened March 1967, on the site of No.32, which was built as the Vicarage for Holy Trinity Church and was a large house with a Gothic porch and some stained glass.

St. Andrew's Road leads to Peacock Street, a name not associated in any way with the bird of splendid plumage, but again preserving the name of another director of the building company, Mr Deputy Peacock of the City Corporation, a Bishopsgate baker. A public house with the title *The Peacock* stands on the corner of St. Andrew's Road. On the right, Peacock Street does not join with Parrock Street as do the earlier streets noted, but runs into Waterloo Street, a roadway which led to Milton barracks.

Once again we turn left down Peacock Street, and crossing Saddington Street, proceed in the direction of Milton Road, in order to observe what was at one time a school, known as Smith's Modern School, where a good-class commercial and general education for boys was obtainable. It was originally opened as Milton British School, in 1846, an elementary school for Nonconformist children, who otherwise had to attend one of the Church schools, education by the state not having been sponsored as today; on one side there was the master's house, on the other a residence for the Methodist Minister (Bagshawe 1847). It had accommodation for 400 children and was used also as a Sunday School. It was after it was taken over by Mr C. Hooper Smith, who had been appointed headmaster about 1874, that its reputation rose so rapidly and so justifiably, and tuition at the school was eagerly sought by parents for their sons. As higher standards of education were attained by state schools towards the close of the 19th century, privately-run schools were less patronised, and after 'Gaffer' Smith had relinquished his interest in the Middle Class school, which was later conducted by H. Waldegrave, it was closed and became for a time a dancing academy run by Mr and Mrs Freeborn. Then for a time it was a repertory theatre, which survived the Second World War as The Playhouse, but its fortunes fluctuated and it was closed in 1950 and was then occupied by Lewis and Sons, printers and bookbinders. Now it is a greengrocers and provision merchants.

J. Kendal junior ran a brewery at 10 Wellington Street from c.1850, then L. Laslett. In 1854, it was taken over by Alexander Walker and in 1893 Walker and Sons. This was acquired by the large London brewery firm of Charrington's in 1905, who continued brewing there until about 1928, after a fire at Barton's timber yard had damaged the premises and turned the beer sour; it had to be pumped out by the fire hoses, and the building was demolished in 1936 and the site used as part of *The Jolly Drayman*, better known as the *Brewery Tap*, or colloquially as *the Coke Oven* in Love Lane. Charrington's offices on the west side of Wellington Street were later taken over by Alan J. Smith, a tool merchant, and are now used for car sales, opposite the old brewery site.

Parallel with Wellington Street on its eastern side, with the high wall of the former Barracks on one side and the back gardens of the houses in Wellington Street on the other, is a wide passage that in earlier years justified its title of Love Lane. With open country views over sloping ground towards the river on one side and the aspect of the town on the other, it ran between low hedges from Milton Road to the base of Windmill Hill, and was much favoured by youth of both sexes for sociable walking out. The title of Love Lane was bestowed upon it as a nickname, it being first known as Gurnett's Walk, from having been a public gift in perpetuity to the town of Gravesend by Thomas Gurnett 'to provide a pleasant walk to

Windmill Hill from Milton Place'. In addition to the previously-mentioned names, it was also known as Pennywick Lane, Pennycoat Lane (a variant of Petticoat Lane), and as Melancholy Walk. That it was a popular path to Windmill Hill is confirmed by a voucher of Milton Vestry expenditure of 1830: 'Paid to W. Webster, To writing 144 inches on the gable end of Mr Amos's house "Love Lane leading to Windmill Hill" at 1/2d per inch, 6/-. To painting ground 1/6.'.

Milton Barracks were built in 1863 on land purchased from the South Eastern Railway Company in 1860. It was occupied by various regiments, and in summertime was the quarters of troops undergoing musketry training, who marched in columns of four to the butts at Shorne Mead. It was finally closed in 1971. The site has now been redeveloped with a new Trinity School at the west end and residential development. A new Sikh Temple is now being built on part of the Barrack's site.

Site of The Playhouse, Peacock Street, later Lewis the printers

Chapter 17

MILTON AND PARROCK MANOR HOUSES AND ENVIRONS

THIS CHAPTER DEALS with the area bounded on the north by Parrock Avenue, on the west by Parrock Road, on the south by Old Road East and on the east by Denton parish. Assuming that the perambulation set out in the previous chapter ended at the top of Wellington Street or Love Lane, only a few yards of Parrock Road have to be covered before the north-west corner of the area is reached, the top of Parrock Avenue. Most of the houses here are modern, and a comparatively few years ago this was pastureland or farmland.

A recent development on part of what were playing fields is Bronte View. Mention must be made of Plum Pudding Lane, a pathway leading from Parrock Road to Church Walk (see Chapter 10) on the north side of Parrock Avenue. This was as much sought after in the early years of the 20th century by courting couples as was Love Lane 80 years earlier. It was at one time called 'Arnold Walk'. Meadowland stretched from Parrock Road, guarded by an iron fence down to a large house, which in the 1890s was known as 'The Home Boys', it being the hostel of an organisation connected with the Homes for Little Boys at Farningham, elder lads being employed upon the farm and a dairy business carried on with the house as a centre.

Actually, 'The Home Boys' was the manor house of the manor of Milton, and it still stands, a large 18th-century house in Joy Road, divided into freehold flats, still preserving some of the features which graced it when it was built in 1761 by Peter Moulson, then lord. of the manor of Milton. Milton Manor House was known at various times as 'Figges', 'Sir Thomas Wyatt's Place', 'Milton Place' and, quite erroneously, as 'Lower Parrock'. In the early 19th century the present house was the property of, and was occupied by, Thomas Dalton, a colonel in the West Kent Militia, and Groom of the Bedchamber to the Duke of Gloucester, who was commander of the regiment. It was here that Col. Dalton entertained the Duke, his officers and men when the regiment returned from service on the Continent after the Napoleonic Wars. Col. Dalton (who died in 1827, and to whom there is dedicated a tablet in Milton church and a hatchment) was the last lord of the Manor of Milton to reside in the manor house, the manor becoming the property on his death of members of the Raphael family (although the house was sold elsewhere). Richard Barham, author of *Ingoldsby Legends*, frequently stayed here with Col. Dalton (he was his wife's nephew) of whose property he was an executor, and it was, during his visits that he wrote some of the poems which have a local reference. (Cruden's history of Gravesend [1843] contains much of interest regarding the manor of Milton, including some farm accounts of the 14th century.) After the Kent and Essex Land Company developed the area and laid it out for building, George Sharland at one time lived in the house, with a small area surrounding it for gardens. He was Clerk of the Peace for Gravesend and a local solicitor, his father having been part-time Town Clerk. He married Alice Edmonds, whose father was Mayor. His executors sold the property to Captain Lionel Seymour, the last person to occupy the whole house. He in turn sold it in 1925 to the builder William Hopkins, who laid out Joy Road and turned the building into flats.

There is yet another manor house within the area dealt with in this chapter, that of Parrock, to whose owner in 1268, Robert de la Parrok, was granted a market and fair. It is this charter which is referred to in an inscription at the entrance to Gravesend market today (see Chapter 2), the Corporation of Gravesend having bought the manor of Parrock from George Etkins in 1694. The de Gravesend family, members of which became Bishops of Lincoln and of London, were lords of the manor of Parrock in the 14th century and may have resided there in the manor house of that time.

The present Parrock Manor house is approached from Echo Square and its south front encases a timber-framed building, the roof having principal rafters with collars and butt side purlins of two storeys with attics built 1620-30. There is a brick chimney at each end and a fine chimney-piece with shouldered arch, floral spandrils and a lintel ornamented with paterae and halved Tudor roses. The brick chimney at the other end of the house was the kitchen. On the first floor is a similar fireplace of simpler type. The present false front was added about 1775. In 1830, a large new block, now known as Parrock Manor or 'North House', was added. It has a porch with Tuscan columns and a low slate roof with deep Tuscan eaves. The house

Parrock Farm circa 1900

Milton Manor House (now at the bottom of Joy Road) and Old Road East.
Watercolour, Gravesend Library Collection

Top picture: The entrance road to Milton Hall later Pine Avenue, with the Lodge House far left

Middle picture: Milton Hall

Bottom picture: The Arnold family at Milton Hall

was bought by John Russell junior in 1907. When he died in 1938 the south part of the house and Byre House were sold to Francis Tolhurst, and Edmund Southwood bought 'North House'. The old 'Byre House' is now two residences, and until 1952 there existed a barn, relic of the days when the property was known as Parrock farm. An interesting detached weatherboarded building in the grounds of the old manor house was a granary. It has a wood-lined upper storey where the grain was stored. Charles Smart, after whom Smarts Road was named, was a one time tenant of Parrock Farm.

In the 16th century the old manor house of Parrock was known as 'Spryvers Hache', a name that has an echo of a deed of 1456 which refers to the house of John Sprever which stood where now the old town hall stands in High Street, with the market behind. The manor of Parrock does not appear to have possessed a continuous area of landed property, its holdings being scattered in the parish of Milton. The farm lands which went with Parrock Manor House and stretched from Sun Lane to Wrotham Road were mostly bought by the Gravesend Land Company in 1907 and they laid out the roads between and developed most of this area between the wars.

Christ Church, Milton, is the successor of the earlier Christ Church mentioned in Chapter 15. Much of the material from the old church was taken down, marked and erected on the new site. The architect of the new church was G.E. Clay. The foundation stone was laid by Florence Dowager Countess of Darnley on 16 October 1934, and the church was consecrated on 14 September 1935. The clerestory was added by George Clay and makes the church much lighter. The original had a flat plaster ceiling and was very dark. It was extended by two bays to the east c.1867. On rebuilding the short tower had battlements added instead of a saddleback roof (Carpenter had designed a spire). J.M. Newman describes it as 'original and effective' and Goodhart-Rendel commented, 'All detail and intensely Kentish and local'. It has a very fine east window (stained glass, 1867, by Ward and Hughes, at a cost of £150) and architecturally is the best Victorian church in Gravesend.

On the rising ground to the east of the district, where now Pine Avenue and Milton Hall Road are built, there stood from 1873 to 1930 the mansion built by George Matthews Arnold, solicitor and Mayor of Gravesend eight times, bearing the name of Milton Hall (architect, Geo. Summers Clarke). The 'Building News' for 28 August, 1874, contains a lithograph of the house and brief description. It had 'a baronial hall, reception room 40 feet by 24 feet and 34 feet high and the cloak room was lit by a lancet window'. In its extensive grounds Mr Arnold established a museum of antiquities in which were housed objects of local interest, including prehistoric flint implements excavated from chalk quarries in the neighbourhood, fossils, Roman remains from Springhead and Higham, and various articles with local historical associations. These, after Mr Arnold's death in 1908, were dispersed, some finding a place in the Maidstone museum, others in Gravesend public library, in whose reference library some of the documents are housed. Mr Arnold was also the donor of two statues of Queen Victoria to the town, and of land near the river for the extension of Gravesend promenade and the Gordon Memorial gardens (see Chapters 2, 12 and 13). Pine Avenue was the drive which led to the mansion. Pine trees flanked the drive, these were cut down in May 1984. The first house on the west side, now much altered was the Lodge which still has the two Arnold lions (one from each gate pillar) in the front garden. In the back garden of 30 Pine Avenue are the columns of the old Gravesend market, presented to G.M. Arnold in 1898 when the present market hall was erected. Bernard Arnold, his only surviving son, occupied the house from his father's death in 1908 until his own death in 1925.

PART THREE

Chapter 18

MILTON PARISH SOUTH OF OLD ROAD EAST

WE START THIS CHAPTER at the junction of Old Road with Windmill Street on the north and Singlewell Road on the south, reminding ourselves again that the parishes of Gravesend and Milton have their boundaries along these thoroughfares. While we are waiting for the traffic lights to change (and at this corner were the first traffic lights erected in Gravesend in 1929), the not-so-old may glance obliquely to the left down Devonshire Road and reflect that this and Central Avenue into which the former leads follow roughly a path across cornfields to Singlewell, known as 'Singlewell Fields' and which followed the left-hand footpath in Devonshire Road and the right-hand one in Central Avenue, hence the reason for the two carriageways not being opposite each other. When I first remember Devonshire Road in the 1920s it was a grass track used by the dustcarts and the residents of the first block of houses in Singlewell Road for their grass cuttings and bonfires. Singlewell Fields was a favourite summer evening walk until the early years of the twentieth century. Here until 1929 was the terminus of the Windmill Street tram service, the car stopping in the middle of the crossroads to unload and load and for the conductor to walk the arm round and, at an earlier date, this was the turning point of the donkey rides from the Tivoli. It was also the limit of the one shilling cab fare from the town.

We cross to Singlewell Road, known for many years until building increased as Singlewell Lane, a narrower roadway than now, and less well kept as regards its surface. The first houses in Singlewell Road were those on the west side which, together with the cottages running south from Hammonds Corner, were built from 1883 onwards. The row on the east side were not built until 1906. Prior to this date the triangle of land between Singlewell Road, Devonshire Road and Cross Lane East was from 1879 the Cemetery Nurseries of William Badman who lived at Springfield House, Old Road East. He formerly occupied nurseries near the cemetery. On his death in 1900, his son Frank Badman took over the nursery business, but the triangle of land between Singlewell Road and Devonshire Road (formerly the footpath to Singlewell) near the *Old Prince of Orange* and the frontage to Cross Lane were sold for development. The rest of the nurseries remained but were gradually built on, the last plot being built on c.1955. The block of houses nos. 2 to 24 Singlewell Road were built on the site by Philip Martin Senior. They were one of the earliest blocks in the town to have electric light installed when built, but some of them had gaslight as well, as a precaution against current failures. It was in the back garden of no.12 that the twin-chamber Denehole, described in Philips' History was found in 1905, opened up again after the floods of 1958. The dene hole was found when Albert Edward Chapman, known as 'Dick', one of Philip Martin the builder's workmen, was digging a cesspool; the side of the cesspool collapsed and he fell into one of the twin chambers. The original shaft could not be found. When the main drainage was installed in 1930 a pipe went through the chamber; this burst in 1958. It was 'Dick' who took A.J. Philip down in 1905. He suffered from numerous jokes about his trip to Australia.

At the beginning of the 19th century there stood on the north-west corner of Cross Lane and Singlewell Road Mount Pleasant, the residence of James Leigh Joynes, brewer, banker, estate developer, whose enterprise was responsible for the planning and building of The Terrace (see Chapter 9). Outbuildings occupied part of the Cross Lane frontage, and meadowland, with small plantations of trees, backed the whole as far as Old Road, to which there was a carriage drive. Unfortunately Mr Joynes' incursions into so many business fields led to financial misfortune, and Mount Pleasant and its surrounding buildings were sold to Col. Thomas Dalton (see Chapter 17), who already owned a large proportion of the land southwards from Old Road. Col. Dalton demolished the house about 1822 and turned the estate into market garden land. Later the site became Hammond the baker's garden and his flour store, built up to protect it from rats and the flooding which used to affect the crossroads because of defective surface drainage pipes.

For older Gravesenders, the right-hand corner of Cross Lane and Singlewell Road will always be Hammond's Corner, for here, from 1884 until 1967, was the bakery and sweet shop established by Humphrey Hammond, formerly the manager of a bakery at the corner of Bath Street. The business was continued by his son, Herbert Charles Hammond (who died in 1967) and two daughters, Daisy and Annie, the latter of whom died in 1975. The shop is now used for the sale of ladies' clothes. The opposite corner at the south east was until about 1898 occupied by the playing fields of Gutteridge's school at Clarence House. This was developed as Warwick Terrace, the houses on the south side of Cross Lane East and the west end of Portland Avenue.

From this corner the road rises southward until Watling Street, known to motorists as the A2, is reached a mile farther south. The row of cottages on the west side ends with a parade of shops built in 1934, and thereafter three roads, Hillingdon Road, The Fairway and Dennis Road, laid out in the 1930s, which link Singlewell Road with Upper Wrotham Road.

Beyond these roads is the 18-hole course of the Mid-Kent Golf Club, opened in 1909 by A. J. Balfour and the Hon. A. Lyttleton, M.P., who were partnered by John Braid and Harry Vardon, two ex champions. Mr. C. E. Hatton was the first secretary, and which at one time extended northwards as far as the cottages beyond the Central Parade. The old clubhouse was on the east side of Singlewell Road at the corner of Ascot Road. Across the southern part of the golf course the former southern boundary of the parish of Gravesend runs from the 'hamlet of Claphall' in Upper Wrotham Road to Gypsy Corner, at both ends of which the old parish boundary stones could still be seen until recently. A loop roadway between Gypsy Corner and Ridgeway Avenue, now overgrown, still remains to remind present-day citizens of the quiet, narrow lane to Singlewell which preceded the modern road (built in 1920). There was another boundary stone on the east side of Singlewell Road, above Windsor Road, and the parish boundary continued across fields as far as Lamorna Avenue, the land farther south of both Gravesend and Milton being portions of the parishes of Northfleet and Ifield previous to 1935.

At this point it is well to return to Hammond's Corner, and sketch lightly the developments on the east of Singlewell Road between it and the next north-south road, Whitehill Road. The first on the left (Portland Avenue issues from Cross Lane) is Ferndale Road. The first houses on the north side of Ferndale Road appear in the 1909 Directory. A solitary house appears on the south side in 1911, occupied by William Badman, brother of Frank, who ran a market garden at the rear on the site of the first block of houses in Lingfield Road. At its intersection with Central Avenue was St. Faith's Hall, which before the building of the new Christ Church was a 'mission' church opened in 1907 for that part of Milton parish south of Old Road East. It was closed in 1935, when the new Christ Church was opened, and was used for parochial activities of a social nature as well as for meetings of associations having social welfare as their aim. It was replaced (1975) by a new hall adjoining Christ Church, and has been demolished and the site developed for housing. Lingfield Road was a 1930s development..

Between Singlewell Road and Sun Lane is a maze of residential roads which was served by two licensed houses, *Central Avenue* hotel and the former *General Gordon* hotel (closed 1976 and burnt down 1992) and two schools, Kings Farm primary in Cedar Avenue, and the former Southfields secondary, now a nursery school. When the *Central Avenue* Hotel was built in 1932 the brewers Trumans agreed to lay out a large area of ground to the south and west as a sports ground. This was used by the Gravesend Rugby Club in the winter and the Gravesend Sunday Cricket Club in the summer. Cricket was not allowed on the Bat and Ball on Sundays at this time. In addition at the west end of the ground behind the Golf Club House were two tennis clubs. The pavilion of one of these was used by 'Z' company, 16th Kent Battalion as its headquarters in the early years of the Home Guard, later moving across to 8 Ascot Road and when this property was bombed, to 28 Singlewell Road. The O.C. was Major H.F. Tuffee. The sports ground has recently been developed for housing including the frontage to Ascot Road, but a small part fronting Central Avenue has been left as a children's play area and recreation ground. The whole of the area between Old Road East on the north, Sun Lane on the east, the boundary line of Milton with Northfleet on the south and Singlewell Lane on the west was known in the late 18th century as Punchbowl Field. In the early 19th century, when it was the duty of 'highway surveyors' to compel property owners to repair the roads of the parish (or pay a highway rate), the southern part of this area was the source of much material in the form of flints collected from the surface of the fields by boys and women which were carted from

King's Farm and Christian's Fields, two names which still survive, and laid as foundations of the thoroughfares in the older part of the town to make water-bound macadam roads.

With the exception of the western end of Portland Avenue and Ferndale Road, which were opened before the First World War, all these roads were laid out and built up in the 1920s and 1930s. The area to the south was known as Craggs Farm (although the farmhouse was in Singlewell) and that to the north was Parrock Farm; it was all developed by the Gravesend Land Company on land bought from the Raphael family in 1907. One of these roads, Malvina Avenue, was originally the 'allotment estate' providing small market gardens and allotments with detached small houses and bungalows, but since the last war it has all been built up.

King's Farm Estate was the first council estate built to rehouse the inhabitants of the area between Church Street and West Street, when this area was demolished under slum clearance. The land was bought by the Corporation in 1919 from Alfred Tolhurst's Trustees. George King was the farmer who gave his name to the estate. The farm house was on the south west side of Sun Lane, near its junction with Kitchener Avenue. Mr Christian, who had a cottage in Whitehill Lane, farmed the land to the south. Kings Drive was the first road to link Singlewell Road with the new estate c.1924. In that year a small airfield was established south of Kings Drive from which Sir Alan Cobham ran trips at 5 shillings a time. In 1931, a Roman burial site with several grave goods was found in the back garden of 27 Kings Drive. The first council houses were erected at the top of Whitehall Road and in Sun Lane, and Cornwall Avenue and Jellicoe Avenue were cut and houses built in the early 1920s. The Mayor, W.S. Harrington who later lived in Kings Drive, cut the first sod on 6 January 1921. He was a grocer in Wrotham Road. Ridgeway Avenue and Northridge Road were cut early in 1929.

The area became part of Christ Church parish in 1935 and a new church, the Church of the Holy Family, was built to serve this area and dedicated by Bishop H.C. Read in June 1959. It is now a separate Parish joined to Ifield.

The next perambulation of this southern part of the parish of Milton starts at Echo Square. Here it will be noted that two roads run south, Whitehill Road and Sun Lane. Of these Sun Lane is the older, having been originally a lane leading to Cobham; it joins into Whitehill Road again at the top near the junction of Sun Lane and Kitchener Avenue. Whitehill Road Schools opened in 1927 on a site occupied by Ashenden's Nurseries who moved to Singlewell Road, a site on which Southfield's School was later built. Beyond this point southward was known until shortly after the Second World War as Whitehill Lane or 'the lane to the Sanatorium'. At the junction of Sun Lane and Cross Lane there stood until about 1900 a building formerly the *Sun* inn or beerhouse, from which the lane took its name. To this Pocock refers in his Chronology, where he records that a suicide named Knight was buried 'in the four-went way near the Sun public-house, now a private house' (1797). It is worth noting that Pocock records a four-went way where there are now six. Whitehill Road was a footpath until 1853, the road was at first known as 'Parrock Road Fields', and Old Road joined Cross Lane in a 'T' junction at the western end of Elnathan Cottages prior to 1795, when the turnpike commissioners altered the road to its present course and later sold the 'sandbank' between the roads and the cottages were built in 1884. Sun Lane was also called 'Old Sun Lane' and 'Sun Pond Lane', the latter from the pond shown in old maps which was in the depression on the left-hand side opposite the end of Portland Avenue. Beyond Elnathan Cottages were a row of high elms and until the 1960s a large rookery. Before 1914, an annual rook shoot was held to keep down their numbers. Until the 20th century the West Kent Hunt used on occasions to meet at Echo Square. About three-quarters of the way along Whitehill Road on the right beyond Canterbury Road may be seen a pair of tall iron gates leading to two houses where formerly stood the residence of Mr. G.E. Sharland, Town Clerk of Gravesend for many years. These gates stood prior to 1901 at the London Road entrance to Rosherville Gardens. On the opposite side of the road stood Canterbury House, at one time the residence of W. Edmonds, a dentist, and a one-time mayor and alderman. This was said to be the first house in the town to have electric light from current generated by a small steam engine installed by his son, Hubert Edmonds, a marine engineer. William Smoker in his reminiscences says that the first house in the town to have 'a carbon burning electric light' was that of a doctor in Darnley Road. The house was painted white in 1892.

The houses in Sun Lane (east side) and Whitehill Road date from the middle of the 19th

Top picture: Pine Avenue
February, 1984

Bottom picture: St Faith's
Church and hall, Central
Avenue, 1962

Bomb damage Ascot Road, corner of Gatwick Road

The *Echo* public house, Echo Square

century with later ones filling the gaps and replacing some of the older houses, which had large gardens.

On the left of Whitehill Road, Laurel Avenue and Hollybush Road lead to a maze of new residential roads similar to that between Whitehill Road and Singlewell Road, most of which date from the 1930s and some of which are of post-Second World War construction. This area was part of Parrock Farm.

Several deneholes have been found in this area, including a large one at the rear of the Echo public house, on a site now occupied by garages.

To close this chapter, we return to Echo Square in order to complete the survey of Old Road East within the Milton territory leading to Denton, and note on the right-hand side at the corner of Old Road East and Whitehill Road the *Echo* public house, built as a beerhouse in 1865, becoming a full public house in 1869. For many years it belonged to the Brown family as a 'freehouse'. The drinking trough in the middle of the Square was erected in 1903 with a legacy to the memory of Frederick and Annie Martha Gibbon. From 1979 to the middle of the 1990s the trough had been sited at the junction with Cross Lane West, where it had been rebuilt and restored after its previous demolition by a lorry at its earlier central position. It was in 1979 that the central position of Echo Square became a roundabout with circular garden. Hillside Drive, at the end of which is St. Joseph's convent and chapel, which was formerly 'Hillside', and from 1894 the residence of Mr John Russell (the elder), Alderman and brewer of the town and Milton churchwarden, and built in 1882 by Edward Fooks (a son-in-law and partner of G.M. Arnold) on a small spur with views over both the river to the north and the open country to the south. Downham, now the Convent Preparatory School was formerly for many years the residence of A.J. Shade, a local baker with shops at 36 Stone Street and 13 High Street. He was Mayor in 1926. One of his daughters was very active in local dramatic and dance productions and kept her scenery and props in a store at the rear of the Stone Street shop in Garden Row. Opposite the end of Pine Avenue was a large late Georgian House known as Milton Grange, its frontage being straight onto the road. In the 19th century it was known as Ivy Cottage and was for many years the only house between the *Echo* and Bell Cottages. It was demolished in 1958 when the Yews estate was built on its site and that of the old cherry orchard. In the 18th century Bell Cottages were said to have been a small beerhouse but they are described as two cottages in 1833, when the bounds were perambulated.

Milton Grange, Old Road East

Chapter 19

THE PARISH OF DENTON

THE PARISH OF DENTON, which from 1895 had been part of Strood Rural District Council, became part of the Borough of Gravesend in 1935, and has almost lost its identity as roads within its boundaries are continued into the parishes of Milton and Chalk; but the fact that this volume is concerned with the historical as well as the topographical aspect of the township demands that an account be given of the boundaries of the old parish and its principal features as well as a brief survey of its past.

From north to south, Denton is long as compared with its breadth, its west and east limits ending in a point towards the south-east, similar to the tip of an old pen nib. Its western boundary is also the eastern boundary of Milton, as its eastern boundary is that also of Chalk on the western side of that parish. Like all riverside parishes it extends theoretically into the centre of the Thames, its shore on the north being a matter of about 1000 yards from a point West of 'Woodville Cottages' (built in 1883, and were said to be the first working class homes in the area to have fixed baths which could be filled from the copper after the water had been used for washing clothes but most of which have been demolished), to a spot beyond the former Port of London Isolation Hospital to the east (opened in 1884, closed 1974 and now demolished). The training ship *Cornwall* was moored in the river opposite Woodville Cottages from 1925 (having been moved there from Purfleet) until 1940, when it was sunk by a German raider on 24 September, when Hitler claimed to have sunk one of our warships called 'Cory Wall'.

From the western point the parish boundary crosses the railway and runs to the north of Waterton Avenue, and follows Elliott Street to the London-Rochester road, where it swings round in a south-easterly direction towards Rochester. Thence it heads in a south-south-westerly direction to Hillside and Lamorna Avenue, which it follows to cross Valley Drive and make the pen-point mentioned above. The eastern boundary runs roughly north from this point, leaving St. Dunstan's Drive and part of Hampton Crescent within the parish, to Old Road East, where it turns along the road to the junction with Rochester Road and thence skirts Ingoldsby Road and pursues a somewhat zigzag course, which was dictated by the marsh ditches, to the riverside again below the former hospital. Within the borders of Denton parish on the marshes is Gravesend Corporation Sewage Disposal Works, main drainage being installed in the 1930s. Denton Parish was probably part of the Minster Parish of Northfleet and came from Milton. Its church, dedicated to St. Mary (an early dedication), is very near the Milton boundary.

Like the southern portion of Gravesend, Milton and Chalk, the southern portion of Denton has been thickly built over. Until the 1930s, the only part occupied by domestic dwellings consisted of a number of short streets on the north side of the London-Rochester Road. Lower Range Road was the most important of these, gaining its name from the fact that it was by this road that troops housed in Milton barracks proceeded to the butts at Shorne Mead for musketry practice. There was a level crossing over the railway where from 1906 to 1961 was Denton Halt at which only the Hundred of Hoo line trains stopped, being closed when this service was withdrawn. A large castellated house called 'The Poplars' was built in Waterton Avenue c.1909. On the riverside T.F. Wood built a wharf for unloading explosives, later taken over by I.C.I. On the sea wall a public house called the *Ship and Lobster* was built about 1813. A new one was built c.1890. An inn at the turn of the road was called *The Markers' Retreat.* A school, Denton primary, stood at the corner where Empress Road leads from Lower Range Road and was built in 1909 to cater for Denton when it lay outside the Borough. It was closed in 1976. Where now is Baltimore Terrace there was formerly a group of weatherboard dwellings known as 'the five houses'. One of these was, in the 1890s, the cottage-shop of 'Mother Kirk', whose home-made toffee, manufactured in little patty-pans, was one of the locally appreciated sweetmeats. A little farther along on the left was the prosperous dairy of W.J. Champion (later Maclean and now the United Dairies office). W.J. Champion was a staunch supporter of Milton Church nearby, his son, Harold, being for some years its talented organist, who also had the organ renovated in 1936 at his own expense as a memorial to his parents.

The *Ship and Lobster* Tavern, Denton

The Poplars, Waterton Avenue

Denton Halt

A little farther along on the left-hand side, its west wall only a few yards from the footway, is a Roman Catholic chapel, built by G.M. Arnold in 1901 on the site of the former parish church of Denton (architect F.A. Walters, F.S.A.): the ruins of this ancient church were incorporated in the newer edifice. (Reference to this church and the manor of Denton will be found in the historical matter at the end of this chapter.)

Until 1936, there stood to the south-east of the chapel Denton Court, built in 1791 by Nicholas Gilbee, on the site of the ancient manor house of Denton. It long had a large board outside saying 'Site for Empire Paper Mills', but they were never built here.On the demolition of Denton Court the site was cleared for building, the name surviving in Denton Court Road which occupies part of the site. Mr Gilbee also built a smock windmill on the waterside on a site adjoining 'Woodville Cottages' in about 1790, as well as building a 'Freecoal' wharf there in 1791. He overspent himself and went bankrupt in 1816. His wife was Miss Ann Cruden, a sister of the historian. The mill was pulled down by 1877.

The earliest reference to Denton in documents is to be found in a will of 950 AD, in which Byrhtric, a Saxon thane of Meopham with Aelfswiths his wife, bequeathed land at Denetune which belonged to her, in order that masses might be said for the souls of himself and his wife. Domesday Book 1086 AD refers to Danitone and its church, and at intervals during the following two centuries the manor, its dues and possessions are set out in various documents. Henry VIII settled the manor and advowson on the Dean and Chapter of Rochester where it remained until bought by G.M. Arnold. The Domesday spelling of the name has played a part in the belief that it refers to possession at some time by Danish settlers (Dane town), but modern philologists favour the derivation from 'denu', a Saxon word for valley which certainly describes the parish.

With the very small and probably decreasing population that Denton had it is not surprising to learn that services ceased to be held in Denton parish church after 1650 in the Commonwealth period. No record of a priest holding the living is existent after the incumbency of John Stace in 1536. Burials continued in the churchyard until 1678, but the ecclesiastical parish was no longer a reality: its revenues appear to have accrued to the diocese until 1879, when part of them was allotted to the rector of Milton, and Denton was amalgamated with that Parish. Earlier the adjoining parish of Chalk was recognised as being the church for banns of marriage and so on, in the late 18th century and the early 19th century, the registers of 1788 referring to a bridegroom as being 'of the extraparochial place of Denton', and another as being of 'Denton, having no church or chapel standing'.

The old churchyard of Denton extended in a westerly direction, including land through which the present roadway on the Milton side was cut when the 'turnpike', now Rochester Road, was made. The ruins of this church were the site of the imaginary Ingoldsby Abbey in the Rev. R.H. Barham's poem 'The Ingoldsby Penance' in the Ingoldsby Legends, where 'A full choir of monks and a full choir of nuns shall live upon cabbage and hot cross buns'. Ingoldsby Road and Abbey Road derive their names from this poem in the Ingoldsby Legends.

Other places of religious congregation include a Community Centre and place of worship belonging to the Shaftesbury Society and a 'Full Gospel Church' in Valley Drive,

Further particulars of the parish are to be found in Denton, by G.M. Arnold, F.S.A., published in 1902 by Caddel & Sons, a copy of which can be seen in Gravesend public library.

Mention should be made in this section of the vast housing estates on either side of Valley Drive, all built since the Second World War. The upper part of Valley Drive was formerly part of Whitehall Lane and on its east side in The Warren were the isolation hospitals and sanatorium of Gravesend and Strood councils (built in 1887), Denton and Chalk parishes both being formerly part of Strood Rural District. A proposal to use these hospitals for a maternity hospital is commemorated in the name of a public house established in one of the former hospital buildings and called The Stork at Rest. This pub was completely rebuilt in Stacey Close in 1957. There is a cottage on the south side of Old Road East formerly known as 'Laundry Cottage' where the washerwoman for Hillside House lived and did the families' laundry. Near here was the farm or settlement of Upper Denton.

When the Council built the estate of council houses to the north of Rochester Road the brewery built a new public house called The Dickens on the south-west corner of Dickens Road and Rochester Road in 1934. This became the Colonial in 1986, it was closed in 1992 and demolished in 1996.

Denton Court, circa 1900

Chapter 20

THE PARISH OF CHALK

AS LATE AS the early years of the 20th century Chalk was a village remote and separate from Gravesend. Its few houses on the old main road to Rochester and the sparsely-set cottages and farmhouses on the Lower Road to Higham were only seen by those Gravesend inhabitants who indulged in a Sunday afternoon walk in that direction, or by youthful cyclists and later motorists out for a country spin. Taken into the Gravesend Corporation area in 1935, Chalk has become, so far as its south-western portion is concerned, a huge housing estate. The former Gravesend airport opened as the Gravesend School of Flying in 1932, from which Amy Johnson started her record flight and which became a war-time fighter station, was sold to Dolphin Development in 1957, and is now covered by the River View Park Estate.

Most of the traffic through Chalk passes along the wide highway constructed between Gravesend and Strood in 1921 and officially opened in 1923 under one of the Unemployment Relief Acts. This work gave rise to a very serious railway accident at Milton Range Halt, on Filborough Marshes, which was being used for workmen from London under this job creation project.

Two trains of workmen left Charing Cross and New Cross each morning with men who walked from the Halt to their work. On 24 August 1922, there was a thick fog and the first train overran the platform and, before the driver could set back, the men began to get out and cross the up-line to get to work in time. There was no bridge in any case. A light engine from Strood emerged from the fog and killed one man and carried two others along the track who later died in hospital. The driver was unaware of what had happened. By now the New Cross train had arrived at Gravesend and the driver missed a signal there. Denton signal box was not yet open and the second train ran into the first. The passengers remaining in the first train, hearing the second approaching, jumped out, some into the canal, and the force of the impact smashed coaches and knocked them into the canal and two more passengers were killed. (See *South Eastern and Chatham Railways*, Adrian Gray, p.137 for a full description and illustration.)

This road leaves the former turnpike road on the left at the Lion Garage and only joins it to absorb it about seven-eighths of a mile farther east. If we take this older road at the roundabout which was completed in 1972, we pass a building which was formerly the malting premises of Charrington's brewery formerly Wood's (its twin towers were taken down in 1957). It was later used for educational purposes and then for small businesses. At present it is boarded up and empty. Almost opposite was the Chalk tollgate, set up by the Turnpike Commissioners who, under a series of local acts, the first of which was granted in 1711, maintained the main road between Northfleet (later extended to Dartford) and Strood. The site of the Chalk gate was originally further east, but was moved to this spot when the road was straightened in 1777. The turnpike trust was wound up in 1871, when the County took over responsibility for this main road.

On the right of the road at the corner of Forge Lane, which in older days extended southward to the extreme southern boundary of the parish, is the forge from which Charles Dickens drew some of the features of the forge in his novel, *Great Expectations*. Oscar Mullender, who used to operate the smithy, knew Dickens well. The last smith to operate the forge was A. Mann, who retired on 4 November 1953.

Opposite a lane led down to the marshes and the house 'West Court', one of the Chalk manors. It was built in 1739 as a typical two-bay Georgian house, facing south with a central front door and entrance. In about 1870, it was extended to the east with another bay in similar style and three ground floor wooden bay windows added. It had extensive curtiledge buildings, including thatched barns, stables, cart house, granary and single oast with drying floor. The manor was purchased by Sir Joseph Williamson, then living at Cobham Hall when sold to pay the debts on the death of the last Duke of Richmond and, on Sir Joseph Williamson's death in 1701, it came into the possession of the Darnley family. It was included in the 1925 Darnley sale and bought by the then tenant farmer Thomas Barr Maclean. Much of the land was, over the years, sold off for development. The house remained as a private residence until 1988 and after two disastrous fires it was demolished in 1991. An excavation by Pre-Construct Archaeology in 1997, prior to the redevelopment of the site, revealed evidence of the mediaeval manor house c.1150 and of a later period c.1270-1350. (See *Archaeologia Cantiana CXIX 1999* p.353.) The Brooke family were tenant farmers from 1886 to 1918. They collected the town refuse and had a 'dust hole' near the upper part of Forge Lane. Mr. Brooke supplied the horses for the trams and fire engine (usually taken from a tram when the fire bell was rung). In the late 19th century, horse sales were held outside the *Nelson Hotel* in New Road, by George Brooke and John Brann from Great Clayne Farm, Chalk. At the junction with Lower Higham Road was Malthouse Farm, the house latterly used as two cottages. A little farther on stood the former *White Hart* inn (1604-1937) and the site is now occupied by a new house. A new inn with the same name was built on the newer road some distance in the rear in 1937. It in turn was demolished in 1999 and a Harvester Restaurant was built on the site.

The village school building (built 1866) is now at the rear of the newer village hall used mainly for social functions and the youth club.

Just past the junction of the road to the left, which leads to Higham, Cliffe and other hamlets in the Hundred of Hoo, is a cottage on which there is a bust of Charles Dickens, by Fitzgerald, with a tablet stating that it was here that Dickens spent his honeymoon. The tablet was erected by the local Dickens Fellowship in 1911. This house is usually known as 'Craddock's Cottage', from the name of the 19th-century tenant, who let lodgings and was 'identified' as the honeymoon cottage by the late Mr A.J. Philip. Previously the house at the corner of Vicarage Lane, now known (quite incorrectly) as 'The Manor House', and formerly as 'The Old Parsonage' (this was probably the residence of the farmer of the Rectorial tithes, in lay hands from the Reformation) was claimed to be the honeymoon cottage on the authority of Mr. E.F. Blanchard, a contemporary of Dickens, who lived at Rosherville. The claims of 'Craddock's Cottage' were never accepted by the London Dickens Fellowship, and shortly after the Fitzgerald bust was erected a letter written by Dickens on his honeymoon from 'Mrs. Nash's' at Chalk was found. This cottage (No.18 Lower Higham Road) was further west on the south side, next to the old *White Hart*, and was demolished in 1957. Mrs Mary Nash appears as a resident of Chalk in *Bagshawe's Directory* of 1847.

The second public house in Chalk village was *'The Lord Nelson'* (from 1806 to 1923 when it was closed as an inn) earlier *'The George'*, *'The Blackboy'*, *'The Round House'* and *'The King of Prussia'*. It stood opposite the junction of Lower Higham Road from 1715 to 1923. The building was demolished in the 1950s.

Vicarage Lane is so called from the vicarage which was built in 1870 and stood on the east side. It was demolished about 1968 and a small estate and new vicarage were built on the site. An earlier vicarage was, in 1822, a small jetted two-bay house with an outshott illustrated in *Some Kentish Houses, Kentish Sources V* by Elizabeth Melling and Anne Oakley, p.70. Situated in Lower Higham Road, it was at one time used as a school. Great Clayne Farm was a refronted early 18th-century house, of the same style and period as 'West Court', with red bricks and flared headers and weather boarding at the rear. It was demolished in 1963. As earlier noted the village road continues to loop into the main road which leads to the parish church of St. Mary. Prior to 1777, the main turnpike road to Rochester proceeded down Lower Higham Road to the corner of Vicarage Lane, then up Vicarage Lane and left opposite the Parsonage (now Old Manor House). The Chalk Turnpike was situated opposite the Old Parsonage (The Manor House) in Chalk Road. In 1777 the Trustees cut a new road from the present junction with Lower Higham Road to join the road at the parsonage and moved the Tollgate to a site to the west of the Forge.

Near Via Romana were found in 1961 the remains of a large Roman villa. A narrow roadway on the left, Castle Lane, leads to the Lower Road and a new estate, and at the corner of this road stood until the Second World War *The Lisle Castle*, Chalk's third inn. This was destroyed by an aerial mine on 22 September 1940 and it remained in a derelict condition until totally demolished in 1956, and a new house built on the site. In this lane were a row of cottages known as 'Golf Cottages', from the fact that the second Gravesend golf links was laid out there.

Top picture: The Forge, 1979

Middle picture: Nash's Cottage.
Lower Higham Road

Bottom picture: Golf Links
Cottages, Chalk, 1959

Great Clayne Farm house, Lower Higham Road, Chalk
The walkers are in Vicarage Lane. Circa 1959

Through the trees the Victorian Chalk Vicarage circa 1962

The church of St. Mary is largely of Early English date, with a late 12th-century north aisle. The dormer windows in this aisle are 19th-century work, the roof previously sweeping down to a low north wall. The 13th-century lancets in the chancel have been much restored. A later south aisle was destroyed in 1759 and the arcade arches filled in. The tower is a typical Kentish 15th-century one with projecting stair turret, and the porch with its quaint tippling figures which so intrigued Dickens, is of the same period. The porch cornice is Victorian; previously there was a pointed roof. The church suffered from a drastic Victorian restoration and lost its screen of 1660. It underwent further considerable restoration in the early 1950s. It has a nave of three bays with north aisle, the western end of which is now a vestry for choir and priest. On the south side of the chancel is a 13th-century sedila and piscina with shelf. Inside the west door is a stoup.

On the east side of Church Lane is 'East Court', another of the Chalk manors. The present house dates from the 18th century. This part of the parish east of Castle Lane is still largely unbuilt on and was always quite separate from Chalk Street at 'West Court'.

Of its farms, that of Filborough is the oldest, being mentioned as early as 1220, when it was bought from John, son of Hugh de Nevill, by John, son of Henry de Cobham. It later passed into the hands of Henry VIII, who let it to James Reynolds of London, joiner, in 1545. A brass to a member of a family occupying Filborough, William Martyn and his wife Isabella, was placed in Chalk church after their death in 1416. They left money for 'the fabric of the church' and the porch figures may be connected with this. The house itself was an open hall with cross wing and inserted chimney and crown posts in both the main part and the wing and was restored by G.M. Arnold. The present building dates from the end of the 15th century (see Anthony Quinly, *Kent Houses,* p.138 and, for a detailed description and plan by G.M. Arnold *Archaeologia Cantiana XXI* p.161). It originally consisted of an open hall and detached kitchen, later joined to the main building by a brick addition. Mr Arnold found smoke-blackened rafters from a central fire in the hall, later replaced by a brick chimney. It seems to have been the residence of the Marten family (sometimes spelt Martyn or Martin) at one time and, although described as in 'East Chalk', it seems to have been associated with the small manors of Raynehurst and Timberwood. Opposite the house is Little Filborough a 19th century house and an interesting listed granary. West Filborough was an 18th century house which stood on the south west corner of Castle Lane and Lower Higham Road, demolished in 1959. All three Filborough houses occupied old sites.

A prominent feature of the marshes is the National Sea Training School building and the mission centre of the Mission to Seamen. The school was moved here in 1967. It is now used, together with the adjoining ex-army ranges, as a training school for firearms for the Metropolitan Police and other security organisations. The architects for the Sea School were Lyons, Israel, Ellis and Partners.

Another ancient house in Lower Higham Road is 'Readers', probably dating from the 17th century. It was the home of the Reader family and later of Mr Louis Grewcock (known as 'Peg Leg Reader') until 1959, when it was bought and restored in 1965 by Mr. Cecil Stroud.

A member of the family of Lovelace, which was that of the poet of that name, designated himself as a 'gentleman of Chalke, where I was born'. His wish to give something to the poor of Chalk and his desire to be buried there do not seem to have been carried out.

Chalk is mentioned in Domesday, but this is not the earliest mention of the parish, there having been a 'witan' there shortly after 700 AD to confirm the Wilmington Charter of that year devised by Archbishop Berhtwald. It would appear that, in 1390, Cobham College, then an abode of monks, owned land in the village, John Long being appointed vicar on the presentation of the Master and Brethren of the College. A John Pottkyn and his wife Constance are mentioned in records of wills, John's wife having formerly been the wife of Robert Martin, who died in 1456.

The area of Chalk before its incorporation into Gravesend was 1835 acres, its western boundary being for a considerable length that of the eastern boundary of Denton, but extending farther south to border Ifield before it turns east for about 1200 yards to cross Thong Lane and leave the southern part of the lane in the parish of Shorne. To the east of Thong Lane the boundary line turns north for about 200 yards, then north-east irregularly for 1000 yards to pass below the church at Deadman's Bottom (so called from the name of a local farmer) at about 250 yards on the eastern side, and so to the riverside 300 yards more or less from Shornemead fort. Chalk's boundaries included two detached parts of the parish, one on the Essex shore opposite and one sandwiched between Shorne and Lower Higham, known as 'Chalk Extra'.

In that part of the Chalk area more recently built over, a Church of England church was built in 1962, dedicated to St. Aidan (architects, Northover and Northover of Tenterden) now a separate Parish. The foundation stone was laid by Lady Tristram Eve, the wife of Sir Malcolm Eve, First Church Commissioner, on 3 May 1962, and dedicated by David Saye, Bishop of Rochester. The land had been set aside in 1951 and a hall built on the site in 1954-5 (architect George Clay, builder Jury and Co.). Services were held here until 1963, when the new church was consecrated, used for the first time on 11 May that year. A parish hall was also built in 1965. A Pentecostal Church was established in the late 1940s for which a new church was erected in 1972.

In 1920 the London County Council purchased estates at Chalk, Thong and Shorne Ifield (later taken over by the Kent County Council) from the Darnley estate under Lloyd George's Homes for Heroes' Act (five acres and a pig!) and built a series of detached and semi-detached houses with small timber barns and a number of these were erected in Castle Lane, Church Lane, Thong Lane and Shorne Ifield. Most of the houses and a few barns have survived but without the smallholdings.

The Leisure Centre of Cascades was laid out on the east of Thong Lane, the pavilion being built in 1969, the sports hall in 1974, the swimming pool in 1975 (it replaced the pool in Ordnance Road) and a squash court in 1979.

The *Lord Nelson* public house

Chapter 21

THE PARISH OF IFIELD AND THE VILLAGE OF SINGLEWELL

WHILST IT IS POSSIBLE to convey to a reader a tolerably clear idea of the shape and place upon a larger map of the parishes of Denton and Chalk, the parish of Ifield offers no such easy depiction. It was no doubt created out of Northfleet and the puzzling manner in which parts of the parish of Northfleet were left and separated one part of Ifield from another had always been difficult to follow. The village of Singlewell was included within the Gravesend municipal boundary in 1935, the rest of Ifield including the church then becoming part of the civil parish of Cobham; all is now of course part of Gravesham. A map of Ifield before that date suggests a section of a patchwork quilt, with the eastern part of the parish running north and south across Watling Street, and divided from the western part north of Watling Street by a strip of Northfleet territory on the east side of Singlewell Road, which broadens out south of Watling Street, only retreating to the west sufficiently to allow Ifield church and rectory to preserve a place just inside the parish border.

Thus the ground upon which Harman Avenue, Orchard Avenue and Golf Links Avenue are built and the southern part of the golf links on the west side of Singlewell Road are in the old Ifield parish, whilst the land on the east side of that thoroughfare, including the former Southfield school, and the former Westfield and Craggs farm are, or rather were, in the parish of Northfleet, as far as the eastern portion mentioned above. Craggs Farm was bought by John Wood in 1872. It had a large barn parallel with the present Hever Court Road and was just round the corner from Singlewell Road, It was demolished in 1971 and the site developed. Beyond the barn were a row of Georgian cottages and beyond them a row of weatherboard cottages known as 'Jubilee Cottages', which were demolished before World War II. The Miskin Memorial Hall probably occupied their site. John Wood ran the brickfield between Wrotham Road and the end of Park Road and he built a large stock brick house called Westfield near the top of Singlewell Road. After being used as offices, this has been demolished and a new estate built. The lodge, much altered, still survives in Singlewell Road. John Wood, who also had a brickfield at Lower Halstow, was one of the founders of Eastwoods brickmakers.

Except for the church and rectory of Ifield, most of the parish was in common parlance Singlewell, a name arising from the old public well (properly 'Shinglewell') which, with its winding gear, stood a few yards from the older Watling Street at the junction of Church Road and Hever Court Road in the middle of the road. The well was filled in and domed over in April 1914 and in 1935 a granite slab was placed there to record its earlier existence, and inscribed 'Site of ancient well Shinglewell Parish of Ifield'. This slab was removed in 1952 by the Kent County Council as road authority. (The widely-held opinion that the village was named 'Singlewell' because there was only one well in the parish was entirely erroneous, there being others in the district.) A legend of a miracle performed here by St. Thomas of Canterbury, whereby a panic-stricken girl, Salerna, was saved from drowning by the saint's intervention, may be taken as witness of the well's antiquity. The legend, translated from two Latin MSS by the Rev. K.M. Ffinch, rector of Ifield, 1912-38, is printed in *The History of Ifield and Singlewell* from Mr Ffinch's notes. A stained glass window illustrating the Salerna story was placed in Ifield Church in 1954 in memory of Stuart Miskin.

The houses on Hever Court estate were erected in 1957. Until these changes were wrought the thoroughfare was a narrow lane with a pond on the north side of the roadway overhung with elms. 'Hever Court', opposite Orchard Farm, which gave its name to the road, was for many years the most imposing house in the village, itself standing upon the site of an earlier 'Hever Court', the original house of the Hever family, who removed to Hever, near Tonbridge, in 1331. The later 'Hever Court' was a 17th century house of brick which bore over its dining-room window 'P.R.E. 1675'. During the Second World War it was occupied by the War Office as a barracks, and during that occupation a fire caused great damage to roof and walls: as a result it became derelict and was demolished in 1952. It had been formerly the property of Sir James Fergusson and Sir Thomas Colyer-Fergusson, his son. It was the manor house for Ifield Parish, Ifield Court being a separate manor in Northfleet Parish.

Opposite Church Road, to the east of the site of Hever Court, is a pathway leading to Gravesend across what was for many years arable land, and known as Singlewell Fields. (See also p.67 for the Gravesend end of this path.)

On the south side of the road, unsuspected by many who have passed it by through the years, is what remains of an old chapel which may date back to the period of the Salerna legend. The stucco front of the farmhouse, Chapel Farm, gives no hint that the lower walls are some 2 feet 6 inches thick. The south wall, away from the road, is exposed and of flint and ragstone with a doorway and stone quoins of two windows which have been filled in. There are some written references to this chapel, and a fuller account is given in the 'History' mentioned above.

A few yards farther east is the *George* inn, previously the *Crown and Three Horseshoes* (1715-64) which, during the 19th century, was a favourite house of refreshment of Gravesenders, who found it a convenient walking distance from home on summer evenings. An extension on the south in the 1930s opened its patronage to the coaches and lorries on the A2, or the 'New' Watling Street opened by the Prince of Wales (later the Duke of Windsor) on 19 November 1924. This in turn was replaced by a dual carriageway road opened in August, 1966, by Alderman Simmons, Chairman of the Kent County Council Roads Committee. The new *George* Travelodge, opened in 1999, is now reached by a loopway from the A2. In 1966, Church Road was cut in two and an underground pathway provided as a link to the rest of the road leading to the church. The building of the high-speed rail link in 2000 has now cut off this road from the church which can only be reached by a new road from Henshurst Lane.

Beyond the *George,* where now is the Manor House restaurant and hotel, was a pond and thatched cottage (demolished c.1928) at one time Singlewell Post Office, later moved to the shop in Church Lane next to Corner Cottage. Opposite the *George* was the Fair Field in which a fair was held by Royal Charter of 20 January 1331 which granted a weekly market to Thomas de Hevre every Monday at his Manor of Singlewell and a fair every year on the Vigil and day of St. Lawrence (10 August). The fair was held in this field until about 1870. The fact that it was held on St. Laurence Day may give us some indication of the dedication of the chapel opposite. At the rear of the field was Hever Farm, built on the site of the former 'good house' which in the 17th century belonged to the Parker family and was probably demolished about 1836 (it appears on the Tithe Map) when Hever Farm, for many years known as 'New House', was built and occupied by the Solomon family. It was demolished in 1977 and replaced by the new Hever Farm house in Church Road. The whole site has since been developed.

On the south side of the busy road the former Church Road, a narrow thoroughfare of some antiquity, led to the tiny parish church of St. Margaret. While it has no great architectural pretensions, it is attractive in its isolated rural setting. From its dimensions and the thickness of the walls it would seem that Ifield church is probably a small two-cell Norman fabric like Denton, Dode and Paddlesworth, but roughcast and interior plaster have concealed all the early features except the remains of an inserted low side window on the south chancel wall. A reference in an early 19th-century painting in the K.A.S. collection at Maidstone refers to lancets in the chancel. The present windows date from 1845, the cusping and tracery may have been copied from the 15th-century window at 'Ifield Court'. The previous church windows were also square-headed. The former rectory on the right-hand side of the lane was built in 1865 on the glebe land and was sold by the church in 1978 when Ifield was joined with the Church of the Holy Family for ecclesiastical purposes.

'Ifield Court', reached by a drive on the right, is a Georgian house rebuilt in 1791 by John Tilden (who had bought it in 1766), standing on the site of a former manor house, a small fragment of which in ragstone with a three-light triple-cusped window, exists at the east end of the present house. Further mediaeval work was demolished in 1907, but, unfortunately, no illustration of this seems to have survived. In the reign of Elizabeth I it belonged to Sir John Garrard, Lord Mayor of London. There were formerly three manors of Ifield Court, Wells and Cossington, all in Northfleet parish. Earthworks in Cossington Wood probably mark the site of a deserted village or hamlet, and Wells Field was to the south of the church. At the end of Church Lane, where the road branches for Nurstead, Sole Street and Cobham, was Toltingtrow Green, the meeting place of the Hundred of Toltingtrow, of which Northfleet,

The well at Singlewell (Salerna Legend)

The *George*, Singlewell, April, 1963

Hever Farm, Singlewell, circa 1962

Craggs Farmhouse, December, 1962

Chapel Farm, Singlewell, c.1930

Ifleld, Gravesend and Milton formed part (Denton and Chalk were in Shamel). The meeting place for the Hundred of Shamel seems to have been Gads Hill, where there is a 'Court' Wood. In the 18th century the Shamel Hundred met at the *Duke of York* at Shorne.

The Glebe land of the parish of Ifield on the north end of which the Rectory was built in 1865 (sold in 1978 for £46,000) stretched to Ifield Court Drive where are now two bungalows. The road from Ifield Court Drive to the church and the triangle of grass in front of the churchyard (formerly a small chalk pit) on which the war memorial stands was in Northfleet Parish with the land on either side of the road being in Ifield Parish.

PART FOUR

Chapter 22

THE PARISH OF NORTHFLEET

IN THE LAST CHAPTER we dealt with a small part of the parish of Northfleet, which was intertwined with the parish of Ifield, and in this chapter the bounds of Northfleet parish will be dealt with, including its organisation. It immediately adjoins Gravesend to the west, but is of considerably greater area, about 3000 acres, and extends far to the south. Its western boundary commences from a point in the River Thames in Northfleet Hope where a sweep to the north in the course of the river leaves a large tract of marsh. The eastern part of this marsh, known as Botany Marsh, is in Northfleet, the western part being in Swanscombe. The boundary runs across saltings and then along a track known as Green Manor Way, and thence along the Lower Road to the main road which it crosses, and then to the railway, when it turns east, then following what was the old or former course of the river Ebbsfleet to Springhead, taking in the easterly part of the gardens once famous for their watercress. It then runs along Watling Street to a point about a quarter of a mile east of Springhead Road, then turns south and runs more or less parallel with the New Barn Road to a point near the reservoir of the Medway Water Board to the south of Fawkham Avenue. From here, it turns east and runs to a point on the Wrotham Road just to the north of Nurstead Wood, where it crosses the road and runs between Nurstead Court and Nash Street and, taking in Cossington Wood, runs to Church Lane, Ifield, just to the north of Toltingtrow Green. The boundary then runs into the field opposite, to include Wells Field before turning north to run with Cobham and Ifield, and thence to Singlewell village. It will be seen that, in addition to Northfleet 'town', the parish includes such hamlets as Northfleet Green and Nash Street, the old built-up area of Perry Street and the new estates at Shears Green, Istead Rise and Downs Road. Professor Alan Everitt in his book *Continuity and Colonization,* dealing with the evolution of Kentish Settlement (1986 page 194), suggests that Northfleet was the Saxon Minster Parish between Hoo St. Werburgh and Dartford and, applying his criteria, it would seem that Gravesend, Milton, Denton and Ifield, of those parishes dealt with in his book, were originally part of Northfleet. It seems more likely that Chalk was a part of Shorne, a sub-minster of Hoo St. Werburgh. The Northfleet Urban District Council, which was merged with Gravesend on 1 April 1974, was set up under the Local Government Act of 1894, and its predecessor, the Northfleet Local Board of Health, was constituted at a meeting held on 9 July 1874. In that year the local board had their offices in Lawn House at the south-east corner of Lawn Road. In 1884, they moved to a purpose-built office on the Hill, next to Granby Place (later the Co-operative shop) staying there until 1920 when they moved to Northfleet House (quid vide).

We will now deal with the older part of Northfleet parish by following the main roads in a pattern similar to that adopted for Gravesend.

A view from the area at the north end of Burch Road before any development.

131

Rosherville Church, showing the angels which adorned the spire
before their removal during the repairs carried out in 1896.

Boorman's Mill, at the end of Rural Vale

Chapter 23

LONDON ROAD FROM THE GRAVESEND BOUNDARY TO THE 'LEATHER BOTTLE'

IMMEDIATELY AFTER CROSSING the parish boundary from Gravesend the name of the road changes from Overcliffe to London Road. To the north lie Pier Road and Burch Road, which were laid out as part of a scheme for Rosherville New Town in 1830, by H.E. Kendal. A prospectus of the period states that 'this spot will ultimately become to Gravesend what St. Leonards is to Hastings and Broadstairs to Margate'. The houses with porches with Corinthian capitals at the south ends of these two roads and the Italianate houses in Lansdown Square date from this period.

On the south side of the London Road opposite Pier Road and Burch Road were the two entrances to Rosherville railway station. The station, built to cater for the visitors to the Rosherville Garden, was opened in 1886 following the construction of the new Gravesend branch line of the London, Chatham and Dover Railway to West Street. The station was closed in 1933. The stationmaster's house stayed until c.1991 when it was demolished to make way for Thames Way, as was the employment exchange that had been closed in 1973 when new offices were opened in The Grove, Gravesend.

St. Mark's vicarage, which stood on the corner of Burch Road until 1964, was a charming ragstone Gothic conceit in the same style as the church. Built in 1855, St. Mark's church was designed by the architects Messrs H. and E. Rose, and the cost and endowment were borne by the Rosher family. Mr George Rosher was the patron, who also paid for the vicarage. The church was built of Kentish rag and Caen stone quoins and carvings. The rag weathered very badly and extensive repairs were carried out in 1896 under W. and C.A. Bassett Smith, when the four stone angels which stood on supports round the spire were removed. The restoration of the spire was completed in 1901. St. Mark's was demolished in 1976 and replaced by the modern 'Church centre'.

The land opposite the church now occupied by the bus depot (built in 1938) and the houses in Marina Drive and the adjoining roads, was until about 1930 a small dairy farm known as Johnson's. On the north side of the road were large houses built in the 1830s as part of Rosherville new town and they were later demolished to make way for the large number of modern residences. Fountain Walk marks the site of the London Road entrance to Rosherville Gardens (see also Chapter 24). This entrance was opened in 1864, when a tower was built containing a clock with chimes on which tunes could be played. The clock was later removed and replaced by circular windows. The tower was demolished in 1938, but the entrance remained with its wall plaques until 1965, when the site was cleared. Any remains of the Upper Walk at the end of Fountain Walk, which contained urns and statues that formed part of the ornamental gardens, have now disappeared mainly owing to vandalism.

Rural Vale was the first of the small roads to be laid out on the south side of London Road, the houses on the west side being built about 1845. At the end of Rural Vale was a brick-tower windmill, built in 1840 by Richard Young, which was 50 feet in height. It was acquired in 1858 by William Boorman, who with his sons was a corn merchant in Milton Road, Gravesend, and was usually known as Boorman's mill. It ceased work in 1894 and was pulled down about 1916. The remaining roads in this area were laid out in the 1880s.

At the top of the rise are Rosherville schools, built in 1871, as church schools by the Rosher family: it became in 1937 a junior mixed and infant school. It is built of flint with brick dressings, as is the schoolhouse next door.

The houses between Rosherville schools and the *Leather Bottle* were built in the 1830s as part of the Calcraft-Ryder estate of 'Upper Northfleet'. 'De Warren House', about halfway along, was at one time the residence of Thomas Bevan, the cement maker, and his initials figured in the iron railings. He was unseated as Liberal M.P. for Gravesend in 1881 because he gave his workers a day off with pay on election day to vote for him. Some of these houses were demolished in the 1970s but survivors include 'Fernbank', a private house that became Northfleet's first full-time Public Library, operated by Kent County Library in 1940. An early 19th century illustration shows a sawpit and carpenter's yard on this site. The library has now moved to a new site at The Hive and 'Fernbank' is up for sale.

Chapter 24

THE RIVERSIDE FROM THE GRAVESEND BOUNDARY TO GRANBY ROAD

AT THE FOOT OF BURCH ROAD on the west side stood the *Rosherville Hotel*, also built by H.E. Kendal. This hotel hosted many of the celebration dinners that followed the launching of numerous ships built in Northfleet in the early Victorian period, and also played its part in the Gravesend Yacht Week. It was used as a hospital during the First World War and then became flats and was demolished about 1968. Also at the foot of Burch Road was Rosherville pier, built in 1840, for the Rosherville Garden's traffic. For many years there was a ferry from this pier to Tilbury in the mornings and return trip at night to cater for the 'commuters' who lived at Rosherville and travelled to London by the London, Tilbury and Southend railway.

At the south-west corner of Lansdowne Square was the entrance to Rosherville Gardens, laid out in 1837 by George Jones in a disused chalk pit leased from Jeremiah Rosher, lying between Crete Hall Road and London Road. They were a place of surpassing beauty and a favourite resort of Londoners. Adorned with small Greek temples and statuary set in the cliffs, there were terraces, an archery lawn, Bijou theatre, the Baronial Hall for refreshments, and at one time a lake. At night the gardens were illuminated with thousands of coloured lights and there were firework displays and dancing. Famous bands such as the American Sousa were engaged during the season. The 'Black Blondin', a trapezist, performed on a tightrope stretched across a chasm in the cliffs. In 1857 as many as 20,000 visitors passed through the turnstiles in one week. Henry Rose was the original architect for the gardens. He received one thousand £1 shares as his remuneration. By 1880, the gardens had reached the peak of their popularity and thereafter began to decline. In 1901, they were closed and came under the hammer. However, there was a brief revival in 1903 when they reopened for the summer season only until 1911. They were then used as a location for some early films, and the archery lawn became a football ground. The grounds were also occasionally opened for the local hospital fetes which had been held there since 1857.

On the north side of Crete Hall Road facing the river and to the rear of the *Old Sun* was Old Crete Hall, with its park. Built by Benjamin Burch in the 18th century, the property was later occupied by Jeremiah Rosher (son-in-law of Benjamin Burch) who, in 1818, built Crete Hall. George Sturge purchased the western portion of the property, including the lodge, c.1860, where he built a house known as the 'Mount'. The rest of the property remained in the Rosher family until the eastern portion was sold in 1891 to Edwin Thomas. Thomas lived there for a few years and endeavoured to promote a paper-making company to occupy the park site, but this effort was unsuccessful. However it was sold in 1899, and the Harmsworth printing works, that later became known as the Amalgamated Press, was built.

W.T. Henley's Telegraph Works Ltd. acquired the remainder of Crete Hall estate in 1905, and erected their cable works in the grounds, the first length of cable being produced in July 1906. In 1921, they added the tyre and rubber works. Crete Hall became the residence of their local manager, the last to live there being Mr T. Wright, and it was later used as a canteen and offices, being finally demolished in 1937.

In 1926, Henley's acquired part of the then derelict Rosherville Gardens and in 1938 they purchased the remainder to expand the factory. There was, however, one last fete held in the remaining part of the gardens in 1936, before the area was cleared and the cliffs cut back for the new offices and factories of Henley's, now A.E.I. During the Second World War Henley's played the leading part in the production of the PLUTO (pipeline under the ocean) project and in the war against magnetic mines.

In the 1880s, the 'Mount' was sold and the 'Northfleet Foundry' was established on the site. But the factory did not prosper for any length of time and Alfred Tolhurst's Red Lion Cement Works were built here at the end of the 19th century. The Red Lion Cement Works also incorporated the area neighbouring the Mount that was at one time a residential area with a group of streets with such names as Sheep Head Hill and Bullock Cheek's Row, and when the old *Red Lion* public house occupied a site on the river bank.

In 1894, Tolhurst built the Deepwater Wharf, a wooden T-shaped structure jutting 230 feet into the river, which for the first time enabled a large sailing vessel to be taken off a Thames

A view from an old engraving of Rosherville Gardens, 1841

Crete Hall, 1937

Granby Road, Northfleet

Published by Godfrey John Baynes.

Northfleet Dockyard. Kent.

Northfleet Dockyard

wharf at dead low tide. Next to the Red Lion works was the Imperial Cement Works which had been established a few years earlier.

However neither of these works survived for very long, both the Red Lion works and the Imperial Cement Company's works being closed during the First World War, although the Deepwater Wharf continued to be used for mooring ships.

During the 1939-1945 war the concrete floating fortresses called 'Maunsell Forts' after their designer were built on the site of the old Deepwater Wharf. The forts were towed from Northfleet into the Thames Estuary and coastal areas before being fixed to the seabed. In the 1960s some of these structures became pirate radio stations. The Deepwater Wharf site was finally cleared in 1951, when the South Eastern Electricity Generating Station was built on the site of the old derelict Red Lion and Imperial Cement works. However, the site is now derelict again, since the generating station was shut down and demolished c.1988.

There was a road leading from London Road (opposite the Fox and Hounds) to Crete Hall Road, known as the Coach Road. This was the private carriage drive to Crete Hall and a Lodge at one time stood at the London Road end.

Proceeding along Crete Hall Road towards Northfleet we come to the area between the road and the river which was the site of Pitcher's dockyard. Thomas Pitcher started building his shipyard in 1788 on ground levelled as a result of chalk workings.

The first launch (1238 tons) for the East India Company charters took place on 2 November 1789. Many more ships were built over the next two decades for the East India Company, plus frigates and 74-gun warships for the Royal Navy. From then on the yard worked mainly on ship repairs until Thomas's son William modernised the yard and started to build wooden hulled paddle steamers in the late 1830s, followed later by propellor-driven ships.

William Pitcher built ships not only for British customers like the Royal Mail Steam Packet Company and the Royal Navy, but for many foreign customers such as Russia, Italy, Chile, Portugal, Greece and Australia. When William Pitcher died in 1860 the yard had built over 160 ships in a period of 72 years. The yard struggled on under the Official Receiver until 1864, when C.J. Mare purchased the yard to build four blockade runners for the American Civil War and two Mersey ferries, before he sold the yard in 1865, when it finally closed.

In the 1830s, Pitcher built a castellated house and gate known as the 'Castle' using material from Old London Bridge, which survived until about 1924. Alongside the dockyard was a street of terraced houses called Dock Row, built by Thomas Pitcher c.1790, which incorporated *The Royal Charlotte Inn*, named after the first vessel launched from the yard. An annual fair and sports known as Royal Charlotte Fair were held here in the 1830s.

A scheme for much larger docks on the same site, including a dock large enough to take the *Great Eastern* was featured in the *Illustrated London News* in April 1859, but nothing came of it. There was no major development of the site until Bowater's built their paper mill in 1925. Bowaters became firmly established in Northfleet, specialising in the production of newsprint paper. Their importance was highlighted when, during the general strike of 1926, the government installed troops to ensure that production continued during this troubled period.

On the south side of the road there stood until 1955 a mass of chalk and clay (known as Caley Bank, or the Camels Hump) some 80 feet in height, which had been left by the early chalk diggers. When the dockyard was in operation a flagstaff stood on the top with a small cannon which was fired when launches took place. In this area was the Northfleet brickfield which in the late 1870s was worked by Messrs Gay and Blackman. It later belonged to George Austin who had a small wharf at the foot of Granby Road. It is on this site that in 1955 Bowater Scott built their large tissue paper mill which still operates today under the name of Kimberley Clarke. Running north-south to the east of the brickfield was Portland Road, built in 1869. A curious brick building at the bottom of Granby Road, demolished in 1954, known as the 'Mill House', was apparently erected as a building to house a stationary engine used to haul chalk trucks along rails by means of a cable and pulley system.

Between Dock Row and Granby Road was a gathering of houses known as Lower Northfleet, which included the Undershore that fronted the river. In the 19th century Lower Northfleet was the commercial centre of Northfleet. The community had a complete range of shops and businesses, including the first post office in Northfleet. The area was well served with inns and beer houses including *The Shipwright's Arms, Half Moon* and the *Staff of Life.*

The non-conformist Christians first established themselves in Lower Northfleet. The first attempt to preach the Gospel in Northfleet was made in 1764-65, by a Mr Morley, an Itinerant, who was preaching at the Tabernacle, King Street, Gravesend. The minister and his friends were met with strong opposition from some villagers and were stoned and driven out.

It was not until early in 1807 that a small room in a dwelling house occupied by a Mr. Venus in Lower Northfleet was acquired and the Rev. William Kent held the first Non-Conformist religious service in Northfleet. The worshippers moved to various locations in Lower Northfleet including the Engine House, until William Pitcher, the owner of the dockyard, erected a wooden building 36 feet by 24 feet specifically for the chapel. It was located behind the Undershore at the rear of Dock Row. This new building was opened as a chapel and Sunday school on 24 June 1829.

By 1834, the Sunday school at the Chapel on the Shore, Northfleet, had 200 pupils, according to the *Gravesend and Milton Journal,* 13 September 1834. By 1836, the popularity of the Sunday school had increased to such an extent that a gallery was built in the east end of the chapel. The 21-year lease on the chapel building expired in June 1850 and, because of a desire by the congregation to build their own chapel, a plot of ground was purchased in Dover Road and a new chapel built. On Wednesday 20 June 1850, the new chapel was opened for worship.

The Engine House, Granby Road

Chapter 25

SPRINGHEAD ROAD AND DOVER ROAD

LONDON ROAD JOINS Dover Road and Springhead Road (formerly Leather Bottle Lane) and then sweeps to the right to become The Hill. At the junction of Dover Road and Springhead Road stands the *Leather Bottle* (sometimes spelt *Bottel*) whose licensees' records date back to 1706.

Trade must have been good in the 19th century as the *Leather Bottel* was patronised by up to 36 coaches a day passing through on the then London to Dover Road. It had extensive gardens, notable for a fine walnut tree and stables at the rear.

Abutting the *Leather Bottle* in Springhead Road was the old parish lock-up. Latterly used as a cottage it was demolished about 1960. The land between Dover Road and Springhead Road was acquired by the government in 1806 (although troops seem to have camped here as early as 1763) and became known as Barrack Field. It was formerly called Harp Field. Here during the Napoleonic wars troops were quartered. Later in the mid-19th century houses were being built in the Shepherd Street, Tooley Street, Buckingham Road and York Road areas.

At the rear of the houses on the west side of Springhead Road is an area known as Church Field. It was here that the Northfleet United football team played between 1893 and 1905 on a pitch that was known as 'the roof' because it had a steep slope from one touchline to the other: and it was here that the Saxon cemetery was found in 1899 when the ground was excavated by the cement companies for chalk. Saucer brooches, a few weapons and cremation urns were among the finds and are in the local museum collection. An inspection of these finds by a researcher into Angle settlements recently showed they were from a settlement of Angles probably from East Anglia or Dorchester on Thames and not Saxons.

A little further down Springhead Road at Snagg's Bottom on the west side is a timber-framed hall house, known as the 'Old Rectory'. It was probably the residence of the steward of the Rectorial Tithes which belonged to the Priory of Rochester. According to Sarah Pearson the hall had a large kitchen with a smoke bay and a dendrochronology date of 1488/89. It was restored by G.M. Arnold (see *Arch. Cant. Vol XX, 1890*, p.71). It is now restored and used for offices.

The Northfleet Industrial Estate was laid out in 1984 and the first businesses arrived in 1986.

On the opposite side of the Springhead Road was Brookvale Farm which covered an area of 170 acres. In the early 19th century it was owned by Thomas Harman and farmed by William Whiskin and, from 1839, it was owned by the Hubble family.

Further south is Northfleet cemetery, opened in December 1893, and beyond that is Northfleet Recreation Ground. Opposite the cemetery is the Springhead Enterprise Park, opened in 1986 and further over in the Ebbsfleet valley is Northfleet Sewerage Works.

Continuing on the eastern side of Springhead Road, abutting the cemetery was Springhead Drill Hall. Built in the 1930s for the local Territorial unit it became a popular Saturday night dance venue, following the Second World War, hosting many nationally known dance bands, In the 1950s it became Northfleet's sports centre before it was finally demolished and the present housing estate built on the site.

Between here and the old Gravesend West to London Victoria railway was an orchard on which pre-fab houses were built to ease the housing crises following the Second World War, although they were only designed to last ten years they exceeded that forecast by several decades before they were replaced by new houses.

Waterdales was the second council estate to be built by the Northfleet Urban District Council, and the building of the adjoining streets in the mid-to-late 1930s expanded this estate.

Finally, there is Sainsbury's supermarket at the top of Pepper Hill, that opened on 3 July, 1992. This store was built on the site of Wingfield Bank Farm, whose history is known to date back to the 12th century. Thomas Harman and Colyer-Fergusson, well-known gentry, were owners during the 18th and 19th centuries.

Returning to the Hill, the Dover Road, which was the route of the London to Dover stage coaches, runs eastward to the boundary with Gravesend.

The Northfleet Traders' Association building was originally a brewery built by W. Pope in 1889. It was known as the Northfleet Brewery and the adjoining public house was the *Brewery Tap*. The brewery changed hands and names several times before it was closed in 1921.

Nearby is the Northfleet United Reform Church that opened for worship on 20 June, 1850. The first Non-Conformist church in Northfleet was Wycliffe Church in Perry Street, which was opened in 1846. The previous chapel had been a wooden building built for the Non-Conformists by William Pitcher in Lower Northfleet.

The first houses built along this part of Dover Road date back to the late 1830s and early 1840s. The *Dover Castle* was built in 1854, originally having a yard and stables at the rear. Behind the houses on the other side of Dover Road a small estate comprising Lime, Plain and Robina Avenues, was built between 1933 and 1935.

Electric trams operated by the Gravesend and Northfleet Electric Tram Co. replaced the old horse-drawn trams in 1902 and the company built a new tram depot behind the *Bridge Inn*, although the *Bridge Inn* was not built until 1907.

Almost opposite the *Bridge Inn* is the Northfleet Dover Road Junior Mixed School. Built in 1901 it was the second 'Board' school to be built in Northfleet. Originally known as the Dover Road Board School, it changed its name to Dover Road Council School in 1911, and it was not until 1966 that it was given the present name.

Decorated for the coronation in 1937
Brookvale Farm, Springhead Road.

The Old Rectory, Snaggs Bottom

BARKWAY & HITCHCOCK,

Brewers, Wine and Spirit Merchants, and Maltsters,

NORTHFLEET, KENT.

Branch Offices and Stores:

10 High St, Maidstone (Wine & Spirit Vaults); 34 Jeffery St, New Brompton;
54 High St, Grays ; Greenhill House, Wrotham ; and 3 Lombard
Court, London, E.C.   Maltings, Long Melford.

Telegrams, " BARKWAY," NORTHFLEET.   Telephone, No. 47, GRAVESEND.

Barkway and Hitchcock's Brewery in Dover Road which became the
New Northfleet Brewery Co. in 1902. It closed in 1921. The Brewery
made 'Last Drop Beer'.

142

Chapter 26

THE HILL

NEXT WE COME TO 'THE HILL'. This area has been regarded as the centre of Northfleet probably since the days when the first Saxon Church was built on this hill which is one hundred feet above sea level. At that time the ground sloped from The Hill area down to the Thames on the north and to the Ebbsfleet on the south but chalk excavation during the 19th century around The Hill has left the church and local shops and houses standing on an isolated pinnacle of chalk.

Nowadays, although strangers passing through the Hill on the main road do not appreciate it, many of the buildings stand precariously on the edge of 80-foot-high cliffs, the access to the Hill being limited to the main roads, Granby Road, and a footbridge over the chalk pits to the south-east corner of St. Botolph's church.

We will start where the London Road meets Dover Road, with our back to the house that until recently was the Northfleet London Road branch of Kent County Library, closed in December 2000.

Until the early 19th century, in front of where the Catholic Church now stands stood the village pound and stocks. The pound was a square brick building with tiled roof, and to the south of the pound, facing the *Leather Bottel*, were the stocks where the parish Beadle administered punishment to those who had misconducted themselves, either at church or at the workhouse. It was also on this spot in 1860 that a tollgate was erected by the Turnpike Commissioners as an additional gate to try to increase the income from the tolls for the road which had been falling since the opening of the railway. The toll gate-house stood on the west side of The Hill about five yards to the south of the road leading to the back of St. Botolph's Church. The location of this toll gate annoyed the traders on the Hill who had to pay a toll every time they wished to go to London Road, Dover Road and Springhead Road, in which direction some of their best customers resided. The women residents also complained about this 'new fortress' erected at the turnpike gate, because the gap between the posts erected on the footpath at the tollgate was too narrow to pass through for women wearing crinolines. The gate was financially successful but only lasted until 1871' when the Turnpike Commissioners' Trust was wound up.

In June 1883, a horse tramway was opened from the *Leather Bottle* to St. James Church, Gravesend (later extended to Milton Place). It was of 3 feet 6 inches gauge and had five small single-deck cars, one of which was an open 'toastrack' for summer use for Rosherville Garden patrons. The depot was on the site of the present Roman Catholic church, the offices and manager's (Mr. Kipping) house being the present Roman Catholic presbytery. In 1888-9 Dick Kerr and Company built an electric extension to Huggens College on the series system, but this was only used for experimental purposes. It was closed in 1890 and the equipment removed and the horse service extended to Huggens College. In 1898, the Company purchased four open-topped double-deck cars. The service continued until 1901, when it ceased so that work for the new 4 feet 8.5 inches gauge electric tramway could be carried out (for details see *The Tramways of Kent* by Invicta, Vol.1, 1971, page 13).

It is here that we see the Roman Catholic church which nowadays is the prominent feature as you approach The Hill from Gravesend. It was built in 1914 on the site of the old Northfleet horse-drawn tram depot, which was closed in 1901, plus an adjoining plot of land given by Mr. Alfred Tolhurst. It had been originally planned to make a public appeal for the funds to build the church, but the children of the late Mr and Mrs A. Tolhurst provided the necessary money (about £8000) as a memorial to Mr A. Tolhurst. The architect was Sir Giles Scott, and the tower foreshadows that of his Liverpool cathedral; the local building contractor was J.B. Lingham. The opening ceremony was held on Tuesday 15 June 1915.

On the opposite side of the road leading down to the bottom of the cliff was a wooden staircase, erected in 1860 for the convenience of the newly formed 20th Kent (Northfleet) Volunteer Rifle Brigade to reach their 200-yard rifle range and drill ground. The firing practice always created an audience at the top of the cliffs.

On the corner of Church Road where the new block of flats now stand was no.4, The Hill,

Penny, Son and Parker's grocer shop, which served the public from 1898 for over 50 years. Next door, nos. 5 and 6 are two brick built shops, called Alma Cottages, built about 1860 on the site of two old weather-boarded houses, one of which had been used as a fancy bazaar and newsagents. Before it was demolished this had been the only place in Northfleet where newspapers could be bought or *The Times* loaned for one penny.

On the south-east corner of the triangular area that was once the village green stands no.7, now a chemist's shop. This was a butcher's shop for over one hundred years, having its own slaughterhouse at the rear during the 19th and early 20th century. The old rails for hanging the meat can still be seen in the shop and on the wall outside. Mr Holker refurbished the building in 1791, when he replaced the wooden weather-boarding frontage with brick.

The houses between the chemist and the lych gate are probably 19th century. In one house, now no.10, lived William Skews, confectioner, and a Waterloo veteran who had lost an arm in that battle. He also had a stall in Gravesend market selling sweetmeats and he was the last remnant of the fair that had been held on The Hill every Easter Tuesday. On that day he would set his chair in the middle of The Hill and on the table in front of him would have varieties of sweets and a disc with numbers round and central pointer which when spun decided the quantity of sweets received. From 1886 until the present day, no.10 has been an undertaker's, run by Richard Fisher until the First World War and since then by the Horlock family. Later the business was sold to Hythe of Sittingbourne although they retained the name of 'Horlocks T.S. & Son'. Recently the firm has been bought by Mr Martin Bourne, previously a manager at Hythe's, and he too has continued to use the Horlocks' name.

Outside the lych gate stood the *Dove Inn*, one of the ancient inns of Northfleet. It was burnt down in 1906 and finally demolished in 1907. At the rear of the inn stood several cottages in an area known as 'Dove Yard'.

The church, dedicated to St. Botolph, is one of the largest in Rochester Diocese and was a wealthy living, frequently held by an absentee incumbent. It dates from the early 14th century in the decorated Gothic (with the exception of the two nave windows, which are perpendicular), and consists of a six-bay nave with north and south aisles and chancel. The tower was built in 1717 inside the one which fell in the previous century. At the south-west corner is evidence of the original Anglo Saxon church, with long and short work on the quoins. Inside part of the arcade is 13th century work. Perhaps the most interesting interior feature is the chancel screen which is early 14th century, the same period as the church. It retained its solid wooden doors until about 1830.

The chancel arch and the harsh sedila in the chancel are both the work of E.W. Godwin in 1862, but there is an attractive piscina and sedila in the south side, which are original, although the sub-deacon's seat was damaged in 1790, when W.H. Burch built a family pew here with 'a warming machine'. The altar dates from 1922 and the screen was erected in 1937 as a memorial to George Snelling and Charles Kean. The floors of both nave and chancel were raised during the Victorian restoration, and the well-known brass of Peter de Lacey (1375) lost its canopy and now has a small modern border. Northfleet at one time had at least 13 brasses, but of these only three remain, the other two being William Lye (1391) and William Rikhill and his wife Katherine (1433). All have been moved and mutilated (see *Archaeologia Cantiana, Vol. XXXII,* p.36, for a full list of the lost brasses at Northfleet).

The chancel was refurnished and fitted between 1861 and 1879. The Victorian stained glass was restored and rededicated on St. Botolph's day 1992 after six years' work at a total cost of £30,000. According to Martin Harvison, the author of *Victorian Stained Glass* (1980), the east window is one of the major 19th-century windows, being a fine example of collaboration between E.W. Godwin, the architect, J. Miller-Allen and Favers and Barnard, the glaziers. It was completed in 1863 as a memorial to Prince Albert. It was designed by Miller-Allen (for a detailed description of this and the other Victorian windows at Northfleet see *The Windows of St. Botolph's Northfleet* by Michael Camp and Keith Hill, 1992).

The window tracery was restored in 1852 by Brandon and Ritchie, who seem to have copied what was there with the exception of the second window from the east on the north side (see John Newman, *The Buildings of West Kent and the Weald,* 2nd edn 1976, p.436). The east window of the south side is a good example of Kentish tracery with split cusps.

The St. Botolph's National School was opened in 1838 and was situated on the south side

The Hill circa 1895. Behind the group of children is the well
and behind that the building with the high pitched roof is The Heritage.

The *Dove* public house, lych gate and row of 17th century terrace cottages
The Hill, Northfleet

Northfleet Manor House, 1878, which stood on the site of the car park
to the rear of the *Coach and Horses*.

Middle picture:
Nos 34 and 35
The Hill, the grocers
shop of James Fox,
c 1892

Bottom picture: The Vicarage,
Northfleet c. 1960,
just before it was
demolished

of the churchyard, adjoining the chalk pit. On 1 February 1869, the Infants' School was opened. Previously all ages had attended the one school, and the infants paid 2d per week to attend. The school continued unchanged until February 1936, when the 11-year-old senior boys and girls left to attend the new Secondary Schools. From 1936, the school was a Primary (Mixed) School, as we know it today. It was not until June 1938 that electric light was installed. In 1977, a new St. Botolph's school was built on a new site in Dover Road which offered superior facilities, including eight classrooms, four practical areas, a television/music room, two library and resource areas, a large hall, normal offices and a kitchen, set in large grounds.

Leaving the church by the lych gate you are faced by a triangular car park that was once the village green with at its north west corner a well. It is believed that the three annual fairs were not held on this green until around the late 18th century when the fairs were diminishing in size and importance, but in two fields on the periphery of the Hill that were known as 'The Hill Market Field' and 'Little Market Field'. The mediaeval fair was more than sideshows and amusements, though these were included; it was a market on a large scale, and was beneficial to the Lord of the Manor who exacted dues from the traders. In 1201 archbishop Hubert gave King John four palfreys in return for the privilege of holding a ten days fair at Northfleet, and the Royal Charter for a fair to be held in May is still extant. The two other fairs were one on Easter Tuesday and another on St. Botolph's Day (17 June). The May or Whitsuntide fair continued to be held until the end of the 18th century. As late as 1803, we read in the Rev. S.H. Cook's *History of Northfleet and its Parish Church* (1942), 'these fairs though of no great note are still kept up', and, as recorded above, William Skews maintained the tradition of the Easter Tuesday Fair well into the Victorian period.

On the village green had stood the cage or lock-up afterwards moved nearer to the *Leather Bottel* plus a weighbridge, a wooden erection on which vehicles and cattle were driven, their weight taken and toll exacted. It was removed when the toll gate was introduced and the weighbridge afterwards stood in the backyard of no.33 The Hill for several years.

In the late 19th century the 'green' was paved over, and in 1923, a War Memorial constructed from Portland Stone was erected to commemorate the 259 Northfleet servicemen who died during the First World War. It was originally situated in the middle of the open area at The Hill, close to the London Road, surrounded by lawn and flowerbeds in an iron railed enclosure. The memorial has now been relegated by the Council to the back corner of the 'green' in deference to the car.

On the north side of the 'green', where the Northfleet Veterans Club now stands, stood a row of 17th-century terrace cottages that were demolished in 1958. On the corner, the *Coach and Horses,* said to date from 1572, and the betting shop adjoining, were apparently part of a timber-framed house.

There was a custom of nailing a hot cross bun to a beam each Good Friday in the *Coach and Horses* and varnishing it. Hot cross buns were traditionally made from the residue of the dough used for making the Host for Easter Sunday and given to people unable to take the sacrament. They were said to partake of the Divine Nature and to be imperishable (in fact probably because of the spices used) and were hung up as good luck charms for the ensuing year. This Northfleet custom was seen to be a possible relic of this pre-Reformation custom, as the building dates from the early 1400s. Today there is a home-made buns competition and the winner receives a free pint of beer a week for one year and has the honour of nailing his or her hot cross bun to the beam.

Behind the *Coach and Horses*, where the disused toilets in the car park are located, Northfleet's first purpose-built fire station was built in 1910. It was 25 years earlier that the Northfleet Volunteer Fire Brigade was formed. In 1941, like all other units, Northfleet Fire Brigade was incorporated into the National Fire Service.

On the northern side of the entrance to the car park stood the second council offices in Northfleet. The local Urban Sanitary Authority that came to be known by the term 'Local Board' built them in 1884. The 'Local Board' continued until 1894, when the Local Government Act of 1894 provided that all the urban sanitary authorities should be reconstituted 'Urban District Councils'. In 1920 Northfleet Urban District Council moved to Northfleet House (now St. Peter's Nursing Home). Thomas Sturge, descended from an old

West of England Quaker family, lived there until his death in 1866. The Sturge family played an important part in abolishing slavery. Thomas's father was Deputy Chairman of the Anti-Slavery Society. In 1929, the Co-operative Society who had purchased the property, extended the frontage of the old council offices closer to the road (evidence of this can still be seen in the brickwork) and moved their business to this building from their old shop in Dover Road. Above the shop was a hall that was used for social events such as weddings and dances. Until very recently this building and the buildings behind were used by Deaves (replacement windows and doors).

Behind Deaves' workshop and Granby Place (nos. 1 and 2 High Street) stood Northfleet Manor House. It was enclosed by a high red-brick wall with a drive and entrance gates (between Deaves and Granby Place) facing the high road. Its date of origin is uncertain; the earliest so far confirmed recorded date is a map from 1726. William Crakelt, the curate, resided and ran a boarding school there for some time, prior to his death in 1812, when Robert Hewetson took over. In 1819, the Manor House became Northfleet's workhouse, which it remained until Northfleet became one of the 15 parishes which formed North Aylesford Union in 1835, and the workhouse was removed to Strood. The North Aylesford Union was divided into two divisions for administration purposes and Northfleet became the administration district for one of those divisions; Mr Henry Heath of Orme House was elected Chairman. About 1860, a further attempt to run a boarding school here was tried by the Reverend F. Davis but as it failed to make a profit, he then established a private asylum for the 'mentally deficient'. What seems now an odd occupation for a curate is explained by his very low salary, which he was obliged to augment. The garden of the Manor House was incorporated into the churchyard in the 1880s and it was about this time that the Manor House disappeared. The site was finally cleared in 1909.

On the third side of the triangular 'green', the east side of the main road, stands another of the old coaching inns the *Queen's Head*, previously *The Crown* (1636-1718), which had extensive grounds and a bowling green at the rear. About the year 1830, a fire broke out in the house which nearly destroyed it. The building was renovated and it appears that it was about this time that the bowling green disappeared and the cliffs were cut away for the chalk. The *Queen's Head* was rebuilt again in 1909.

In the 1880s the Honeycombe family ran the post and telegraph office at nos. 36. 37 and 38 The Hill until 1890, when Richard Fox took over the business. The Fox family ran the sub-post office until at least the Second World War. Nos. 34 and 35, built on the site of the old *Queen's Head* gardens are where James Fox ran a successful grocery business from the 1880s until 1923. On the 1838 map the brick houses are shown set back from the road but by 1890 an extension was added onto the front and used as the shop while the rear was the living quarters.

The oldest house now standing is no. 31, a private house called 'The Heritage'. It is believed to be the remaining part of a much larger house dating from c.1500 Its earliest history is not very clear but it was the *White Hart* and then the *Plough Inn.* (1715-1830). In front of the inn stood a signpost and horse trough and, to the rear, before the cliff was excavated, there were stables and a back passageway leading towards the *Leather Bottel*.

At the start of the Victorian era there lived on the site of no.30 another of Northfleet's old personalities, Isaac Bocking, known as 'Old Isaac', an eccentric character who adopted the name Bocking from the village in Essex where he originated. This man was a shoemaker and over his door he put up the following verse on a board for the enlightenment of the public:

> Isaac Bocking lives here who will not refuse
> To make or mend both boots and shoes.
> His leather is good, his prices just
> For ready money, but no trust.

After the death of this worthy man the premises were pulled down and Mr Eric Wiseman erected the present house and shop on the site that for several years was used as a butcher's shop by him.

There were three known forges in Northfleet, Newby's High Street, Leving's Old Perry

Street and 29 The Hill, which is believed to have been the oldest. Thomas Grey was the smith at this forge from the 1880s until 1929. His 15-year-old son was tragically killed while assisting at the preparations of the vault for the Reverend Southgate's burial in 1885. Charles Dyke purchased the business in 1929 and it remained in use until 1946.

The forge was next to an inn named the *Marquis of Granby* that was situated at the top of Granby Road. It was built in 1885 and continued until 1925; the building was demolished when the new Labour Board Offices were built on the same site in the 1950s.

St. Botolph's Parish Church of Northfleet

Chapter 27

THE MAIN ROAD FROM GRANBY ROAD TO THE PARISH BOUNDARY WITH SWANSCOMBE

THE HIGH STREET, or Bow Street as it was formerly known, commences at the junction with Granby Road and continues as Stonebridge Road (formerly Fishermans Hill) to the parish boundary at Botany Bay, where it continues on as Galley Hill, Swanscombe. Bow Street must have been quite a rural road in the 18th century, with cherry orchards, farmland, meadows, detached rusticated dwellings and rural cottages scatted irregularly on both sides. The coming of the cement industry led to masses of workers' terraced housing and the necessary retail shops which totally changed this rural scene in the latter three decades of the 19th century.

Leaving The Hill, Northfleet High Street starts almost opposite Granby Road where once stood the entrance gates to the Manor House, the drive to the house coming onto the High Street between Deaves and Granby Place.

Before the 19th century the high road did not follow the same course as at present. When approaching The Hill from the High Street it continued straight to the top of Granby Road, passing to the north of a farm, associated with the Manor House, including the Parson's barn. It then turned sharp right towards The Hill through a narrow passage between some cottages and passing over the village green to join the Dover Road at the *Leather Bottel*. In 1800, the Turnpike Trustees had two cottages demolished to improve the road and in 1828 the remaining two old cottages (that stood in front of the present Granby Place), were pulled down and the road was altered to its present course.

The Borough of Gravesend Electricity Works supplied the first electricity for street lighting of the main road in Northfleet in 1908; previously it had been lit by gas and oil lamps. All of the street gas lamps in Northfleet were not finally replaced by electric lamps until after the Second World War.

On the north side of the High Street, on the cliff edge close to Granby Road, was 'Tel's' cafe (previously 'Pete's'), first established in the late 1930s. During the war a signalling system was set up between the cafe and the underground air raid shelter at the bottom of the pit. Before the chalk was excavated from the site of the Northfleet cement works the fields sloped down to the riverside.

Lawn House or Northfleet Lodge stood on the eastern side of Lawn Road at the junction with the High Street. Francis (Paddy) Wadman commenced the construction of the house but it was still not completed at his death in 1814. The Whitehead family lived there for many years and it was later used for Mechanics Institute meetings, social events and political meetings. It was used by the local authority from 1876 for their monthly meetings until they built their own offices in 1884 (see Chapter 26). It was demolished in 1900 and, in 1912, Mr Hextable of Herne Bay made an application to Northfleet Council to erect a cinema on the site, but this was rejected.

Returning to The Hill, on the south side, are nos. 1 and 2 High Street called Granby Place. This is a Grade II listed building, built in 1831, originally as two houses but later converted into a single residence. It was built soon after the main road was altered to its present course.

In August 1848, the 'London Society for the Protection of Young Females' preferred bills of indictment at the Middlesex Sessions against George Joseph Murray (alias Bradley) and his wife Ann (who was the daughter of the notorious Mrs. H.). He lived in a splendid manner at Granby Place, keeping a livery carriage and servants and supposed by the inhabitants to be a gentleman of the highest respectability. On being issued with the 'preferred bills of indictment' he fled from Northfleet and the society offered a £10 reward for knowledge of his whereabouts. He was accused of keeping 60 houses for improper uses, in places ranging from Gravesend to Mayfair, Piccadilly, Holborn, Bishop's Gate and Southwark. Murray was accused of furnishing these houses, in a style according to their location, and installing a person in them who paid him £1 a day, which left them to derive their money from all receipts above that sum.

Alfred Horlock, who built the steam locomotives, also lived at Granby Place at that time, but Granby Place is mostly remembered as bring a doctor's surgery for the past 150 years.

Between Granby Place and the grounds of the Old Vicarage is a car repair garage formerly belonging to the Horlock family. At the front there remains an old-style petrol pump. Part of the wall between the garage and the old vicarage grounds is mediaeval and is the surviving wall of the farm that occupied the area around the garage and Granby Place in the 18th century.

No records have been found relating to the vicarage before the 18th century, but at this time, as a result of the non-residence of the incumbents, the building suffered from neglect. In 1834, it was so dilapidated that a new vicarage was built which the Rev. Southgate later enlarged. The vicarage was demolished in 1961 when the present residential estate was built in the grounds and 'Glanfield House' in the High Street became the vicarage until the new vicarage was built on the site of the old church school.

To the west of St. Botolph's Church was at one time a cherry orchard in what was called 'Vineyard Field', a reminder that the Archbishop of Canterbury had a vineyard at Northfleet in the 14th century. This field was dug out for chalk in the 1860 to 1870s.

In the 1920s, to the west of this quarry, were built the first council houses in Northfleet. Earlier Thomas Sturge purchased the land on which the estate was built when it came up for sale in 1844. It then included the nearly completed new house that became known as Northfleet House. Thomas Sturge lived there with his sister, Esther, both of whom remained single, until his death in 1866. The house was noted for a magnificent pair of entrance gates, made from whaling harpoons, which stood opposite the present Lawn Road School. Alfred Tolhurst, also a cement manufacturer, who gifted the site of the Roman Catholic church on The Hill, Northfleet, later occupied Northfleet House for 25 years, until his wife died in 1911. In 1920, Northfleet House was converted into offices for the Northfleet Urban District Council.

The Northfleet Primary School (Lawn Road School) was the first Board School built in Northfleet. The first meeting of Northfleet School Board took place in December 1884 and within two months they had purchased a large area of land between Lawn Road and Factory Road, including the sites of the *King's Head* and *Marquis of Granby,* two inns which almost stood side by side. Both inns were demolished and a new *Marquis of Granby* was built on the Hill. Lawn Road School opened on 18 October 1886 and was extended in 1893 by the adding of new buildings, including the clock tower - the first public timepiece in Northfleet. The clock tower was badly damaged in the 1987 storm and was subsequently demolished.

On the west corner of Factory Road stands The Factory Club (later known as the Blue Circle Club) which was opened on 31 July 1878 and built at the expense of Thomas Bevan (architects Parr and Strong). It took three years to build at a cost of £11,000 and was built in honour of Bevan's eldest son, Robert's, coming of age. Before 1945, the club was open to all members of the public and was the cultural centre of Northfleet. Two halls, games room, sports facilities, a library and the headquarters of the Northfleet Choral Society plus numerous other local societies were all accommodated. Amongst various other features added over the years was a bowling green and an outdoor swimming pool which was opened in 1907.

From here to the top of Stonebridge Hill was the main retailers' area of Northfleet from the 1880s until the 1950s. Northfleet High Street was a thriving area serving the large number of inhabitants who lived in the numerous workers' houses built on the adjoining streets. These were the days when convenience foods, refrigerators and cars were things of the future, and the community was dependent upon the High Street shops for their daily needs.

Rayner's Court replaced the block of shops that were built in the High Street in 1883 between the Factory Hall and Hive Lane. Built in the 1960s, it took its name from one   well-known family of retailers, an oil and paint shop, that had served the community for about 60 years. There were other well-known retailers who prospered for years, such as Fred Waters, tailor, who also formed the 2nd Northfleet Scouts in 1907; Mr Frederick Ware, sweet and tobacconist shop; and, Lincoln's the chemist, with the great pear-shaped carboys in the window on the corner of Hive Lane. Many more could be recalled.

Hive Lane was originally the drive to a large house and grounds called Hive House. At the High Street stood two octagonal lodges either side of the drive entrance. The estate was eleven and a half acres, extending from the High Street almost down to the river and between College

Road (then known as One Tree Lane) and Lawn Road. The house itself was a large three-storeyed house with a basement, built of brick with stone quoins. It had ten bedrooms on the two upper floors, a large entrance hall, library, dining room, breakfast room and so on with butler's pantry and kitchen below, enclosed in its own walled gardens with carriage house and stables, the whole set in park-lands and orchard.

About the middle of the 18th century the house was the residence of Thomas Chiffinch, a barrister, and he was followed by Major (Paddy) Wadman who had married a niece of Mr Chiffinch. Wadman died in 1814 and Mr and Mrs Kirwan leased the estate until c.1830, when a Mr Gibbons opened it as a boarding school. The estate was sold by auction in 1838 and purchased by Thomas Sturge, who in 1853 built the Knight Bevan and Sturge cement mill on part of the property.

At the top of Hive Lane, opposite Lincoln's chemist shop, was the green tiled public house called *The Little Wonder*, named after the 1840 Derby winner. Between the *Little Wonder* and the Sturge school building were the shops built c.1850 when Samaritan Grove and the terrace houses in Hive Lane were also built.

In 1858, the population of Northfleet had reached 5700, and George Sturge, a Quaker, saw the demand for and financed a Non-Conformist school, 'Sturge's British School' which was built on Thomas Sturge's property in Northfleet. The school was located on the north side of the High Street opposite the entrance to Wood Street. It was built mainly of flint with a slate roof. It consisted of one large room and a small office located just inside the main door. A small playground was located at the rear of the building enclosed by a low flint wall, and at the front was a small drinking fountain which had a small brass or copper cup attached to the wall by a steel chain. By the start of the Second World War the school had closed and, in February 1942, it was opened as a 'British Restaurant'. After the war, in 1945, it became the headquarters of the 1st Northfleet Scouts.

Under the High Street were several disused railway tunnels that were utilised as air raid shelters during the Second World War. At first they had sand bags to form the blast walls at the entrances but later brick blast walls and electric lighting were provided. They were 80 feet below ground level and were virtually bomb and soundproof. Residents took their bedding there every night during the Blitz, being assured of a good night's sleep. People made their own entertainment during the evenings, including 'housey housey' (a form of bingo) and community singing, and of course, women had their knitting and children their toys.

Returning back up the High Street, Bow House was built on the south side about two hundred years ago opposite the later site of the Factory Hall. 'Paddy' Wadman built it, intending to open it as a bazaar, but due to its failure it became known locally as 'Paddy Wadman's Folly'. The building and grounds were leased to local farmers and eventually demolished prior to the site being put up for auction in 1842. Thomas Sturge purchased the land and it became part of the 'Northfleet House' estate.

Lower down the High Street, now the site of the second-hand car sales, was where, in about 1912, the 'Northfleet Cinema' was opened. It remained in use as a cinema until December 1929, when a more modern cinema was built next door. It then became known as 'The Astoria' and continued mainly used as a dance hall until it was pulled down in 1957, along with the cinema that had been built to replace it, and then known as 'The Wardona'. The 'Wardona' changed hands several times during its lifetime and had been previously known as the 'Strathconer' and the 'Star'. Until the 1840s, about 50 yards south of the cinema site stood a windmill, about which very little is known.

A few yards back from the High Street, in Rose Street, were Moody and Windiate's garages. Mr W.J. Moody, motor job master, was noted for his 'charabanc' (motor coaches) business started in 1919. His father started the business in the 1880s, but in his day, of course, people were taken about in horse-drawn cabs.

Court Mews was formerly the Northfleet Police Station and was built in 1866. Until then the old Parish Lock-up was in Springhead Road, behind the *Leather Bottel*. The Magistrates' Courtrooms that were at the rear of the police station were opened on 29 October 1887.

Wood Street ran downhill from the High Street to Station Street and in 1875 Wood Street Primitive Chapel was opened, providing a place of worship and also at one time schooling for the young children. The building remains but is no longer used for worship.

North side Northfleet High Street, looking east, in the early 1900s

North side, Northfleet High Street, looking east, 1962

Northfleet Police Station, 1962

The original gates, Huggens College

In 1871, the population of Northfleet had increased to 6500 and the Roman Catholic community, who established the St. Joseph's school on the south side of the High Street between Station Street and Rose Street, provided some of the school accommodation that was sadly lacking in the town. The building served as a church on Sundays and as a school during the week. The infants school was held in the basement of the premises, the main school on the upper floor. The licence for holding marriage ceremonies was transferred to the new church on The Hill in April 1916. However, the school continued in the building until April 1932 when St. Joseph's moved to a new site in Springhead Road.

From the High Street, Station Road led down from the *Ingress Tavern* to Northfleet Railway Station. On the corner with Station Street were the Mission Rooms, built in 1882. They were used as a temporary boys school by the Northfleet Education Board in 1886 and 1887 while the new school was being built at Lawn Road. The Northfleet Silver Band practised in the Mission Hall for many years. Jack Jackson, the son of the band conductor, played the cornet as a boy in the band. He later became one of the BBC record presenters in the 1940s to 1970s and was the forerunner of the modern disc jockey.

The railway station was opened in 1849 at its present location although there was not a great population in this area at the time, nor had the huge cement industry as yet developed. The original station building perished in a fire and was rebuilt in the late 19th century. Railway electrification took place in 1925. The underpass between the 'Up' and 'Down' platforms was utilised as the main access to Ebbsfleet Park, which was situated between the railway and the Ebbsfleet river that skirted the park's southern boundary. The park was opened on 12 May 1909 and in the early days children used to paddle and play in the clear water of the Ebbsfleet, but after the construction of the sewerage works the stream became dangerously polluted. The park had a bandstand, which was frequently used prior to the Second World War, swings, roundabouts and a slide for the children, plus a putting green for the adults. There was a brick park keeper's hut just inside the main gate, along with a drinking fountain. Ebbsfleet Park was closed in about 1971 when the new railway sidings for Northfleet Cement Works were built on the site.

From the junction with College Road, the High Street becomes Stonebridge Road, commonly known as Stonebridge Hill (formerly Fisherman's Hill). On the north side of the road lies Huggens College, built in 1847 by John Huggens as almshouses, with its own chapel and croquet lawn. The architect was Mr. W. Chadwick. The original college was demolished in 1968 and new bungalows and a chapel were built on part of the site, the remainder being sold to the Council, who built blocks of flats known as Wallis Park. The chaplain's house, which is all that survives of the former college, was originally a farmhouse.

At the foot of Stonebridge Hill was the 'stone bridge' over the river Ebbsfleet, built in 1634 to replace an earlier one of unknown age. The bridge was angled slightly to the north and not directly towards Stonebridge Hill. The reason may have been that the lower road round by the Creek and along to the *India Arms* was the established route, at that time, to Gravesend. It was on 1 June 1648 that this was the site of a Civil War skirmish, when a force of six hundred Royalists, under Major Childs, were defeated by four hundred Parliamentarians, mounted and foot soldiers, under Major Husband. A second brick bridge was aligned to Stonebridge Hill, built many years later alongside the old bridge. In 1775, the Trustees of the Turnpike Road issued instructions that a sheep wash was to be constructed in the space between the two bridges. This fell into disuse in the 19th century and became known as Plough Pond and at the end of the 19th century it was filled in and the Ebbsfleet diverted under the road through a pipeline.

The field on the opposite side of the road from Gravesend and Northfleet Football Ground was known as Plough Marsh. In the north west corner was a lake with small islands which had resulted from clay digging at the turn of the 18th/19th centuries and was described in the late 1840s as being part of the beautiful view from Huggens College. By 1870, it was known as the 'mud hole' and during the next two decades became the scene of many drownings. Eventually the council forced Mr Bevan to fill it in during the 1890s. The field which was known locally as the 'Meadow' was used by the travelling fairgrounds and circuses when they set up in Northfleet and in the Second World War a barrage balloon was sited here during the time of the doodlebug raids. The area is now part of an industrial estate.

The Gravesend and Northfleet Football Ground stands at the bottom of Stonebridge Hill. Prior to the Second World War it had been the home of Northfleet United founded in 1890, but the team had played at other venues before moving to this site in 1905. In 1946, the Gravesend and Northfleet Football Club was formed and they have continued to play on the Stonebridge Road ground until the present day.

On the parish boundary between Swanscombe and Northfleet was the Britannia Cement Works, or Macevoy and Holt's works, built in the 1870s and located at the bottom of Galley Hill at Botany Bay. They became a member of the original Associated Portland Cement Manufacturers group of companies in 1900.

The Northfleet Paper Mill, most of which lay in Swanscombe, was erected between 1884 and 1886 for Carl David Ekman (1845-1906). Ekman was a Swedish chemist who invented a process of pulp making by cooking wood by the sulphite process. However, economic problems coupled with a lawsuit against Ekman over the disposing of some sulphite waste into a nearby quarry, causing the formation of sulphurous acid, ended his business. The New Northfleet Paper Mills Limited took over Ekman's business in 1903. In 1923, the company became a part of the Inveresk Group. The buildings were cleared in the 1970s and the site was developed into the present-day industrial estate.

The Manor Way runs from the bottom of Galley Hill through to the bottom of Craylands Lane, Swanscombe. On the north side are the Botany Marshes and the Broadness Peninsula and on the south side the rising ground was excavated for chalk, forming the pit where the New Northfleet Paper Mill had stood. This ancient right of way also formed the boundary between Northfleet and Swanscombe.

According to the *1907 Directory*, R.D. Pembleton at Deep Water Wharf was a millstone maker (he was at one time a local councillor). When the site of the New Northfleet Paper Mill was being developed a number of millstones were dug up and one was set up at the entrance to the estate. Pembleton may have produced millstones for cement grinding as well as for windmills. They were used for grinding the cement clinker prior to the introduction of rotary steel drums with steel balls, now used for this purpose.

There was a scheme by the government during the Napoleonic War, in 1805, to build a naval dockyard on Botany Marshes to replace the Royal Dockyards at Deptford and those at Sheerness and possibly Chatham. The peace in 1815 put an end to these schemes and no work was done; the land was purchased but subsequently disposed of.

Ebbsfleet Pleasure Grounds

Chapter 28

THE RIVERSIDE FROM GRANBY ROAD TO SWANSCOMBE BOUNDARY

THE ROAD NOW KNOWN AS GRANBY ROAD was once a busy road from the riverside community of Lower Northfleet to the Hill and church, which was known as Upper Northfleet. In early Victorian times the road was known as Chalk Hill, with a side road called Chalk Hill Court.

At the lower end of Granby Road beyond a scattering of cottages was Howard Square, a small square of late 18th-century houses occupied at one time by customs officers and watermen.

On the waterside, to the west of Howard Square, stood 'Howard House', a red-brick Queen Anne house, built about 1717 for Francis Mackreth. Mackreth owned much of the land on both sides of Granby Road, and was involved in chalk digging and lime burning. The house takes its name from Jeremiah Howard, a lime merchant, who purchased the house following his marriage to Elizabeth Pitcher in 1800.

Howard House was described as, 'a perfect little gem of the architecture of its period'. In the late 19th century it was occupied for many years by Mr James Weeks, formerly a railway man, who was manager and cashier of Bevan's Cement Works in its early days. It then became the administrative offices, and by the 1930s it was divided into flats and let to cement workers. It was demolished in 1956 and the site developed by Gravesend Welding, later D. W. Rewinds. Close to the rear gardens of Howard House was a row of 14 cottages known in the 1840s as Horlocks Row. Later they became known as Belle Vue cottages but were demolished in 1868 to make way for the erection of a new cement works built by J. C. Gostling.

Further up river stood another large house with gardens, called Cliff Cottage. It was located close to the Ship Inn and built on relatively high ground. It was the residence, at least from 1828 to 1840, of William Gladdish and then, in 1841 Henry Ditchburn. It was demolished circa 1956 for further expansion of the Bevans Cement Works.

The land between Howard House and Cliff House became the site of J.C. Gostling Cement Works in 1868. However, on 12 June 1875, Mr John Cubit Gostling, the managing director, was called upon to surrender and stand trial for misappropriating and embezzling large sums of money, the property of the company. In 1876, a limited company was formed, J.C.Gostling & Co. Ltd., but later that year they built a new works at Frindsbury, and sold the Northfleet works to the London Portland Cement Works, who made the Lighthouse Brand of cement.

In 1889, the London Portland Cement works built a new shaft that was called 'The Shah of Persia's Chimney'. It was built during the visit of the Shah of Persia to Queen Victoria and the top was made to look like his fez. It was known locally as 'The Shah's Hat'. It was demolished c.1924. The London Portland Cement Works was a founder member of the original APCM group of companies in 1900.

Close to Cliff Cottage stood the *Ship Inn*, which dated back to 1710. It was situated at the foot of Galloper Wharf, and was described as 'an old time hostelry to gladden the hearts of the lovers of the riverside'. It was closed in the early 1930s and converted into offices for the APCM lighterage department, but was demolished about ten years later.

Between the *Ship Inn* and Lawn Road was the Crown Cement Works, owned by Messrs Lawrence and Wimble, and built in the same era as the London Portland Cement Works.

Before the Crown Cement Works were built, Poynder and Hodson worked the quarry during the first half of the 19th century. Here they built a foundry, called the Northfleet Iron Works, behind the *Ship Inn*. This foundry was leased by Alfred Horlock in 1846, and in 1848 Horlock built two 0-4-0 tender locomotives for the Padarn Railway, North Wales. They were named the *Fire Queen* and *Jenny Lind*. In 1886, *Jenny Lind* was dismantled, but the *Fire Queen* was retained by the Quarry Company and was locked away in a small stone locomotive shed. It was seen only occasionally by privileged visitors down the years. In December 1969, at the age of 121 years, this unique locomotive was rediscovered and put on display at Penrhyn Castle. The survival of *Fire Queen* in original condition makes it a valuable piece of engineering history, for it shows how locomotives were actually built in 1848, not how the experts think they were built, as does a restored locomotive.

Alfred Horlock went out of business 1853 and, at the outbreak of the Crimea War in 1854, Messrs Schlesinger and Wells took over the lease. Schlesinger's manufactured 35 million cartridges for the Turkish Government. The factory was then used as a limelight works by Messrs Holmes and Warner, and then for making patent fuel before it was taken over by Lawrence and Wimble for the cement business. This quarry between Granby Road and Lawn Road is now the site of the new Northfleet Cement Works built in 1970.

At the foot of Lawn Road was the *India Arms*, that dated from the 1830s and was demolished in 1979. It is believed the latter building was erected on the foundations of an earlier inn of the same name, circa 1770, which had strong connections with the East India Company. Adjacent to it, before the Northfleet Gas Works was built, there was the ruin of a small fort dating back to the reign of Henry VIII. In the 19th century there had been a public landing place between Wood's Wharf (or India Arms Wharf) and a wharf that later became known as Gas Works Wharf.

Northfleet Gas Works, built around 1900, was located at the rear of the *India Arms*. The Northfleet Gas Company's Wharf was formerly extensively used for the landing of coal which came down from London by barge, but when the gas works were merged into one of the big London companies the wharf was abandoned and finally purchased by the APCM.

There are two lighthouses on the Northfleet Shore, the Lower and the Upper, designed to act as leading marks for all ships coming up Gravesend Reach. The former was established in the 1860s on the India Arms Wharf. The Upper Light on Bevan's Wharf is of a later date.

Between Lawn Road and College Road was the works of the Knight, Bevan and Sturge Cement Company formed in 1853, and later to become Bevans Cement Works. William Aspdin appears to have had some involvement with Thomas Sturge and the new factory in 1851/52, before Sturge formed his partnership. Thomas Sturge was a big local landowner who was shrewd in seeing opportunities for the development of his land. The cement works being built on his own property, formerly part of the Hive Estate.

Bevans became the dominant cement factory in Northfleet. The factory was modernised in 1925 and the new concrete jetty was built, having a frontage of 600 feet and a water depth of 26 feet. The factory, which was reported to be the finest in Europe with a weekly output of 10,000 tons, was started up in the spring of 1926. It was finally closed when the new Northfleet Works were built in 1970.

When K.B.&S. expanded their cement works in 1872 they demolished a notable old house known as Orme House. It was built on the bank of the Thames close to the Creek. In the 17th century it was described as a beautiful house with an avenue of trees running down to its water gate. Close to Orme House was a small riverside community with streets such as Park Place, Warwick Place, The Creek and York Terrace. All have now been demolished; the last building to survive was the *Huggens Arms,* which was demolished in 1976.

Robins & Cox, which became Robins Cement Co. in 1865, was sited on both sides of the Ebbsfleet River where it flowed out into the Thames at Northfleet Creek. It was here that James Parker, the inventor of Roman Cement in 1797, and which according to some experts was the first true modern cement, established his cement mill. He formed a partnership with James Wyatt and they built their cement mill at the site of an ancient watermill, which they used to drive their machinery. Although a watermill at Northfleet was first mentioned in the Domesday Book, the site of that mill is unknown. But a watermill on this site had certainly existed from the 15th century. Roman cement was made from septaria (concretions with cracks filled with calcite or other minerals) nodules of London clay and chalk formations found on the shore on the Isle of Sheppey and on the Essex shore at Shoeburyness, and presumably brought to the Creek by barges. Parker's patent was granted in 1796 (see *A Hundred Years of Portland Cement 1824-1924,* by A.C. Davis (1924, p.61) and *The Cement Industry 1796-1914; A History,* by A. J. Francis (1977, p.20). The resulting clinker from burning was ground in the watermill on the Creek, possibly the site of the Domesday Mill - see reference to the watermill being used to make stucco (which may refer to Parker's patent) for building (*Hasted octavo edition Vol.III* p.314, 1797) and reference in Pocock's diary of 10 August 1812, 'Walked to Northfleet and got some stone from the cement mill' (*Robert Pocock* by G.M. Arnold, 1883 p.79). Roman cement was used by Marc Brunel for his Thames Tunnel (the first tunnel under water) and for this reason was popular. It was made at White's Cement

The *India Arms* Tavern, Northfleet

Orme House which was on the east side near to the entrance to the Creek, Northfleet.

The Public Landing Place on the Creek at the bottom of College Road, 1910.
In the distance can be seen a visiting American warship.

Works, Swanscombe until circa 1890, long after Portland Cement had replaced it. The Saxon water mill recently discovered on the Ebbsfleet is higher up, near the Roman Villa excavated by H. Stedman and does not appear to be the mill referred to in the Domesday survey.

In 1846, Maude and William Aspdin purchased Parker and Wyatt's cement mill to produce Aspdin's father's patented Portland Cement. Aspdin demolished the ancient watermill and replaced it with a steam engine, and built new bottle kilns, one of which has survived. It was damaged in the last war, but it has been restored and preserved by Blue Circle. Modern cement was used for the restoration of the kiln, not the original lime mortar.

About 200 yards from the *Plough Inn*, along Grove Road stood a grand house, known as Grove House. Henry William Wyatt, who was a partner in Wyatt and Parker Cement works, built the house in 1838 and named it 'Wyattville'.

In 1932, Grove House became the headquarters of the Northfleet Royal Engineers Territorial Unit that comprised mainly workers employed at Bevans cement works. This unit had a distinguished record during the Second World War. Their most notable feat was the blowing up of the oil storage tanks along the Dutch and French coastlines during the retreat in 1940.

Further up river is Northfleet Marshes. It was here in 1871 that the Northfleet Coal and Ballast Company built their deep-water pier. They imported coal from the Tyne as well as exporting chalk and handled other people's goods. They owned the chalk quarries on either side of Galley Hill Road as well as the railway track and private sidings to Northfleet Railway Station. The company opened a branch at West Thurrock, further up river on the Essex side in 1904, and the Northfleet property was sold in 1921.

The Northfleet Coal and Ballast Company supplied the small cement works round the Creek with chalk from their quarry between London Road and the railway, which they also used for ballasting their ships. They also supplied the Britannia Works, a small cement factory near the junction of the Lower Road and Stonebridge Road. The quarry was usually known as 'Kirby's' from the name of the manager who occupied Galley Hill Farm House.

Next to the deep-water pier William Goreham constructed a cement factory that was originally known as Goreham's Works. Mr George Butchard, the well known Gravesend shipbuilder and engineer, bought the works on the open market for £3850 in 1881. He ran it as his own for a short time, but he then remodelled the machinery and formed a small limited company, the 'Tower Portland Cement Company', which made Tower Brand cement.They were among the founder members of the APCM, and Mr Butchard became one of the Managing Directors. In January 1912, a tin-smelting company acquired the premises, and extensive structural alterations were made to adapt the premises for their new purpose.The factory was later occupied by the Britannia Metal Company, specialists in lead and silver.

In the early 1860s, James Weston, who earlier made Roman cement in a factory at Millwall, built a new factory at Northfleet. It was known as the 'Weston Cement Works', and was located on the bank of the Thames above the Creek. It was the furthest west of all the cement factories at Northfleet. It was later renamed 'The Onward Cement Company', and was also a member of the original APCM group of companies in 1900.

The Botany Marshes are protected from flooding by a sea wall. The first account of marshland on the south bank of the Thames being put in the care of persons authorised by the King to take care of them dates from 1312. From this date there were several Commissions held almost yearly through several reigns, and granted to several different persons, the aim of these being to inspect and repair the several breaches made by the tides, and the defaults in the walls and sewers occasioned by the neglect of the owners and occupiers of the marshes from London Bridge as far as Gravesend. There were no applications made to Parliament regarding river defences of the marshes after 1607, and it is presumed that the river defences between Lumbarde's-wall and Gravesend-bridge had been completed. This would indicate that the bank, or causeway, at Stonebridge, Northfleet, was probably erected before this date.

Chapter 29

COLDHARBOUR ROAD, WOMBWELL HALL AND OLD PERRY STREET[1]

HISTORICALLY PERRY STREET is something of a local history black hole, but the next few pages should help to fill this gap in our knowledge of the area.

The district that we think of today as old Perry Street is roughly that from the crossroads by Coldharbour Road library along the Old Perry Street road to the Murrells, thence east to the *Earl Grey* inn and westwards to the Vale Road crossroads with Colyer Road and Park Avenue: probably came into being during the first half of the 18th century, but Perry Street as an entity has been in existence for hundreds of years before this time.

The earliest reference for the district that we have is from 1278, when the village was called 'Pyrie' - meaning the place of pears - a reference to the main industry of the area, fruit growing, an activity which continued right up to the outbreak of the SecondWorld War.

Shears Green, which lies about half a mile to the east of present-day old Perry Street, is first recorded in 1357, and it seems likely that Perry Street first began to develop as a farming community between these two points at a time a little before these dates, probably as part of the Old Manor of Durndale.

The earliest know habitation in the area, though, is not at either of these places but a little further east along Coldharbour Road where Morrison's Superstore now stands. This store was built in 1993 and their town centre shop in the 'Anglesea Centre' (now Wilkinson's) closed in April 1996.

As those of you who are familiar with the district will know, much of the countryside from New Perry Street to the Watling Street has been covered by housing since the end of the Second World War, without as far as I am aware any archaeological survey work being carried out, despite the clear potential of the area. Consequently the answers to the many questions about Perry Street's past now lie buried under the bricks and mortar that cover the ancient green fields and orchards.

Excavations were undertaken about 10 years ago at the Morrison's site, when a Bronze Age settlement was found, dating back to 1100 BC. This discovery, coupled with the finding of the Iron Age Fort on the site of the Tollgate Riding Stables in the late 1990s, by surveyors working for Union Railways, and earlier discoveries along the south side of the A2 between this point and Spring Head, all point to the countryside hereabouts being occupied from a very early point in history.

Coldharbour Road, or Lane as it used to be called, along which we will journey for the first part of our tour, dates from at least Roman times and could in fact be a part of an ancient straight track which ran from the Five Ways Went at the Tollgate to the Hill area of Northfleet, and on to a ferry crossing to Tilbury Ness. Present-day Coldharbour starts a little way up the Watling Street from the Tollgate, but until very recently there used to be an old cart track which, commencing from a point very near the junction, ran in a straight line eastwards until it joined the present road about where the Lions Hospice now stands. This track was probably the original route of the road. Though marked clearly on maps as far back as the 1700s, it has in recent times been ploughed out. The foundation stone of the Lions Hospice was laid on 5 October 1990, and opened on 12 April 1992.

Immediately to the west of the superstore and the hospice the housing estates begin. These do have a history of their own, but we do not have the space available here to give them any more than a fleeting mention. Council housing began in the 1930s, when part of Snelling Avenue and the Crescent were built. Though the outbreak of war curtailed this activity for a while, peace brought with it a resumption of house building. When Newton Abbot, Hartshill and part of Harden Road were built, much of the labour was provided by German prisoners of war. From this time construction has gone on relentlessly until all the countryside north of Watling Street has been built over, except for the farmland on the western side of the Wrotham Road, between St. George's School and the Watling Street. .

The first road junction that we come to as we journey along the road westward is the Five Ways Went at Shears Green. Five-way crossroads were often in times past places of execution. Whether this ever occurred here as it did at the Tollgate, is unknown, but another derivative

---
[1] This chapter was written by David Jewiss

162

of Shears is Sherrifs, which would seem to imply that executions were once enacted here.

Here three ancient lanes converge with Coldharbour - Newhouse, Hog and Durndale. Newhouse and Hog are parts of a much longer ancient route that used to run from a point about where Echo Square now is, all the way to Northfleet Green and Southfleet. Cross Lane seems to be an older road than Old Road East as, before the turnpike road was altered to join what is now Echo Square direct, in 1795 it made a 'T' junction with Cross Lane East to the west of Elnathan Cottages, and it would seem possible that Lower Higham Road, Old Road East to the rest of Echo Square, New House Lane and Hog Lane (now Hilary Avenue) may have been a Roman road leading from the Roman potteries on the marshes near Higham to Vagniacis, Springhead (see *Kentish Sources, Some Roads and Bridges,* by E. Mellivy, p.44, and *The Road between Dartford, Gravesend and Strood,* by R.H. Hiscock, 1968, *Arch Cant. Vol.LXXXIII*, p.235). The late David Tassell used to say that, as a boy in the 1940s, he was able to climb through the old elm trees all the way from New House Farm to Shears Green without once touching the ground, so thickly did the trees grow in the hedgerow.

At the bottom end of Hog Lane, at its junction with the Watling Street, there was found a cache of Roman coins in 1923. I think this was while the main arterial A2 road was being laid. In more recent times there were rumours of further finds on the site and stories of people wandering about with pockets full of Roman gold coins.

Durndale Lane, though only of short length, connected Durndale farm with Shears Green and The Watling Street, taking its name from the Old Manor of Durndale, the forerunner of the Wombwell Hall Estate. Very little is known of the early history of the Manor, though it is believed to have been in existence from at least as far back as the 13th Century. The name Durndale is old English for secret, hidden or obscure, which is a good description of the position of the farm, sited as it was, tucked away under the scarp of the rising ground below Shears Green.

It is thought that Durndale Manor got its name from an early owner, a John Derendale. By the reign of Edward III it had come into the possession of William Wangdeford, commonly called Wainford, whose son was a Sergeant at Law and a good benefactor of Rochester Bridge (see *Hasted Octavo,* 2nd Edn, Vol III, 1797, p.300) for further information on Durndale and Wombwell Hall). Since his time, local usage has corrupted the name repeatedly: Durndale, Dundale, Durnle etc. Whether there was ever a Durndale Manor House is not known, as to whether it stood on or near the site of the farm, or nearer to Wombwell Hall, only an archaeological survey could discover, and there seems little likelihood of such a thing being practical in the foreseeable future.

On a lighter note, Durndale Lane, which was little used except for farm traffic, played the important social role of lovers lane for the district, and vied with the kissing gates in New House Lane for first place for matters amatorial in the area.

The *Battle of Britain* public house, which stands by the crossroads, was originally built in 1905 as Shears Green House, and stood in some isolation until 1948, when a temporary inn of wooden structure was erected to help slake the thirst of the new council tenants. In 1961, this was pulled down and the house itself became the Inn.

Shears Green was thought of as lonely and remote in the past, although there is evidence to the contrary. Given its strategic position, placed as it is at the highest point of the ridgeway and commanding views of considerable distances in all directions, it seems very likely that some sort of hamlet or defensive site existed here at one time. During the Second World War, the highest point of Shears Green was the site of a barrage balloon detachment and an ack ack detachment.

A little further along Coldharbour Road, where the top end of Bucks Cross Road is now, was Great Coldharbour Farm. The farm, which in more modern times used to form part of Dalton's Coldharbour Nurseries, dated back to at least the mid-18th century. Ted Jenkins once told me that, as a boy in the 1930s, every time he walked past the farm it seemed smaller and more dilapidated. The farm seems to have finally vanished at about the time of the outbreak of the Second World War, presumably so that the ground could be cleared for wartime food production.

On the opposite side of the road, about where the top of Dene Holm Road now is, there used to be, in the 1760s, a group of buildings, suggestive of another farmhouse. These buildings seem to have disappeared by the beginning of the 19th century, but their presence nearly 250 years ago does give some credence to the theory of Shears Green being more populated in the past.

We next come to Struttons, Scruttons or Strattons Farm, the last surviving farmhouse in the village, except for the Murrells. Although now surrounded by modern housing and shorn of its many outbuildings, it was a working farm until at least the late 1950s. Parts of the house are believed to date back to early Tudor times, which, if verified, could make the farmhouse - the Murrells notwithstanding - the oldest building in Perry Street and one of the earliest houses in the district.

In 1698, in a field near the farm a baby boy was discovered. As his parents could not be traced, he was registered in Northfleet and named Perry Street after the hamlet near where he was found. One of the fields opposite the farm used to be called the Mulberry field, so perhaps it should have been renamed the Gooseberry field. Mulberry trees, by the way, were very much a feature of the village. Apart from the one at Struttons, there was another in the orchard of Coopers Cottage, roughly where Thanet House now stands, while in the garden of Kington House still stands a veritable old giant, said to be as old as the house itself, which would in all probability make it the oldest living thing in the district.

A hundred yards further along we come to what could fairly be described as the heart of Old Perry Street. Some 80 years ago Richard Austin Freeman (1862-1943), who is best remembered now as an early detective story writer and whose main character was Dr. Thorndyke, wrote a short story *The Green Check Jacket* which included a descriptive account of a walk from Gravesend Railway Station to Old Perry Street and then on to make the discovery of the real dene hole, in the fields behind Wombwell Hall.

In his story, Austin Freeman paints a picture very much as the village and its surroundings were in the 1920s, and his sentiments bear out very much what older residents have said about the countryside being so lovely. A number of writers from an earlier age, notably Celia Fiennes and Charles Dickens, have also commented on the once great beauty of the countryside to the south of Gravesend.

My great-grandmother, Jane Marsh (1841-1912) who came to Perry Street in 1860 from Essex, recalled how beautiful the district was, particularly in blossom time with the orchards in full flower. When she first lived in Perry Street, at Argent Cottage - best remembered today as Bonds the Barbers - she used to take in regularly holidaymakers, as was the practice with many other villagers.

The idea of the village being a holiday resort may seem a little ridiculous now, but many people used to come to enjoy the quiet peace of the countryside here while still being within reach of Gravesend and Rosherville to the north and the slightly more horticultural delights of Springhead to the south. All of these could easily be reached by means of the horse breaks that plied during the summer season through the village between Springhead, Gravesend and Rosherville Pier on a regular basis.

The dene hole that Austin Freeman mentions was real enough, and today it is still remembered in the name of the main road through the estate, that now covers the golden barley fields that he described. Incidentally the story was first published in 1925, in the author's book *The Puzzle Lock,* which is still available through local libraries.

Dene holes are of course very much a hidden feature of the area, as they are almost anywhere in chalk country. In the last three or so years, some have been discovered in Pelham Road South, Haynes Road and Napier Road, while one can remember in the not too distant past others opening up in Mitchell Avenue and Nelson Roads. In the 19th century a large one was found in an unspecified part of Perry Street Road, which was adapted by the council as part of the new main drainage system. How many still remain awaiting discovery is anyone's guess. I rather suspect it is more than a few.

At about where Milroy Avenue now joins with Coldharbour, there used to be a group of 18th and early 19th century cottages. There are a number of old photographs of these houses; some thatched, some tiled, they made a very picturesque jumble of rusticity, and it seems such a shame that places of such obvious charm should have to give way to progress, as they did circa 1930, when Milroy Avenue and Earl Roads were built. In one of these old cottages used to live Nurse Carr, the local midwife who in the 1920s was something of a legend in the village.

Durndale Farm early 1960

A distant view of Scruttons Farm, Coldharbour Road, 1961

165

The last Wombwell Hall

A view from Hog Lane (now Hillary Avenue) towards Wombwell Hall in the trees, June 1954.

In one of the issues of the *Gravesend Magazine* of 1913, there is a very attractive photograph of the cottages with a very countrified Coldharbour Lane rolling away eastwards towards Shears Green; by the cottages there can just be seen a footpath which used to lead to Coopers Road and on to the back gate of Petham House in Carters Road.This path crossed Coldharbour Road to the stone steps that can be seen on the right of the photograph and then southwards behind Wombwell Hall Gardens, the dene hole and onward via diverging paths to the Downs Road and Southfleet.

Nearly opposite the old cottages used to stand another, Rose Cottage, which survived until relatively recent times, when it was demolished to make way for Coldharbour Branch Library, opened in 1961. As with the group of cottages on the other side of the road, it was probably first built as a home for Wombwell Hall estate workers.

We next come to the present-day crossroads of Coldharbour Road and Old Perry Street, with Earl Road and Hall Road. Circa 1930 this was a T junction, as Earl Road until this time was only a footpath, leading to New Perry Street.

Hall Road, locally known as Park Road in past times, led past Wombwell Hall southwards to Wingfield Bank, Pepper Hill and Springhead. Wingfield Bank was an old farm house, sadly demolished in recent years, to make way for Sainsbury's superstore. In the mid-18th century, a house stood here called Greenfoot Bank. In the 18th century there were a number of other houses in the vicinity, though the only one named on early maps was 'Wellfield', which stood on the western side of Springhead Road, almost opposite where the Drill Hall stood. Number 7 Wingfield Bank Cottages stood in splendid isolation on the western side of Springhead Road, opposite Waterdales.

In any event, Wingfield/Greenfoot Bank is really outside the boundaries of Perry Street, and the building that really concerns us is Wombwell Hall itself which until 1994 used to stand about a hundred yards south from the crossroads by the library in its own grounds. There have been at least three Wombwell Halls, the first known being built by the Wombwell family in 1471, presumably on the same site as the later two, although it is not possible to be certain as no description of this first hall is known to exist.

The Wombwell family who originally came from Wombwell in Yorkshire took over the ownership of the Hall and estate from the Wangford (Wainford) family of Southfleet, who held the Old Manor of Durndale. The family owned the Hall until 1646, when the local branch of the family died out and the estate was purchased by John Forterie, a Huguenot refugee from Lille. He and his descendants occupied the estate until 1774, when they too died out. During their time there the family pulled down the original Hall and built a very fine red brick mansion faced with white stone to take its place. This house was acknowledged by many as being one of the loveliest country mansions in the country, and great was the consternation when in 1860 the new owner, Thomas Colyer, had it pulled down and erected his own Victorian hall.

With the passing of the Forteries, the Hall had a succession of owners and tenants. First George Sanders, a farmer and maltster from Darenth, who made a lot of improvements to the Hall, then a Captain Elliott, before the property passed through the hands of the local Harman and Brenchley families.

Though the old mansion was acclaimed for its beauty, it did have its dark side. In the early 1800s, one of the servants, a young maid, said to have been strikingly beautiful was murdered by a man called Farmer. Farmer, having shot the girl, attempted to commit suicide by cutting his own throat. As Miss Brabazon in her little book (some editions only) *A Month in Gravesend* reported gleefully, 'the blood of murdered and murderer mingled together on the floor'.

Farmer, though did not die; he got off at the subsequent trial by pleading that his pistol had gone off accidentally; later he was transported for his part in a robbery, only to return years later to the town, where he was regarded as a criminal and public nuisance. Eventually he was taken ill and ended his days in Gravesend workhouse - some sort of justice at last maybe.

The Colyer family, and later through marriage the Colyer-Ferguson family, were to be the last lords of the manor of Wombwell Hall. They quickly began to stamp their identity on the village - the second hall was demolished and the third and last building erected. Though history only records three buildings on the site, as previously speculated it is possible that the remains of a Durndale Manor could be found on the site, but, given the circumstances of the destruction of the last of the Halls, it would seem very unlikely that permission would ever be given to search for it.

At the time of their acquiring the Hall and estate, the Colyer family were already very large landowners, having property and land as far away as Farningham and Crayford and a number of other places, principally Southfleet. While under the ownership of the family the estate probably reached its zenith, but with the rapid industrialisation of Gravesend and Northfleet in the later part of the 19th century, artisan housing began to encroach across the once green estate fields, so much so that, by the mid-1930s, housing developments were nearing (in a matter of speaking) the doorsteps of the Hall, and in 1937 the family finally moved out.

During the Second World War the Hall served as a hospital for wounded anti-aircraft gunners from the Tollgate and Green Street batteries. After the war the family finally sold the hall and grounds to the Kent Education Committee, who turned it into a Girls Technical School and later Northfleet Grammar School for Girls. When the school closed in 1988, it was sold to become part of an Old People's Home. As to the hall's final demise in 1994, the then owners of the nursing home sent in the bulldozers and flattened everything, claiming that the Hall was being used as a centre for black magic and pagan worship - claims that rang very hollow with the people living round about, who were unaware of anything unusual going on in the building.

Efforts were made to get the destruction stopped but despite the efforts of historians, councillors and outraged local residents, Wombwell Hall was demolished over the Easter weekend in 1994. Today, only the Lodge, stable block and the old stone boundary wall are left to remind us of what once was. As to the subsequent outcome in the courts, it is very difficult to decide which was the greatest obscenity, the crime or the punishment. A £2000 fine for the destruction of a fine old building and the obliteration of over five hundred years of history seems very cheap.

Before moving on from the Hall, mention should be made of the Park. This was a huge area that stretched westwards from Hall Road all the way to the old Gravesend West railway line, and possibly at one time into Northfleet itself, while from the southern side of Vale Road and Old Perry Street it stretched all the way to Springhead. The Park over the decades served as the village common, where all sorts of events were held from Sunday School treats and school outdoor events to the holding of the first Kent Agricultural Show in 1923.

During the 1930s much of this area was built over - housing in Waterdales, Colyer Road and the Pepper Hill end of Hall Road all date from this time. The first secondary school in the area (The Central School), in Colyer Road, was opened in 1935, and Wombwell Park behind Mitchell Avenue was created. The last portion of this huge area survived as allotments until after the war when the Sports Centre was opened in the 1960s. With hindsight the whole area should have been turned into a really worthwhile country park, something that the urban Gravesham needs, but of course in the 1930s conservation of any sort had hardly been heard of, least of all in civic circles, and the opportunity was lost.

Until the 1890s, the Perry Street Road ran from the *Pelham Arms* in Gravesend right through New Perry Street, to bear away right by the *Earl Grey* inn and on to the 'T' junction at the Murrells in Old Perry Street, where it turns partly back on itself to meet Coldharbour Road at the aforementioned crossroad by the library. In the 1890s, though, Gravesend council decided to annex their part of Perry Street Road and call it Pelham Road South, while in the 1930s, the post office decided that the part between the Murrells and Earl Grey should henceforth be part of Vale Road, leaving the two truncated sections that we have today.

It seems almost inconceivable that there was never a road connecting Roman Gravesend with Springhead and, assuming there was, that it did not form a crossroad with Coldharbour Road somewhere near present-day Old Perry Street and about where an even older Perry Street than the one we know today could have evolved. If it did, though, its exact route has long been lost. The modern route from Gravesend to Pepper Hill, though fairly straight, is not without its twists and turns and does not seem to conform properly to the concept of a Roman road or indeed an ancient British old straight track.

Kington House, built in 1751.

Marlborough Cottage in the 1930s. The building to the right is part of the now demolished Esher Place.

The Murrells circa 1920

The Forge and Wheelwrights Shop with the *Six Bell* public house

There used to be an old track that ran from the junction of Grange Road with Pelham Road in a fairly straight line all the way to roughly where Mitchell Avenue now meets Hall Road, passing the village just to the west of Elm Cottage which was of great age, though whether it could be thought of as a Roman road is uncertain.

Old Perry Street itself deviates from its original line through the hamlet, and at one time ran behind the houses that now stand on the western side of Old Perry Street and Vale Road, from east of Marlborough Cottage to beyond the aforementioned Elm Cottage. The reason for this was the construction of the Murrells farmhouse: once the farm came into being, it began to draw people away from the original road and eventually this small section of the original route became abandoned. As when people left the farm they turned sharp left or right for Gravesend or Northfleet rather than rejoining the original road, so perhaps behind Kington House a small section of the old road still remains, awaiting discovery.

As we walk along Old Perry Street, the first old house that we come to is Marlborough Cottage, which was built circa 1745. Its early history is slightly obscure, but by the 1850s it was a ladies' seminary; from 1900 to the 1920s it was a dairy run by the Baldwin family. Today it is once more a private residence and somewhere in its long and varied existence the cottage has managed to acquire a ghost, known as the White Lady Ann.

Between Marlborough Cottage and Kington House there now stands a modern bungalow but here, until they were demolished in the 1950s, Esher Place stood, a group of very small 18th century cottages, three on one side and four on the other, facing one another across a small courtyard. It is thought that the Old Northfleet Workhouse was situated in the vicinity, possibly centred on nearby Bumble Cottages, and possibly Esher Place could have formed part of this complex, though they were more likely simply estate workers' cottages. In the 1870s, the cottages were the scene of a tragedy when a little boy fell into the well situated in the courtyard, and despite the desperate efforts of the people from the forge opposite, slipped further and further down the shaft until he reached the water and drowned. Sadly this was not an uncommon occurrence in those times.

Opposite Esher Place used to stand the Forge and the Wheelwrights shop. Austin Freeman, in his previously mentioned short story, refers to the Forge/Wheelwrights complex as 'Looking like an out-patients department for invalid carts'. It was certainly there in the 1760s and probably for a long time before that. It probably originated - to use a modern description - as a service centre for the local farms and the Hall Estate. The site closed to trade around the end of the Second World War and today a modern doctor's surgery occupies its position.

Next to where the Forge stood is the *Six Bells*, as with so many old buildings in the area, its age is uncertain. It is claimed to date from circa 1700, and certainly there is a building marked on the site as far back as the 1760s, though whether this is supposed to be the Forge or Inn, or both, is unclear. By the latter part of the 19th century it had acquired a rather violent reputation, as my aunt Minnie used to recall: a great deal of fighting of one sort or another used to go on there.

On the corner of Old Perry Street, facing eastwards towards the *Earl Grey*, standing in its own grounds, is Kington House a fine imposing country house built in 1751. Sadly, it is now, together with the Murrells opposite, beginning to look increasingly out of place amidst all the surrounding urbanisation. A reminder of a more gentle age, it was from 1913 for many years the home of the Southwood family, who ran the nearby dairy.

The Murrells which stands almost opposite, was originally called Craddocks Farm. The name 'Murrells' relates to an Edward Murrell, a 19th century owner. During the 18th century, the house was variously called Perry Street Farm, Beechlands Farm and Steels Farm. The date of 1687 on the front of the house could well be correct, although the discovery of 14th-century pewterware under the floorboards during a recent renovation suggests that at least part of the farmhouse could be older. In the 19th century the house acted as the village Post and Telegraph Office. During the Second World War Murrells was the headquarters of the local home guard, Major Sunnocks, the then occupant, being the commanding officer.

Robert Pocock in his diary for 27 November 1822, writes: 'This morning about 3 o'clock a fire broke out at Mr. Murrell's Perry Street in the nursery, which it destroyed; but the children of Mr. Robinson a clerk in the tower escaped with difficulties by the activity and perseverance of a person at the hazard of his life. The market bell was rung and the town alarmed when two engines were sent over but the fire was extinguished without them.' (*Robert Pocock, p.158*).

Just west of The Murrells, in the vicinity of the present garage, once stood a house reputed to have been of a great age, the structure of which was said to resemble a beehive. I am not sure how true this is since it has long been demolished and there are no surviving illustrations. Also on the site of the garage was a large pond which can just be seen on some photographs of the Murrells. The pond was filled in during the 1930s. Behind Murrells, in 1925, was established the bus depot of the Gravesend and District Bus Company which started a service of small one man red buses between Perry Street and the Clock Tower via Old Road West and Darnley Road. The Watch Committee having objected to their using Pelham Road owing to competition with the tram route. Later another route went from the *Nelson Hotel,* Windmill Street via Wrotham Road, Cross Lane East and Singlewell Road to the Golf Club House, later Putt's corner, and then along King's Drive to Oak Road, later up Oak Road to the *General Gordon* and then to Gloucester Road and Poplar Avenue. A short lived service to Meopham did much to reduce the fares charged on the Maidstone and District Service to Borough Green.

Before the days of heavy traffic it was the custom on Guy Fawkes night to have a bonfire in the centre of the road junction here. Imagine the reaction now if anyone tried to revive the custom!

From The Murrells which stands on the base of the 'T' junction of Vale Road and Old Perry Street, we have to go two ways, which is a bit difficult to do all at once. Firstly we travel eastwards a short distance along Vale Road until we come to the other village inn, the *Earl Grey* which stands near the frontier between the old and the new villages. Said to have originally been two houses, it became an inn towards the end of the 18th century. Though some distance from the river, for some reason the inn attracted the attention of the naval press gangs. According to the landlord there is a brick dated 1677 in the oldest part of the building, which suggests it is ten years older than The Murrells. This method of dating houses is not foolproof, however, since new houses were often built on the foundations of older ones, so we cannot be sure if the date relates to the original building or the commencement of the new one. Between the Murrells and the *Earl Grey* and around the road junction of Perry Street with Coopers Road used to stand a number of older buildings but these, apart from the 'Shrubbery' (see later) have long been demolished.

Moving eastwards from The Murrells but on the other side of Vale Road we come to four modern semi-detached houses which stand on the site of the fondly remembered Bumble Cottages of great, if uncertain, age. They dated from the mid-18th century, if not earlier, and, as previously mentioned, could have been the site of the Northfleet Workhouse. They were demolished circa 1960.

To the west of them still stands Murrell Cottage, although what relationship it ever had with the farmhouse is unclear, as it was in situ long before Mr Murrell ever farmed at The Murrells. The date of 1720 that used to be displayed by the front door is arguable but the cottage is certainly of 18th century origin. The weatherboarding on Murrell Cottage is a new addition, and whether there was ever boarding there in the past is doubtful as photographs of the cottage from the early 1900s show that there were none there at that time. The last old house in the village, Elm Cottage, certainly is old, as is its weatherboarding. Like the other old houses here it dates back to the 18th century and, like Marlborough Cottage, boasts a ghost. One of the past owners recalled, 'I was working in the cellar one day when I felt a hand on my shoulder, when I looked round there was nobody there. I went back to work and the same thing happened again. I never went down into the cellar again.'

Tucked round the back of the old houses with an entrance next to Elm Cottage used to be Southwood's Dairies. Their horses and carts were a familiar sight in the area until well into the 1950s, long after the other dairies had gone over to electrified floats. It is said that Southwood's was the first dairy to commence delivering milk to schools at the beginning of the 1939-45 war. Perhaps they did, but as one who had to drink it, one wishes they had not bothered; but for small boys in the late 1940s their cardboard milk tops were fine substitutes for the fast disappearing cigarette cards as things to play games with, although the convention of wearing them in festoons around one's neck could be a bit anti-social in hot weather.

A short distance beyond the site of the dairy we come to a large modern building which was built in the 1960s as the new Northfleet Police station. It was built on the meadow on which the dairy once grazed its horses. The police station did not last very long and the building is now offices. Opposite, in Colyer Road, stands the Central School, later the Northfleet School for Boys, and now Colyer House. Although this building is not really within the borders of Perry Street, a great many of the older village children attended the school and still do, so it deserves a mention. Opened in 1935, it was built on part of the Wombwell Hall's parkland and the playing fields running down to Waterdales are a surviving fragment of it.

The school was bombed during the Second World War, as were several places around what could be considered the western fringe of Perry Street: Waterdales, Detling Road, Park Avenue and Dover Road East, where a bomb narrowly missed the Dover Road Schools, falling just across the road from it. An unexploded bomb fell behind Hardy Avenue. Perry Street itself escaped relatively unscathed, though for years afterwards I can remember picking up shrapnel in our back garden in Wycliffe Road.

Wooden houses, Wycliffe Road,
photograph dating from the 1970s

Chapter 30

PARK AVENUE, THE OLD ROAD AND NEW PERRY STREET[2]

PARK AVENUE RUNNING between Vale Road and the Old Road forms the western boundary of Perry Street and dates from around 1900, when it is was laid out over the old track, previously mentioned, running between present-day Grange Road and the top of Mitchell Avenue. At its northern end, by Dover Road School, it joins the Old Road at a point that many would consider is the most dangerous crossroads in the borough. The Old Road was part of the London to Dover coach road, one of the busiest stage routes in the country, though what the travellers of the horse age would have thought about today's volume of traffic one cannot imagine.

Dover Road School was opened in 1901 to take pressure off the church school in Carters Road which, by then, was bursting at the seams. A little more about this school later.

Roughly opposite Park Avenue, Fiveash Road is named in memory of the smock mill which stood at its northern end. The mill was built by a John Fiveash in 1795 and continued under various millers until 1878, when it ceased trading, mainly because of the changing farm patterns in the area and the march of urbanisation over much of the surrounding countryside. It was finally pulled down c.1897. During its life the mill had a rather dark reputation. Owing to the very low sweep of its sails, two people had their heads stove in and were killed: in 1830, a young girl called Louisa Loft and on a later occasion a Mr Broad. Both deaths prompted public outcries for closure of the mill but nothing was done. After the mill and a nearby group of little clap-board cottages had been demolished, Fiveash Road was built. The road itself was not without tragedy, as a man murdered his wife here in the 1920s.

Opposite the site of the windmill in Fiveash Road stands a factory site. From 1901, this building was the depot of the Gravesend and Northfleet Tramway Company, until its closure in 1929. Behind the large building in Dover Road, which until recently was the *Bridge Inn* (now awaiting demolition), the tram entrance can still be seen and until recently the tramlines themselves were visible. In 1913, The Tramway Company built a bus depot with a petrol storage tank in Fiveash Road and commenced services to Dartford and Chatham with Daimler open top buses. They also hired out Belsize and Burford single-decker buses for private trips. By 1914, they were operating to Meopham, and to Hoo, West Malling and Cliffe from Chatham. These bus interests were sold to the Maidstone and District Company in 1920 (another company in which the British Electric Traction Co. had a substantial interest) who took over the Tramway and, in February 1929, replaced the trams with 16 low-roof Leyland motor buses.

The Old Road forms the northern boundary of New Perry Street, from Park Avenue to Cecil Road. Just before we reach Victoria Road we come to a group of two-storey houses, known as May Place, which were among the first to be built in New Perry Street. Now private houses, they were from the late 1830s to 1875 a Jewish Academy run by a Mrs Crawcou, the first of a number of such schools in the Gravesend area.

Down the middle of Victoria Road runs the boundary between Gravesend and Northfleet. I consider this small area of Gravesend from Victoria Road along to Cecil Road and round by Salisbury Road to be very much part of Perry Street rather than Gravesend. Not everyone would agree with me, but the spirit of a community is not dictated by political borders and to me this small portion of its bigger neighbour belongs in all but name to Perry Street.

In connection with the above (though one is not sure about people's feelings now) in the past, far from considering themselves as part of Gravesend or Northfleet, the villagers considered themselves to be simply Perry Streetians. If they felt any affinity for elsewhere it was for Southfleet, rather than the two bigger neighbours. This attitude certainly prevailed until the 1950s, probably due in no small part to the influence the Colyer and Harris families once had on the village.

New Perry Street began life in 1830 as a pre-Victorian property speculation which went rapidly downmarket. At this time a number of substantial country houses were built on the Northfleet side of Victoria Road (of which Gotha Cottage and Tolhurst House are the last survivors). In Perry Street itself, four substantial houses were built on the north side, of which

---

[2] This chapter was written by David Jewiss

only Preston Lodge, now the Conservative Club, still survives. The other three houses occupied the site of present-day Baldwins furniture shop and Post Office. On the south side the *Rose* and *Crown Inn*, were built together with the parade of shops between, known originally as Portland Place.

Prior to this time the hamlet was still centred on the area of The Murrells and the *Six Bells*. The New Perry Street countryside consisted mainly of orchards and fields with a few farm workers' cottages dotted about, of which Coopers Cottage, better known as Cockley's Shop, and the two weatherboard cottages opposite Coopers Road, were the last survivors.

By the 1860s, with the growth of industry along Thameside, pressure to provide cheap housing for the workers, became desperate, triggering another rather less salubrious property boom in the Village, so much so that parts of Perry Street at that time could easily have been called 'Jerry Street'.

Towards the end of the Victorian era, however, rather better housing began to be built, particularly on the northern side of the Village and in the Gravesend sector. The resultant mix of the good, the bad and the not really so ugly gave to the village a particular charm of its own and helped Perry Street keep its village atmosphere long after it had ceased to be one in reality.

In the years leading up to the Second World War and those immediately afterwards, much of the really bad housing, mostly situated on the south side of the Village, was cleared away and by the 1960s most of the remaining old houses either had been modernised or could easily have been so.

This state of affairs, however, did not deter the now defunct Northfleet Council from deciding in 1970 to announce that they intended to municipalise virtually all of New Perry Street en bloc. In the event the worst was averted, the wildest aspects of the grandiose scheme being much watered down. Northfleet Urban District Council was merged with Gravesend to become the new Borough of Gravesham, who were left to pick up the pieces and administer the last rites. As a result many parts of the Village designated for an appointment with the bulldozer escaped. However most of the old country houses of Victoria Road were reduced to rubble, along with much of May Avenue, Lansdown Place, Wycliffe, Carters and Garden Roads, Alfred and Walnut Tree Places, the northern side of Newmans Road and the eastern end of Coopers Road. The little streets, narrow alleys and rows of small terraced housing that had endured for a hundred or more years were no more. Modern small terraced houses and flats linked by new narrow alleyways were built and the new tenants moved in and soon dubbed it 'Mugger's Paradise'. Progress indeed!

Sadly space does not allow for more than a brief mention of but a few of the more historical places and buildings that went to make up old New Perry Street but I shall attempt to cover as many as possible.

The oldest house still standing is the Shrubbery, situated between the Parish Church and the junction of Coopers Road and Vale Road. Built in 1820, as a private house, it has had a varied career. From 1871 to 1914 it was the vicarage after which it reverted to being a private house until, in 1928, it became the surgery of Dr Napier, the first doctor in the Village. Today the old part of the house contains a veterinary surgery and the doctors' practice is carried on in a new extension at the rear.

Just about where the toilets are now in Perry Street used to stand a pair of old weatherboard cottages called Rose Lodge and Montpellier House. This type of house became very popular in the late 18th century (from when this pair probably date) and were quite a feature in the Village. There were others in Walnut Tree Place, Napier Road, Wycliffe Road, Perry Street and Vale Road. Today the only genuine old weatherboarded house left is Elm Cottage in Vale Road.

Regarding Rose Lodge and Montpellier House, my aunt Elsie Gregory once told me that the lady of one of those cottages told her the legend that it was believed that a tunnel used to run from her cellar to Wombwell Hall about a quarter of a mile away.

In Wycliffe Road at one time there were a number of weatherboard houses and a story seems to have grown that the ones facing Wycliffe Church, aptly known locally as 'the little houses' were of Tudor origin. In fact they dated from early Victorian times.

Coopers Cottage, previously mentioned, played a leading role in the early history of the Village and was, in many ways, the cradle of religion and education in the district. Probably built towards the end of the 18th century, it is perhaps better remembered as Cockley's Shop, although the shop part was a Victorian addition. In its earliest days it was probably a market garden, for, in the late 1830s, an Ann Cooper is listed as living there, plying the trade of gardener. It is presumably from her or her ancestors that the cottage and Coopers Lane got their original names.

At the beginning of the 1840s there was a great deal of concern about the welfare of the children seemingly running wild in the village. Wycliffe Church Records show that a lady, probably Mrs Cooper, approached members of the Gravesend Princess Street Church about the matter and to cut a long narrative short, a room was opened in Alfred Place, possibly in the home of an 80-year old Mr Cooper, also a gardener and, one assumes, the father or a relative of Ann. This arrangement did not last long before the embryo School/Sunday School was transferred to Coopers Cottage until 1846, at which time purpose built classrooms were opened on the site of what became Wycliffe Church.

This arrangement continued for some time until the then local Parish Church, St. Mark's Rosherville, being concerned about the Non-Conformist church making all the running unchallenged in the growing village, opened its own school at the bottom of Carters Road, in 1856. At this time the day school at Wycliffe closed, although it continued to flourish as a church and it is worth noting that, human nature being what it is, the small rooms and hall to the rear of the church were still referred to as the classrooms and school room right up to its closure at the end of 1979. Coopers Cottage which, incidentally, also at one time boasted a coal yard and laid claim to a resident ghost, succumbed to the demolition men at about the same time as Wycliffe Church, despite the clear case for it to be preserved. To this day nothing has been built on the ground where it stood.

The Church School or 'Little School' as it was affectionately called, served the educational needs of the Village children until 1965, after which it soldiered on for a few years as a youth club, until the police decided it was all getting rather too much of a good thing and closed it down. From its beginnings in 1856 it catered for all ages of scholars right up to 1901, at which time Dover Road School was built and took all the older children from Northfleet. Cecil Road School opened in 1909, duly taking the remaining older children from Gravesend. Quite how the 'Little School' coped with all the children it had before these two schools opened is difficult to imagine, especially considering that this was achieved in what was essentially two classrooms and a small hall. Writing in 1886, J.R.S. Clifford had this to say: 'Here are daily gathered the Village children to the number of 230. The behaviour of some of them out of school suggests that their teachers must have no small trouble in maintaining order within.' Clearly matters had improved greatly by the time I went there in 1945, but then we were not nearly 230 strong. One story about the school is that in Victorian times a number of the schoolchildren were enticed away by a visiting circus.

The Parish Church of All Saints took a little longer to build than the school and was not opened until 1871, since when it has been the dominant architectural feature of the Village. The architect of All Saints was James Brooks. John Newman, in *West Kent and the Weald* (Buildings of England, Pevsner, 2nd edn, 1976, p.437), describes it as 'not an especially large church but an extremely powerful one'; see this reference for further details of the architecture. For very many years the Villagers' spiritual and secular allegiances were divided sharply between the Parish Church and Wycliffe and, despite a number of rather half-hearted ecumenical attempts during the 1950s, there was never a real meeting point between the two. During their co-existence the two churches ministered to the spiritual and material needs of the villagers in a way of which people nowadays, cocooned by the Welfare State, cannot have any real concept.

Apart from the Parish Church, the only place of worship still flourishing is the Pentecostal Church in All Saints Road. At one time there were two other churches in the village - the Rehoboth Hall in St. Thomas's Road, which over the years has had a varied career, as a place of worship, a warehouse for Baldwins Furniture and a Light Industrial Unit, and the Primitive Baptist Church at the top of Lansdown Place.

Over the years the idea has grown that Wycliffe Church was named after John Wycliffe (1330-84) famous for his translation of the Bible. This is only partly true, for the church was named after Wycliffe Church, Stepney, which together with Princes Street Church played an

Mrs. Knell and Mrs Bowen
outside Walnut Tree Place

The Tuffee family
outside their shop in
Pelham Road South

Outing from the *Jolly Gardeners* circa 1905.
The public house stood at the corner of Garden and Coopers Road

H.C. Palmer & Sons, 15 Coopers Road, in the 1930s.
Mr. Palmer is in the doorway. In the window is a prize winning display
in a Stork margarine competition

important role in establishing the Church in Perry Street. This is well documented in the early records of the church, and also in the Rev. Perry's *The Romance of Wycliffe*. Wycliffe Road was established and named before the church was built as a map of circa 1845 makes clear.

In the main, the Villagers' lives have been tranquil ones: a few tragedies, a couple of murders and the odd ghost. Even the two world wars did not intrude as much as they did elsewhere. However, there was one incident in 1871 that shattered the peace and calm, 'The Great Battle of Perry Street'. On the evening of 23 January, a great body of people, 200 strong marched along Coopers Lane ringing sheep bells, waving torches and carrying two burning effigies. At the junction with Wycliffe Road they turned left and marched down to the Village crossroads with Perry Street and Victoria Road. Here a lengthy confrontation with the police ensued, during which many scuffles and fights broke out and fires were lit. At about 10.00 pm more police reinforcements arrived from Northfleet, whereupon more general fighting broke out. The crowd by this time was estimated at over 500, a considerable portion of the population of Perry Street at the time. Eventually a number of prisoners were taken to Northfleet, but it was well into the small hours before peace was finally restored. Nor was that the end of the matter; in the ensuing days there were further incidents in the Village and in Gravesend.

The local papers of the day are strangely unforthcoming as to the cause of the unrest, but it seems to have stemmed from a dispute with one of the butchers in the Village - though quite over what is uncertain. There seems little doubt, though, as to where the sympathy of the Villagers lay. A great many of them attended Northfleet Magistrates' Court to hear the prisoners, all local men, being sentenced, and then marched with them to Northfleet railway station to see them off to prison amidst great shouting and cheering. When the men were released from prison they were greeted by another large crowd of cheering people, all gathered to welcome them home. As for the butchers, they closed down soon after, presumably because they had lost their trade, and the well-known Drake family took over the shop, continuing the business until the 1980s.

Finally, mention should be made of the small streams that are claimed to have once flowed through the smiling orchards and meadows of Perry Street. One is said to have run from near Marlborough Cottage to Waterdales, possibly rising from a chalk spring, although this is not evident now. A second small stream of which there is some geographical evidence is believed to have run from a point just in front of All Saints Church down what is now Brook Road until it met the rising ground near the Old Road where it turned left and ran through the fields to join the Ebbsfleet a little to the west of Brookvale in Springhead Road. On some of the old maps there is a small stream shown at about this point. Although Brook Road was laid well after any stream ran down it, it is probably named after a folk memory of this stream. The third stream is thought to have risen in Istead Rise and flowed down the valley to the west of Wrotham Road and on past the tollgate into what is now Woodlands Park, where meeting the rising ground by the Old Road, it turned left to join the Brook Road stream. Though there is no visible evidence of this stream other than the topography of the ground, Mr Barry Philips tells me that at one point near St. George's School he has seen underground water running strongly. Until recently, at places along its supposed course, there were wet points or ponds. The original meaning of 'Wycliffe' - as in Wycliffe Road which was in existence as a track at least as far back as the mid-1700s - is 'a shallow bank or slope near a river': another clue perhaps to a watercourse in the vicinity in times gone by.

APPENDIX 1

THE GRAVESEND PIERS[3]

WITH THE DEVELOPMENT of Gravesend as a watering place and the coming of the pleasure steamer traffic to the town, the first half of the 19th century saw the development of piers on the river bank.

At the beginning of the century the principal landing place was the ancient Town Quay at the bottom of the High Street, which had long been one of the possessions of the Gravesend Corporation, and from which it derived a certain amount of income from landing fees. This quay was originally part of the Manor of Milton.

In 1827, the Corporation took steps to rebuild the quay and improve its approaches. The inn known as *The Christopher* which narrowed the entrance to the quay was purchased and pulled down, and after public meetings to gain support, an Act of Parliament was obtained giving the Corporation power to build a new quay and to raise £7000 on bonds secured upon a 1d. toll on all landing or departing from the new quay. A new stone-built quay with improved facilities was then built, with the small square and *Pier* hotel occupying the remainder of the old *Christopher* site. The quay was opened in 1829. Passengers from the steamers were rowed to the quay in watermen's wherries at a fee of 4d. per head, which was popular with the watermen, though not with the passengers of the steam companies. A year later 1830, Mr Pitcher, who had a shipyard at Northfleet, opened a temporary pier at Northfleet, which was so successful that Gravesend people began to fear loss of traffic, and a project for the construction of a Gravesend pier was begun. A Bill was presented to parliament for power to build a pier on the site of the quay. This was resisted by the watermen, and finally rejected by the House of Lords. The Corporation then resolved to erect a temporary pier and to promote yet another Bill before parliament. The temporary pier was erected in 1832, and just before its completion was smashed up in a watermen's riot, to be rebuilt by the Corporation at considerable expense. The second Bill before parliament was successful after a compromised arrangement with the watermen, which was to prove expensive, and the Corporation was authorised to build a pier and raise £12,000 to meet the expense again on bonds secured on tolls. The pier was built and opened in 1834, but very considerable extravagance on the part of the Corporation incurred large debts in addition to the £12,000 bonds. The design of the pier was by William Tierney Clark, a civil engineer. The builder was William Wood; the cost £8700.

In 1835, Blockhouse Fort came on the market and was acquired on their own account by some councillors, who immediately erected a temporary pier called the Terrace Pier, in competition with the Town Pier. This was followed by the Municipal Reform Act 1835, under which the old Corporation was ejected and a more or less new body of councillors elected. The new council immediately began litigation with the Terrace Pier party, which was inconclusive, expensive and went on until 1842, when both parties were financially exhausted.

During this time a permanent pier was erected at Rosherville in Northfleet, and another pier with a relatively short life was built at Marine Parade, to the western end of the town.

In 1842, a contract was entered into between the Corporation and the Terrace Pier party for the Terrace Pier and gardens to be sold to the Corporation for £42,500, the sale to be completed as soon as the Terrace Pier Co. had constructed a new and permanent pier. The Royal Terrace Pier was then erected, but through a series of complicated evasions the contract to sell to the Corporation was never completed. The engineer who designed the Terrace Pier was J.B. Redman.

At this stage free competition between the two piers forced landing tolls down to unprofitable levels and neither party was in a position to compete with the railway from London to Gravesend, which was finally opened in 1849. By 1852, Gravesend Corporation was bankrupt, and the bondholders had appointed a receiver of the Town Pier, who was quite unable to make the pier earn enough even to pay the interest, whilst the unsecured creditors levied execution on the Corporation's furniture at the pier and town hall, including its regalia and even the mace, aldermen's robes, and the jury box, and the mortgagees of the other assets

---

[3] Written by A.F. Allen (with additions).

of the Corporation, such as the town hall, put a bailiff into walking possession to protect their security against the other creditors. The Royal Terrace Pier continued for a time to cater for the fading tripper traffic from London, in the teeth of growing competition from Rosherville Pier and Rosherville Gardens.

For many years the Corporation rented back its furniture and regalia from its creditors by a complicated hire purchase arrangement, until the old debts were at last liquidated. The council remained yearly tenants of the town hall until 1881, in which year Mr G.E. Sharland, the town clerk, reorganised the town's finances, bought back the freehold of the town hall for £6250, and redeemed the regalia and movables for £311. On 12 February that year he announced 'satisfaction of all judgments against the Corporation'.

Finally, in 1884, the Town Pier was sold by the receivers with parliamentary consent to the Tilbury and Southend railway for £8600, and in 1895 the Royal Terrace Pier Company went into liquidation, the Terrace Gardens were sold to a speculative builder and the pier was sold to a new company belonging to the local pilots.

The Town Quay Gravesend from an old engraving drawn in 1820

STREET NAMES AND THEIR DERIVATIONS[4]

MANY OF GRAVESEND AND NORTHFLEET'S streets have names whose origins are self-explanatory. There are groups named after tugs, sailing barges, saints, explorers, Dickensian characters, trees, painters, landowners and former members of the two Councils. Others are named after Royalty, Lords of Cobham Hall, eminent politicians and West Country towns. The origins of many older names are more obscure and the source and derivation of some of these are set out below.

Street	Origin
Abberley Street	Mr James Abberley Mitchell, District Surveyor, N.U.D.C.
Abbey Road	The poem, 'Ingoldsby Abbey', from *The Ingoldsby Legends* by Richard Harris Barham (1788-1845).
Abbotsfield	Field name from 1839.
Alfred Road	After Alfred Ignatius, the son of Alfred Tolhurst (1834-1913), solicitor and cement manufacturer.
Anglesea Place Centre	After the Marquis of Anglesea, friend and patron of Henry Eversfield, a local builder and auctioneer.
Arnold Road	George Matthews Arnold (1827-1908), of Milton Hall. Eight times Mayor, a wealthy solicitor and landowner.
Artillery Row	Built on land that had been part of Milton Barracks.
Ascot Road	After the famous racecourse built by Dagnall and J & A Builders.
Aspdin Road	William Aspdin (1815-1864), son of Joseph Aspdin patentee of Portland cement, took over an established company at Northfleet Creek and introduced Portland Cement manufacture to the area in 1846.
Austin Road	J.H. Austin, mayor in 1930.
Bader Walk	Group Captain Douglas Bader, D.S.O., D.F.C., (born 1910), pilot with two artificial legs, air ace during the Second World War.
Baker Hill Close	An old local field name; a rising hill.
Bank Street	Cut through in 1850 after a fire destroyed The London and County Bank in the High Street, Gravesend.
Barham Close	Richard Harris Barham, author of *The Ingoldsby Legends,* who often stayed at Milton Manor.
Barr Road	Thomas Barr MacLean (1889-1976), farmer at Westcourt, Chalk.
Bath Street	Road to the Clifton Baths, formerly Fairfield Road.
Beaumont Drive	The Beaumont family owned land at Rosherville.
Beckley Close	A manor that was part of Chalk, known as Chalk Extra but actually in Higham.
Bentley Street	William Bentley, landowner in 1775.
Beresford Road	Admiral Charles W. Beresford (1846-1919), nicknamed 'Lord Charles'.
Berkley Crescent	William Berkley, landowner and stepson of Michael Bedell.
Bernard Street	Bernard Wiltshire Tolhurst, son of Alfred Tolhurst.
Boucher Drive	J.W. Boucher, butcher and Captain of the Northfleet Volunteer Fire Brigade, and E.W. Boucher, Chairman of the Northfleet Urban District Council 1939-51.
Bourne Road	William Bourne (c.1535-82), Portreve 1571, gunner, mathematician and a Gravesend innkeeper. Author of books on ballistics and navigation.

Brandon Street	Benjamin Brandon, gardener and landowner.
Brenchley Avenue	John Brenchley of Wombwell Hall, Mayor 1808, died in 1857.
Brooke Drive	George Brooke the tenant of Westcourt, Chalk, from 1886 to 1918, a horse breeder and provider of 'horse power'.
Brown Road	H. Hampton Brown, Town Clerk, Gravesend, 1904-48.
Bucks Cross Road	Village in Devon to which Northfleet children were evacuated during the Second World War.
Burch Road	Benjamin Burch built Crete Hall, Northfleet.
Cambrian Grove	Built by Mr Jenkin Jones who lived in Cambrian Villa.
Campbell Road	Sir Colin Campbell (1792-1863), Commander of the British forces during the Indian Mutiny of 1857.
Castle Lane	Public house, the *Lisle Castle* (1776-1940) damaged by an aerial mine 22 September 1940. In 1760, Prettywick Lane.
Chiffinch Gardens	Thomas Chiffinch (1697-1774), of Hive House and later Wombwell Hall.
Christianfields Avenue	Field name recorded in 1403. Mr. Christian lived in a cottage on this site in the 19th century.
Clarence Place	Duke of Clarence (1765-1837), later William IV.
Clifton Grove	John Bligh (1687-1728), Baron Clifton, 1st Earl of Darnley.
Clifton Road	Previously The Old Main (road).
College Road	Huggens College, previously One Tree Lane.
Colyer Road	Thomas Colyer (1809-74), owner of a large estate. His daughter Mary Ann married Sir James Ranken Fergusson.
Coombe Road	William Alexander Coombe, solicitor and landowner.
Coopers Road	Coopers Lane leading to Coopers Cottage.
Cornwell Avenue	Jack Cornwell, V.C., the young sailor and hero at the Battle of Jutland, 1914-1918 War.
Coulton Avenue	W. Coulton, Chairman of Northfleet U.D.C., 1913-36.
Cremorne Road	Famous London Pleasure Gardens.
Crooked Lane	The winding lane at the bottom of Queen Street.
Cross Lane East and Cross Lane West	Lane cutting through from east to west and once called Cut-Throat Lane.
Cruden Road	Robert Pierce Cruden (1775-1847), Mayor in 1817, 1818 and 1831. Wrote a History of Gravesend in 1843.
Cutmore Street	Gardiner More Cutmore, the landowner. Built by George Bench, Edward Edwards and M. Middleton.
Cygnet Gardens	The *Cygnet*, a ship adopted by Northfleet U.D.C. during National Savings Week, Second World War.
Damigos Road	Named after architect involved with Hoplands Development.
Darnley Road	Earls of Darnley, of Cobham Hall. Earlier called Ruck's Lane after Lawrence Ruck, grocer who lived at Ruckland House, now the Masonic Hall.
Davis Avenue	William Davis, a member of Northfleet U.D.C.
Deneholm Road	A variant of dene hole, as one was found here.
Dennis Road	Named by William Hopkins, the builder, after his adopted son.
Dering Way	Edward Dering, maltster of Chalk, who died in 1698.
Devonshire Road	Frank Badman, the landowner, loved the Devonshire country.
Dobson Road	William Francis Dobson, Mayor in 1853 and 1854.
Dowding Walk	Air Chief Marshall Hugh Dowding, hero of the Second World War.
Dudley Road	Part of the Dudley Ryder Estate.
Durndale Lane	Landscape name meaning a hidden, secret or obscure valley.
Eagle Way	*Black Eagle* public house (1866-1967). Once a manor house?
Echo Square	Once a very pronounced echo in an orchard nearby.
Edwin Street	Edwin, Alderman of the Barbican in the City of London, who was another director of the Milton Park Estate Company.

Elliott Street	Thomas Elliott, the tenant farmer.
Elwill Way	Based on part of the name of the developer and his wife.
Enfield Terrace	Alfred Edwin Enfield, Mayor in 1913.
Festival Avenue	Built during the Festival of Britain, 1951.
First Avenue	First of three roads on the original development plan.
Fishermans Hill	Old name for Stonebridge Hill. A fishery was recorded in the Domesday Book.
Fiveash Road	Site of the windmill built by Mr John Fiveash, the miller (1789-1839).
Ford Road	Before the stonebridge was built at the bottom of Stonebridge Hill there was a ford across the Ebbsfleet river.
Fortrey Close	James Fortrye, a Huguenot from Ill, who lived at Wombwell Hall from 1666 until 1745.
Fountain Walk	Recalls a similar walk in Rosherville Gardens.
Freeman Road	Richard Austin Freeman (1862-1943), surgeon and author of the Dr Thorndyke detective stories.
Garden Row	Previously known as Greenhill Road.
Garrick Street	David Garrick (1717-79), actor. After the theatre which stood on the site of Tesco Supermarket.
Gibson Close	Wing Commander Guy Gibson, Pilot Second World War.
Gill Crescent	Mr N. Gill, engineer and surveyor, Northfleet U.D.C.
Grange Road	House called the Grange in Pelham Road.
Granville Road	George L.G. Granville, 2nd Earl (1815-91).
Grieves Road	Mr A.C. Grieves, Chairman, Northfleet U.D.C.,1931-35.
Grove Road	Grove House, built by Henry W. Wyatt, in 1838. Previously One Tree Lane.
Hall Road	Wombwell Hall, Thomas Wombwell built the first Hall in 1471. The family came from Wombwell, Yorkshire.
Hammonds Corner	Humphrey Hammond, owner of the bakery and shop.
Hampton Crescent	H. Hampton Brown, Gravesend's Town Clerk, 1904-48.
Harden Road	Lance Corporal, Eric Harden V.C., who rescued four wounded men on a frozen Dutch battlefield during the Second World War.
Hardy Avenue	Hardy family, who were Council members of the N.U.D.C.
Harman Avenue	Thomas Harman (d.1837) of Wingfield Bank, who purchased Wombwell Hall.
Harmer Street	James Harmer (1777-1853), Alderman of London and a Director of the Milton Park Estate. Rebuilt Ingress Abbey, Greenhithe,
Hartshill Road	Place inWarwickshire to which Northfleet children were evacuated during the Second World War.
Hatton Close	Margaret Hatton (d.1583) who married Thomas Wombwell (1550-1619) of Wombwell Hall.
Havelock Road	General Sir Henry Havelock (1795-1857), who distinguished himself during the Indian Mutiny in 1857.
Haven Close	Built on land which was the grounds of a house, 'The Haven'.
Haynes Road	Mr J. Haynes, Chairman of Northfleet U.D.C., 1921-31 and 1933-49.
Hazells	William Hessill (d.1425), owner of the farm and estate. Brass in St. Botolph's Church.
Hever Court Road	Hever Court, home of the Hever family in 13th century before they moved to Hever Castle in 1331.
Hillary Avenue	Sir Edmund Hillary (b.1919 Auckland, N.Z.), one of the two successful climbers of Mt Everest in May 1953.
Hive (The)	A corruption of 'hythe' or landing place.
Hog Lane	Old English name meaning a ridge.

Holyoake Mount	G.J. Holyoake (1817-1906). Leading member of the Co-operative Society.
Hunt Road	Sir John Hunt (b.1910), Baron. Mountaineer who led the expedition that conquered Mount Everest.
Ingoldsby Road	*Ingoldsby Legends*, by Richard Harris Barham, who frequently stayed with Colonel Thomas Dalton at Milton Manor.
Jellicoe Avenue	Admiral John Rushworth Jellicoe (1859-1935), Commander of the Grand Fleet, First World War.
John Street	Son of Mr L.P. Staff, mayor of Gravesend in 1843.
Johnson Close	Isaac Charles Johnson (1811-1911), cement manufacturer.
Joy Road	Joy Hopkins, the adopted daughter of Mr William Hopkins, the builder.
Jury Street	Cut in 1846-7 between the High Street and Princes Street after a fire. A jury sat to assess the damage and costs.
Kempthorne Street	Charlotte Kempthorne (1722-72), daughter of Thomas Kempthorne, Commissioner of the Navy stationed at Chatham. She married John Wakefield.
Kemsley Close	Mr F.G. Kemsley, farmer and Councillor, N.U.D.C., 1952-8.
Khartoum Place	City in the Sudan where General Gordon was killed in 1885.
Kilndown	Singlewell hopkilns once stood on this site.
King Street	A 'Royal' street. Previously Pelican Row and St. Thomas Street.
Kitchener Avenue	Sir Herbert Kitchener (1850-1916), Secretary of State for War at the beginning of the 1914-18 War.
Lamorna Avenue	The beautiful valley in Cornwall. Built by Mr Ridger and Mr Martin.
Leigh Road	James Leigh Joynes (1746-1803). His house stood on this site.
Leith Park Road	Frederick Leith, Mayor 1867 and 1868. Lived at no.5 Bronte Villas.
Lennox Road	Darnley family of Cobham Hall. Built in 1877. Previously a lane called the New Cut.
Lisle Close	*Lisle Castle* public house. Damaged by an aerial mine, 22 September, 1940.
Longwalk	After Longwalk Cottage.
Lord Street	Benjamin Lord, shipping agent.
Love Lane	Earlier Pennywick Lane or Melancholy Walk. Given in perpetuity in 1742 by John Gurnett, brewer.
Mackenzie Way	William Boyle Mackenzie, Mayor 1934 and 1959.
Malvina Avenue	Name of the nurse who cared for Alderman A. Ramsay during the 1914-18 war.
Manor Road	The Quit Rents of the Manor of Parrock were paid each year under a tree at the western end. Earlier name for Pelham Road after Manor Farm at the junction with Darnley Road. Early name for Ordnance Road which led to St. Thomas Wyatt's Place or Figges.
Mead Road	Field name, Little Mead.
Medhurst Crescent and Medhurst Gardens	Medhurst and Troughton families. Thomas Medhurst, Mayor, 1761; Walter Medhurst, Mayor 1772; Medhurst Troughton, Mayor, 1822, 1836, 1841 and 1860; Medhurst Albert Troughton, Mayor, 1877.
Milton Hall Road	The large mansion built in 1863 and demolished in 1930. The residence of George Matthews Arnold (1827-1908).
Milton Place	Previously called Charlotte's Walk.
Miskin Way	Mr Gerald Miskin, of Ifield Court.
Mitchell Avenue	Mr J.A. Mitchell, Surveyor for Northfleet U.D.C.
Napier Road	Robert Cornelis Napier (1810-90), 1st Baron. British Field Marshall, who directed battles in India and the Sudan.

Newton Abbot Road	After the town in Devon to which Northfleet children were evacuated in the Second World War.
Northcote Road	Sir Stafford Northcote (1818-87).
Ordnance Road	Land previously owned by the Board of Ordnance. Earlier called Manor Way or Manor Road. Sometimes referred to as the Coal Road because it led to the 'free' coal wharves which were in Denton Parish and therefore outside the limits of the Port of London Coal Tax Acts.
Packham Road	Mr S. Packham, Chairman of Northfleet U.D.C., 1931-35.
Painters Ash Lane	Painter: Old English for the end of a shoulder or ridge. The early field name was Partridge Ash.
Palmer Avenue	Robert A.M. Palmer, V.C., D.F.C. and Bar. Acting Wing Commander R.A.F.V.R. Bomber pilot, Second World War.
Park Place	Adam Park (1777-1846) surgeon, brother of Mungo Park the explorer. A Director of the Milton Park Estate Company.
Parrock Street	Old English pearroc: an enclosure or paddock.
Peacock Street	Walter A. Peacock, Deputy of the City of London Corporation. A baker of Bishopsgate, Director of Milton Park Estate Co.
Pelham Road	Another family name of the Darnley family of Cobham Hall. Earlier called Manor Road, from Gravesend Manor Farm at the junction with Darnley Road. Sometimes it was called Style's Lane after the farmer; also White Post Lane after the white posts surrounding the glebe lands.
Pepper Hill	Heathen temple of Pippera or an Old English name for the aspen tree.
Perry Street	Land on which pear trees were grown.
Peter Street	Mr L. Peter Staff, the landowner.
Pine Avenue	The drive to Milton Hall, which was flanked by pine trees. The trees were felled in May, 1984, as they were unsafe.
Pinnocks Avenue	Henry Pinnock (d.1624), Portreve 1597, 1607 and 1613. Gave land on the corner of Windmill Street and King Street for almshouses. These were demolished and new ones built at the junction of Wrotham Road and the Old Road.
Preston Road	Maiden name of the builder's wife.
Ranelagh Gardens	Famous pleasure gardens in Chelsea laid out by Richard Jones, 3rd Viscount Ranelagh. Opened to the public in 1742.
Raphael Road	Lewis Raphael (1822-1907) and Alexander Raphael, the owners of the land.
Riversdale	Thomas Riversdale Colyer Fergusson V.C. (1896-1917).
Robert Street	Robert Smith, the landowner.
Rouge Lane	Rouge Hill an early name for Windmill Hill. Corruption of Rogge Hill or Rugden Hill - a rugged hill.
Royal Oak Terrace	*Royal Oak* public house, 1849-1958, at 18 South Hill Road.
Russell Street	Two John Russells, brewers; father Mayor in 1876, who lived at Hillside; son Mayor in 1898, who lived at Parrock Manor.
Saddington Street	John Saddington (d.1861), Mayor in 1840, 1844, 1846, 1847 and 1852.
Sharland Road	Mr G. Sharland of Coombe and Sharland, later Sharland, Hatten and Sharland, solicitors. He was at one time Town Clerk.
Sheppey Place	Builder of the houses came from the Isle of Sheppey.
Smarts Road	Charles John Smart, farmer of Parrock Manor, The Echo.
Snelling Avenue	Mr G. Snelling, Chairman of Northfleet U.D.C., 1931-34.
Spencer Street	Mr Charles Spencer, chemist and tradesman.
Springhead Road	Leading to Springhead. Northern part once called Leather Bottle Lane. Road at Brookvale formerly Snaggs Bottom, meaning snakes valley or snape - marshy ground.

Stacey Close	Stacey family landowners. John Stacey, Mayor of Gravesend in 1649 and Robert Stacey, Mayor in 1688.
Stonebridge Road	A stone culvert crossing the Ebbsfleet stream.
Stoney Corner	From the field in Istead Rise called Stoneyland.
Struttons Avenue	Name of the nearby farm Struttons or Scruttons.
Sun Lane	After the *Sun* alehouse (1732-1810), which stood at the northern end at Echo Square. Sometimes called Frogs Lane.
Sutherland Close	Capt. William Sutherland, O.B.E., a Capehorner.
Tensing Avenue	Nepalese mountaineer Tenzing Norgay who reached the summit of Everest with Edmund Hillary, 29 May 1953.
The Fairway	Once part of the Mid-Kent Golf Club.
Thistledown	A field of 36 acres in Singlewell that is recorded in 1698.
Thomas Drive	William Evan Thomas, Mayor in 1921 and 1922. A builder.
Thong Lane	A long narrow lane. In 1434 called Longweystrete.
Tooley Street	Tooley Street, London. *Royal Standard* pub in both streets.
Townfield Corner	Townfield in 1796 contained 10 acres 1 rood and 32 perches.
Vale Road	A definite valley, previously Perry Street Road.
Vauxhall Close	Vauxhall Gardens, Lambeth, 1661-1859.
Vicarage Drive	Built on the site of St. Botolph's old vicarage.
Wakefield Street	John Wakefield (1737-1819), a waiter at the *King's Head,* Gloucester, who became a wealthy landowner.
Wallis Park	Mr William Wallis, member of Northfleet U.D.C.
Waterdales	Meadow waterlogged during periods of high rainfall. Name dates back to the 15th century.
Waterton Avenue	Mr. George Albert Waterton, builder, who bought the land from the Raphael family in 1895.
Westcott Avenue	Mrs Violet Grace Westcott, J.P. Chairwoman of the N.U.D.C.
Wilfred Street	Mr Wilfred Charles Tolhurst. *New Inn* Fields were developed by Alfred Tolhurst, resulting in Berkley Road, Bernard Street and Wilfred Street. The last two named after his sons.
William Street	William Staff, son of the landowner L.P. Staff (1807-1881), Mayor, 1843.
Windsor Road	Originally Edward VIII Road but the name changed to Windsor Road after the abdication.
Wingfield Road	Sir Charles W. Wingfield, Liberal Candidate for Gravesend in 1868 and 1874. He was elected M.P. in 1868 but was defeated in the next general election.
Winters Croft	The field immediately to the south of the A.2 near Singlewell; earliest reference in 1680.
Wood Street	The Wood family of Northfleet; Mr J. and Mr B. Wood.
Woodfield Avenue	Part of Parrock Manor Farm. Site of Cottage Field or Great Paddock. John Wood (1818-96) and son William Wood the builder and John's son George developed a brickfield here the Woods were tenants of Lewis Raphael and no relation to George Wood, the brewer.
Woodlands Park	Tadman's Cherry Orchard in the 18th century; Willingtons and Gravesend Orchard in 1840, when it was owned by Thomas Colyer. Bought by George Wood, the brewer from John Wood in 1884. He built the house Woodlands in 1893. Gravesend Corporation purchased the house and meadow in 1933. The house and garden were sold for a hotel in 1937.
Wycliffe Road	John Wycliffe (c.1330-84), translator of the Bible.
Zion Place	The road leading to Zion Chapel in Windmill Street; the Baptist Church built in 1843.

THERE ARE HISTORIES of Gravesend by Robert Pocock (1797) and Robert P. Cruden (1843), still the most useful and informative history up to this date. W.H. Hart (1878) compiled a series of entries from the *Public Records,* in whose office he worked, relating to the area, called *Records of Gravesend, Milton, Denton, Chalk, Northfleet, Southfleet and Ifield* and which contains entries relating to these parishes. It is called Part I, but Part II was never published. *Gravesend in the Very Time of Olde,* G.M. Arnold (1896) is useful for early and mediaeval history. A history written by Alex J. Philip, Vol. 1 (1914) was all that was published plus a one-volume history in 1954. *History of Gravesend* F.A. Mansfield (1922), reprinted 1981, by Rochester Press. The first edition of this history (1976), James Benson and Robert Hiscock, reprinted with additions and corrections 1981. Further histories are: *The Book of Gravesham,* Sydney Harker (1979); *History of Northfleet,* S. H. Cooke (1942); *Chalk,* C.R. Bull (1984), enlarged edition (1992); *An A to Z History of Chalk Parish,* C.R. Bull, 2nd. edition (1992); *Denton,* G.M. Arnold (1902); *Singlewell and Ifield* from a manuscript by K.M. Ffinch revised and edited by R.H. Hiscock (1957). K.M. Ffinch's original manuscript is deposited in the Gravesend Library.

There is a long series of guide books and potted histories, the first printed by Pocock (1817), a later edition printed by T. Caddell. I have the third edition (1824) which contains the print of the Clifton Baths with bathing machines; the *Gravesend Gazeteer* (1840) contains illustrations of the principal streets showing fronts of the shops, houses etc. The illustrated guide of 1844 contains a number of small prints and is one of a series of such guides from London to Chatham. From 1843 (anon.) there is a substantial guide to the area written as a series of letters to a friend and includes poetical effusions; perhaps the best of the nineteenth century guides is Miss E. J. Brabazon's *A Month at Gravesend* (1863), 2nd edn 1864, with many small prints in the illustrated copies. Mention should also be made of William Miller's *Jottings of Kent* (1869), which has a long section on Gravesend and district and was printed locally; see also J.R.S. Clifford's *Gravesend and its Neighbourhood,* a sort of cross between a potted history and a guide book.

The twentieth century produced *The Homeland Handbook for Gravesend* by A.J. Philip, 1st edn 1906-7. I have a 3rd edn (1908). Over the years the local authorities have produced their own guides. There is one undated but circa 1960 with a large number of photographs by Bertrand N. Marshall; one of Gravesham, also undated but circa 1980 produced by the *Reporter* with a large number of illustrations, some coloured. There is also an earlier series of *Official Corporation Guides*; I have one claimed as the 10th edn, circa 1935, with photographs of this period. The *Mayoral Tercentary Souvenir* of 1932 contains a potted history and illustrations and information about the Borough, its regalia and the opening of the Fort Gardens.

There are *Official Northfleet Guides* of circa 1925 and circa 1960, with an historical section by J. Benson. The Library has a complete run of local directories starting in 1849.

School histories: *St. George's,* D.W. Jenkins, 1955; *Milton Mount College,* Hilda Harwood, 1959; *Milton Road,* Glyn Jones, 1976; *Boys Grammar,* Tim Clark and Peter Read, 1993; *St. Botolph's Northfleet,* John Chinery, 1962; *Princes St. Sunday School,* anon., 1902; *St. John's (R.C.)* by Annette Moss, 1999; *Holy Trinity (Centenary Service) Brochure,* A.G. Lacey, 1993; *Northcourt,* C. Bull, 1988; *The Victoria Centre* per W.E.A., Margaret Browne and others, 1993; *Gravesend, Northfleet and District Teachers' Association,* David Collins and others, 1986; *A Brief History of Whitehill Junior School, 1927-2002* E.R. Green.

Church histories: *St. George's,* R.H. Hiscock, 1961; *Pocahontas,* C.A.P. Thomas, 1895; *True Burial Place,* J.H. Haslem, 1897; *SS. Peter and Paul, Milton,* R.H. Hiscock and J.Benson, 1955; *The History of St. Peter and St. Paul, the Parish Church of Milton-next-Gravesend,* R.H. Hiscock, 2004; *Chalk,* M.B. Perkins, 1951, expanded and edited by C.R. Bull, in 1996; *Christ Church Centenary Souvenir,* 1957; *Jubilee of Christ Church,* H. Devereux, 1985; *St. Mary's,* S.W. Johncock, 1964; *St. Aidan* E. Lane, 1988; *Princes Street,*

Lacey Terrace and Old Road East Congregational Chapels D.A. Douglass, 1975; *Roman Catholic Churches* (a collection of items, 1981); and see *Proprietory Chapel of St. John,* R.H. Hiscock; *Archaeologia Cantiana,* vol. XCIII, 1977; *St. Andrew's Waterside Church,* A.O. Pollard, 1965, (there is also a manuscript history by J. Benson).

Miscellaneous: *Three ornamented Bricks at Gravesend* R.C. Cruden; *Old Pubs and Breweries of the Gravesham Area,* E.R. Green, 1989, earlier edition 1987; *Field Names of Gravesend,* E.R. Green; *Gravesend Sailing Club,* Brian Cockle, 1997; ditto by Arthur Allen, John Skellorn and Mark Body 1963 and 1980; *Bat and Ball Memories,* E. Chapman, 1972; Howard Milton, 1999; *The Five Minute Crossing,* J.M. Ormston, 1992; *Gravesend Public Library,* G.M. Arnold, 1905; *The Gravesend Blockhouse and Clarendon Hotel,* V.T.C. Smith and E.R. Green, 2000; earlier booklets; *Defending London's River,* 1985; *New Tavern Fort,* (2), 1998, both V.T.C. Smith; *Gravesend Fort and Milton Chantry,* 1965; *New Tavern Fort,* 1976; *The Gravesend Post* E.W. Tilley, circa 1985 (typescript). There are firms histories of *Porter and Cobb,* 1980 (estate agents); *W.J. Holland and Son* (builders), 1995; *Martin Tolhurst Partnership,* 1986 (solicitors); *Gravesend Reporter,* 1966 (local paper); *Gravesend Trustee Savings Bank,* 1968. *Pinnock Charities,* C.E. Hatten, circa 1935; *Thames and Medway Canal,* C. Hadfield, 1969 (part of *The Canals of South and South East England).* Northfleet histories include: *The Northfleet Roman Villa,* W.H. Steadman, 1913; *Huggens College,* Miss Johnson and the Rev. Hugh McCalman, 1954; Rev. P.C. Collins, 1980; *Springhead,* A.J. Dunkin, 1848; *The Roman Town at Springhead,* W.S. Penn, circa 1965; *The Romano-British Religious Centre of Vagniacis at Springhead Kent,* V.T.C. Smith; *The Imperial Treasure Trove,* R.A.G. Carson, 1965, (for the coin hoard); *Northfleet from 1900* (typescript) J.S. Kean and S.Dyke. Family histories and biography: *Robert Pocock* (based on some of his diaries), G.A. Arnold, 1883; *Memories of Life on a River Thames Tug,* C.R. Haill, Trinity House Pilot, 1928; *Alfred and Sarah Tolhurst and their family,* and their memorial, Church Lady of the Assumption, Northfleet (R.C.), circa 1922; *A Box Full of Rolls,* Frank W. Holland, 1988; typescripts William Smoker; *William Russell,* now printed as *William Russell J.P. 1842-1920,* M.W. Fowler and E.J. Edwards, 1994 (produced by his Masonic Lodge); *Coy Family; F.A.C. Tatham; Notes on Gravesend Personalities,* E. Chapman; *Clarke's Nurseries,* M.W.M. Clarke; *Moss Family,* J. Gainey-Brown; *Gravesend to the Sea,* Frank C. Bowen (October 15, 1936 et seq. *Gravesend and Dartford Reporter* [parts I to LVI]).

Kent County Histories: There are references to Gravesend in most of the County histories. Lambarde, 1576, was the first county history; Harris, 1710, contains a description of the first St. George's; Thorpe's *Registrum,* the monuments in churches with their inscriptions (reproduced in Pocock); Hasted, octavo edition, 1797, vol. III, contains descriptions of all the local parishes; Furley's *Weald of Kent* has a general history of Kent in vol. I, relating local events to national history; Dr Alan Everet's *Continuity and Colonisation,* 1986, breaks new ground with its origins of the Parish system. There is the new *History of Kent* in the process of publication by the K.C.C., the first of five volumes of which has been published. There are also references to this area in vols. II and III of the *Victoria County History of Kent,* only three volumes of which have been published. There is *Kent Cinemas,* Martin Tapsell, 1987; *Kent Care for the Wounded* (particulars of V.A.D. hospitals), Paul Creswick and others, 1915; *Kent Home Guard,* K.R. Gulvin, 1980; all of which contain references to Gravesend; *Estuary,* A.K. Astbury, 1980; *The River and The Downs,* Michael Baldwin, 1984. The library has an extremely useful set of local street directories covering the period 1834-1956.

There are many references and some articles on Gravesend in *Archaeologia Cantiana,* vols. I (1858) to CXXV (2005) and continuing, and in the *Records* volumes; C.H. Fielding's *Records of Rochester Diocese,* 1910, contains lists of the incumbents of the local churches including the Victorian ones up to this date.

The **cement** industry has been dealt with: *100 years of Portland Cement,* A.C. Davis, 1924; *A History,* by A.J. Francis, 1977; and an official *History of Blue Circle* by Peter Pugh, 1988.

There are numerous **railway** histories which relate to Gravesend, the latest comprehensive one being in three volumes by Adrian Gray and there are earlier short ones by Oakwood Press plus separate booklets on the North Kent and West Street lines. The **tramways** were covered at length in *The Tramways of Kent*, vol.I, by G.E. Baddeley and others, 1971.

Gravesend Chronology 2000 which follows and incorporates earlier chronologies by R. Pocock and C. Gunkel is published by the Library (K.C.C.); also *Gravesend, a photographic history of your town,* Dr. Raymond Solly, 2002; *Then and Now Gravesend,* Eve Streeter, 2001. There are also a number of picture books of Gravesend and Northfleet published over the last few years.

END